Deep Water Gold

For my wife Angie,
and daughters Tracey and Kim

Deep Water Gold

The story of RMS *Niagara* – the quest for New Zealand's greatest shipwreck treasure

KEITH GORDON

First published in 2005 by
SeaROV Technologies Ltd
PO Box 1094
Whangarei
email: searov@xtra.co.nz
www.deepquest.co.nz

Designed and typeset by Egan-Reid Ltd, Auckland
Printed in New Zealand

ISBN 0 473 10056 8

A catalogue record for this book is available from the National Library of New Zealand.

Contents

PART THREE: *The Explorers*

PART FOUR: *Revelations*

Author's note

In writing this narrative, I have recorded a number of measurements made in earlier times in the imperial system, whereas today we use the metric system. Converting older measurements to metric would have meant changing the historical record, so I have compromised by keeping to imperial measurements where they are historically appropriate, and as the story advances into more modern times I have used metric. With developments in diving technology, there has been a transition from imperial to the metric system which is now used by many dive-training agencies. However some divers still use the imperial system, so in discussing diving technology I have used metric and imperial equivalents in the text. For unusual or older terms, I have included an explanation in the Glossary.

I have followed the traditional practice of calling a ship "she" and I trust this will cause no offence. I have found there are several theories why a ship is called "she". One claims that during the early days of sailing every ship was dedicated to a goddess, another that crews believed the ship represented their mother. The one that I consider more likely is as follows: at the time of ancient mariners even as far back as 500BC, most were "married to the sea" due to their love of the ocean. The ships were their livelihood, their home and their love. As a compliment to the women they loved they named their sailing vessels after them, saying it would remind them of the ones they left behind for the months and sometimes years they would be gone.

Whatever the reason, a ship is a beautiful creation and even as a shipwreck on the bottom of the ocean, a ship still retains a certain mystery and allure.

AUCKLAND
New Zealand
Poor Knights Islands
Tutukaka Harbour
HMS Puriri
WHANGAREI
NIAGARA
Hen & Chicken Is
Moko Hinau Islands
Great Barrier Is
Little Barrier Is
Colville Channel
Cuvier Is
Mercury Islands
Hauraki Gulf
Coromandel Peninsula
Whitianga
AUCKLAND

Introduction

Shipwreck and gold! Dramatic words that evoke images of adventure and lost treasures. Like an unread book, a shipwreck is a repository of secrets and information that remain unknown until its contents are revealed. A shipwreck's story concerns not only the decaying remains of the vessel but also her life and the lives of those who sailed with her and who died with her. Shipwrecks are fascinating, and the oceans still contain thousands of wrecks waiting to be discovered and their stories told.

In our remote corner of the South Pacific, recorded maritime history spans only a short period of time. From 1642, when Abel Tasman was reportedly the first European to discover New Zealand, until the late 18th century few vessels visited these shores. Further north above the equator, the treasure galleons of Spain lumbered across the Pacific between Manila and Acapulco carrying silver from the New World and the riches of Asia to Europe. On the Pacific coasts of Central and South America, pirates captured Spanish treasure and looted coastal settlements. Numerous ships laden with gold and silver were overcome by ocean tempests, wrecked on coral reefs or lost through conflict.

Tales of such lost treasures on the bottom of the ocean, or buried on remote Pacific islands, stirred childhood dreams. Robert Louis Stevenson's *Treasure Island* and Saturday matinee movies of pirates and lost treasure fermented the fantasies I re-enacted in playtime adventures. As I grew older I absorbed adventure magazine "true" accounts of sunken galleons and of lost treasures waiting on the bottom of the ocean for those brave enough to challenge the depths. In the late 1940s and early 1950s the submarine environment was still a mysterious world inhabited by monsters. Tales of helmeted divers being crushed by pressure, gobbled up by monstrous grouper or attacked by giant octopus did little to entice people to put their heads beneath the surface. But these stories were of faraway places. Unknown to us youngsters at the time, only a few years earlier a group of men had challenged the ocean depths and wrestled from a sunken liner one of the greatest treasures recovered in our times. And it was not in some far exotic remote location, but from coastal waters only some 200 kilometres from Auckland.

I was in my teens when I first learned of the gold-ship *Niagara*. The exploits of Jacques Cousteau and Hans Hass had put human fear of the ocean depths into the past and I was a keen participant in the new sport of skin-diving. Exploring lost shipwrecks offered excitement and adventure. I knew little of the *Niagara* except that she was deep, well beyond the sport-diving technology of the day. And then there were the rumours that the wreck still contained gold bullion. Boyhood images of sunken treasure resurfaced, but for the time being had to remain images of dreams.

A period of working in Samoa and living close to Robert Louis Stevenson's old residence at Vailima, with his grave on the mountain summit above, rekindled past dreams of lost treasure ships. Returning to New Zealand, I discovered that new developments in remote undersea technology had now put deep shipwrecks within reach. Curious about the lost gold-ship close to my home, I embarked on a voyage that would take me into a fascinating world of adventure, technology, history, a kaleidoscope of characters and the story of the ship – RMS *Niagara*.

I have had the privilege of meeting or corresponding with many people who have been associated in one way or another with RMS *Niagara* or with maritime history and exploring the deep. All have expressed an interest in my writing this book and have given advice, information and services which have enabled me to record the events associated with this historic shipwreck. I am grateful to the divers who have dived the *Niagara* and related their experiences to me, and I thank the following people and organisations who have provided such assistance:

Wendy Adlam, John Asmussen, David Apperley, Philip Bendle, Quentin

Bennett, Robert Birks, Christina Campbell, Tim Cashman, Craig Challan, Lynton Diggle, Wade Doak, Russell Ellis, Peter Fields, Percy Ginders, Dr Roger Grace, Gavin Grant, Walter Guthrie, Dieter Haible, Karl Hall, Craig Howell, Keiran Hulme, Chris Hutchison, Gareth Jones, Rees Jones, Allan Kircher, Ian Lockley, Dave Maddox, Alan Martin, Dave Moran, Roy Martin, Dr Simon Mitchell, Jeff Maynard, Peter Mesley, Ray Nelson, Patrick Noble, Patricia O'Shaughnessy, Alister Parsons, Mary Sanson, Dr Deither Schmidt, Mark Spencer, Professor Peter Tamm, Rosemary Tarlton, Jaan Voot, Jack Ward, Hein-Peter Weyher, Jim White, Jeanette Woods.

Archives New Zealand, Bank of England, Commonwealth Bank of Australia, Museum of Wellington City & Sea, National Archives UK, Natural History Ltd, New Zealand National Maritime Museum, the *Northern Advocate*, University of Glasgow and Wissenscaftliches Institut fur Shiffarts-und Marinegeschichte Gmbh.

A special thank you to Ray Richards of Richards Literary Agency for giving me the courage to persevere with publishing this book, and to Mary Egan and the staff of Egan-Reid Ltd who guided me through the necessities for publication.

Websites: www.bismark-class.dk, www.worldconnect.rootsweb.com, www.markspencer.com.au.

PART ONE

The Ships

1

Gulf Raider

She came from the East, a ship with no name. Silhouetted against the grey dusk of a winter's afternoon, the rust-streaked freighter ploughed through the Pacific swell toward the setting sun. Though she bore no name, her yellow funnel, brown-yellow masts and weathered exterior identified her as a ship of the Dutch-Africa line or perhaps even American. The vessel was of neither nationality, nor was she the freighter she appeared to be. Designated Schiff 36 in the German navy, she was a ship of war – the armed merchant cruiser *Orion*.

Kapitan zur See (Captain) Kurt Weyher inhaled the evening breeze – the scent of land invaded the ever-prevalent ocean tang, kindling memories of a homeland half a world away. For the past nine weeks the ocean stretching across horizons had been his world. To the west, silhouetted against the setting sun, the volcanic hills of the New Zealand coastline grew in sharp relief. Valleys washed in purple shadow descended and disappeared beneath the coastal waters that stretched out to meet the on-coming ship. Weyher scanned the approaching North Island coastline, identifying the approaches to Hauraki Gulf, gateway to the port of Auckland, the *Orion*'s target destination.

The tranquillity of the Pacific evening, so distant from the battlegrounds of Europe, was a paradox for the crew. It was difficult to comprehend that they were approaching this isolated outpost of the British Empire to commit an act of war.

To Wehyer and his officers the peaceful evening and clear conditions were of little comfort. They were behind schedule. High seas had reduced the heavily laden ship's speed as they had followed the 40th parallel across the Pacific from Cape Horn. Boiler repairs while rolling in mid-ocean two weeks previously were a setback to their schedule. Engine failure the following week caused further delay. Arriving on 13 June 1940, Wehyer was conscious that their mission would now miss the cover of darkness under a new moon.

On 6 April HSK *Orion*, formerly the 7021-ton *Kurmark* built in 1930 for the Hamburg Amerika Line, had slipped out into the North Sea disguised as the Dutch freighter *Beemsterdijk*. With a crew complement of 377 men, provisions for twelve months, torpedoes, ammunition and a cargo of 230 sea mines, the disguised HandelsSchiffsKreuzer (trade protection vessel) breached the British blockade off the German coastline. Captain Weyher's orders were to sail the *Orion* undetected through the Denmark Strait, slip between Iceland and Greenland into the North Atlantic then down into the South Atlantic, around Cape Horn and into the Pacific.

The Atlantic passage was not without incident. British destroyers, sighting the solitary freighter sailing south, approached for closer identification. The sudden interest from the British warships sent the crew racing to battle stations. Hidden from sight behind screens, gun crews ranged the *Orion*'s six antiquated 150mm guns onto the approaching warships. Aware there was little chance of survival if conflict did erupt, the Germans gambled on disguise and deceit.

To aid the impression of a neutral ship on a routine passage, the bridge crew, dressed as civilian seamen, posed in full view of the British. The cook appeared on deck to add to the charade. Appearing unfazed by the close presence of warships he nonchalantly emptied a load of trash over the side. In the event their ruse failed, the Germans were confident of firing a broadside barrage with the possibility of sinking one of the enemy destroyers. Victory would undoubtedly be short-lived, as British return fire would have no problem penetrating the *Orion*'s unarmoured hull and igniting her heavy cargo of fuel, mines and munitions.

Their deception succeeded. The British, satisfied the Dutch freighter presented no danger, returned to resume escort duty thereby providing Weyher the opportunity to slip away into the cover of an approaching rainsquall.

Following her escape, the *Orion* changed her appearance to that of a

Russian freighter and then, on reaching the Western Atlantic, to that of a Greek tramp steamer. She sailed unchallenged into the mid-Atlantic, then a revision to orders diverted her from her passage south direct to the Pacific. In an effort to draw forces away from Norway where Germany anticipated strong opposition to their invasion of that country, Weyher was to attempt to create confusion among the enemy. He was ordered to attack merchant ships to give the British the impression that a pocket battleship was on the prowl in the north Atlantic – a rather difficult task to simulate for a ship now disguised as a Greek tramp. The only answer was to quickly sink an enemy ship, then transmit a false SOS reporting the presence of a German battleship in the area.

On 25 April, to the east of Bermuda in the hours before daybreak, the shadow of a ship emerged from the night. The *Orion*, with her crew manning battle stations, closed on the unsuspecting vessel. Confirming its identity as an enemy freighter, the *Orion* hoisted her battle ensign and closed for the attack. The initial salvo scored a direct hit. A total of 75 rounds were fired into the freighter, setting the hapless vessel ablaze. Considerable damage was inflicted to the onboard lifeboats and the German commander, observing his enemy's predicament, ordered his ship to heave to. Lowering their cutters, the *Orion*'s crew set about rescuing the crew from the doomed vessel. She was the 5207-ton *Haxby* under the command of Captain Cornelius Arundell en route from Glasgow to Corpus Christi, Texas – seventeen crew went down with the ship. Confined to Hold No. 4 with the remainder of his captured crew, Arundell was resigned to being a prisoner of war travelling on a voyage into the unknown.

Having succeeded in sinking an enemy vessel, Weyher headed south to a prearranged position in the South Atlantic. Arriving at the rendezvous 660 miles from South Georgia, he was concerned to find the tanker *Winnetou* nowhere in sight. Only 50 days fuel remained and it was vital they refuel to continue their mission. High fuel consumption due to the increased speed required to maintain their operational schedule had consumed reserves. In an effort to locate the missing tanker, the Arado seaplane carried aboard was launched into the Atlantic swells. With some difficulty the little aircraft finally managed to break free from the confused ocean to disappear into the grey horizon. Within an hour the aircraft returned and the pilot reported locating the tanker nearby. Refuelling operations in rising seas was arduous as both ships, connected by a floating umbilical pipeline, struggled to remain in position. Sea conditions further deteriorated, bringing a halt to the refuelling operation after pumping 1900 tons of fuel. The ships parted and the *Orion* headed 120 miles south of Cape Horn, to a latitude considered beyond the range of enemy patrols.

Rounding the Horn on 27 May in relatively calm weather, Weyher, in an effort to avoid inclement weather, decided on a northerly route along the 40th parallel across the Pacific to his destination – New Zealand. On 30 May boiler problems required the ship to heave to for immediate repairs. Working under difficult conditions in rolling seas, the engineers toiled to effect repairs. Despite urgency the work caused many hours' delay but with a period of fine weather following, Weyher hoped to make up for lost time. The navigation crew, aware they had missed the opportunity of a full moon, were still optimistic. They should still be able to reach the Hauraki Gulf while conditions remained conducive for concealing their ship in darkened waters. Once more the *Orion*'s disguise was changed, this time to resemble a ship of the Dutch-Africa Line. No name was painted on her black hull.

Stormy seas slowed the vessel's passage westwards across the Pacific. On 8 June the engine failed. The required repairs now ruled out any chance of making up for the lost time. Weyher became resigned to operating in enemy waters while exposed under the first quarter of a new moon.

On 13 June the mines were prepared for launching. Technicians installed the soluble plugs and screwed the lead horns into place. During the voyage, the stern launching platforms had been concealed behind hinged plates, a disguise now removed as the ship was prepared for launching her deadly cargo.

Approaching the New Zealand coast, the *Orion*'s radio operators monitored local commercial radio stations; to their amazement the received transmissions included daily reports on movements of local shipping and aircraft. This outpost of Britain, so distant from the war in Europe, still lived under a false sense of security unaware of the approaching enemy close to their shores. In a speech about this time, the Prime Minister stated that the ports of Wellington and Auckland were considered to be the safest in the British Empire and would play a major role in supplying Britain with food and goods in ever-increasing quantities. Little did he know that the enemy was now at his nation's doorstep.

The radio broadcasts even revealed to the listening Germans aircraft types operated by the New Zealand forces and details of airfield positions. One news item reported the crash of a Royal New Zealand Air Force aircraft – an Airspeed Oxford had crashed into Akaroa township – while another item on the day of the *Orion*'s arrival advised details of an air force exercise over Wellington. With such information and knowledge of aircraft types and performance, it was relatively easy to compute their fuel consumption and range. News of the Wellington air exercise was of some consolation to the invading Germans. Enemy military aircraft operations in the Auckland region were now unlikely during the period of the *Orion*'s mission in nearby waters.

Local radio weather forecasts advised of an area of high pressure that was active, creating the moderate seas and relatively cloudless sky conditions under which they sailed. A light south-west breeze ruffled the coastal waters as the *Orion* sailed west towards Cuvier Island. Sunset that day was at 1640 hours: the final rays of the day streaked into the heavens creating a colourful sunset. Weyher observed the calm of the evening with some concern. In such clear conditions with the moon in its first quarter, there would be inadequate night cover to conceal his ship. Further to his consternation, information gleaned from local radio the previous day revealed that the New Zealand cruiser HMS *Achilles* and British armed merchant cruiser HMS *Hector* were either in Auckland harbour or sailing nearby waters.

Night fell. Visibility in the muted light was reduced to between ten and twelve miles. With concealment now lost and without the cover of a new moon, the original plan to operate well inside the Gulf was aborted. Weyher decided to lay the same number of mines over a wider area, but still to cover the approaches to the inner Gulf leading to Auckland. With any chance for stealth now gone, he decided the best course of action was to brazen it through relying on disguise, good navigation and an unsuspecting enemy. The crew were ordered to battle stations.

The *Orion* on full power headed directly for the Cuvier lighthouse while all available hands set to heaving the mine trolleys along the twin launching rails feeding the stern launching platforms. Wehyer, accepting their approach under the overhead moon could expose the *Orion* to the lighthouse keepers, turned his attention astern. They were also visible to observers on Great Mercury Island where lights could now be discerned among the trees on the island. Closer to Cuvier, the revolving light flashed across the *Orion*, each sweep increasing their exposure to discovery. But no alarm was raised ashore. The strange manoeuvres of the approaching ship went unnoticed or, if seen at all, attracted no suspicion.

Earlier in the year the Japanese vessel MV *Kozan Maru* had been observed acting suspiciously in the Gulf off Tiritiri Matangi island. It displayed no navigation lights and gave no response to signals. Japan was still at peace with Britain and the New Zealand government response to the intrusion was to send the Japanese a warning regarding such movements by their ships in New Zealand waters. So far from the battlefields of Europe, an official recommendation to station patrol vessels in the area had not been considered a priority. Sightings of tramp steamers seemingly unsure of the Auckland approaches were not cause for concern nor considered a danger to the nation.

At 1926 hours the first mine was launched. Plunging into the foam of the ship's wake, the metallic sphere immediately disappeared into the black depths. The crew toiled to maintain the momentum, launching mines simultaneously from port and starboard platforms. The helmsman steered a zigzag course towards Cuvier. Suddenly, brilliance flooded across the port mine-deployment crew. They froze momentarily under the sudden luminance then scurried for cover. The beam of light swept on across the port side then out into the night before returning again to turn night into day. With each sweep of the beacon the chance of discovery heightened. Discovery by another vessel at this stage of operations, especially while illuminated in the beam of the lighthouse, would abort the mission. In the confines of the Gulf the *Orion* would be lucky to escape to the open sea.

By 1955 hours the first barrage of mines was complete, stretching between Great Mercury and Cuvier islands. Another 90 minutes passed. A further field of mines in the Colville Channel, between Cuvier and Great Barrier islands, extended for a distance out to sea beyond Great Barrier. Weyher ordered a new course to take the *Orion* towards the northern entrance of the Gulf.

An urgent warning from the port lookout alerted the bridge as a shadow emerged out of the darkness. The helmsman, reacting to orders, quickly changed heading to avoid the approaching vessel, now identified as a small craft. A short time later came a further alert. Again the heading was altered as the shadow of a larger unlit vessel was sighted. The *Orion* once again slipped away into the folds of night, the crew's adrenalin rush eased as the shadow vessels disappeared.

At 2315 hours Weyher, now aware of local shipping around the Gulf, ordered all possible speed on a course towards the northern tip of Great Barrier island. The mine-laying crews toiled at their task, conscious of the need for haste. Dragging the heavy two-metre spheres onto the launch platform they sent the mines plunging into the channel between the Great Barrier and Moko Hinau islands. Good visibility and lights from navigation beacons around the Gulf aided the Germans in navigating the unfamiliar waters. However, operating under such conditions magnified the danger of discovery.

The night wore on. To the *Haxby* survivors, imprisoned below the mine deck, the continual noise from above made sleep impossible. Listening to the continual rumble of heavy mines being dragged to the platforms, the prisoners maintained a tally of mines as they were launched.

The moonlight diminished as overcast conditions began to settle in and by midnight a light drizzle provided a welcome cloak for concealment. The change in weather conditions helped relieve crew tension. Beacon lights around the Gulf remained visible through the light rain, continuing to aid navigation during the final hours of the mission. Circumnavigating the Moko Hinaus at a distance of six miles, Weyher ordered a new heading and set a westerly course for the mainland past Maro Tiri island.

Conscious of his increasing fatigue, Weyher knew that the physical effort laying mines and the mental stress of night operations in enemy waters was taking a toll on his crew. The danger of discovery at any moment remained constant throughout the long night. The many weeks at sea far from home, without news of family and loved ones, or of the state of the war in Europe, was not the elixir for maintaining his crew in peak battle condition. He took some comfort in his knowledge of the weakness of the New Zealand defences. The South Pacific Dominion, half a world away from the fighting in Europe, had little reason to consider the possibility of an enemy naval cruiser operating undetected within their waters. This false belief in security through isolation was an advantage for the German raiders and greatly lessened their chance of discovery during the mine-laying operations. Even so, lookouts were ordered to maintain vigilance as the weary crew prepared to lay the final ordinance to complete the mine blockade of the port of Auckland.

"Ship lights to port!"

Crew fatigue instantly disappeared as the lookout's warning was relayed through the ship. Tension again invaded the bridge. Focusing his night glasses, Weyher sought and found the lights of a ship. It was sailing towards the mines they had recently laid. Secured to their mooring cables, the mines were positioned approximately eighteen feet below the surface; the approaching vessel drew at least 25 feet of water. Transfixed, Weyher waited, praying that the mines would remain inactive with their dissolving detonator caps yet to bring them to life. An explosion at that stage would place the *Orion* in a hazardous position. There would be little chance of escape from the confines of the Gulf before alerted enemy forces arrived on the scene. Suddenly, lights of another vessel appeared from the night. The two nearby ships galvanised Weyher into action. To delay further the laying of the final mines would position the *Orion* close to shore, exposing her to the increasing light of dawn. Deciding to cast caution aside, Weyher ordered the mine-laying operation to continue. In the upper shadows of the now darkened wheelhouse the ship's motto, carved into a wooden beam, invaded the thoughts of some: "Wir segein mit klaram Blick, am Ruder die Faust und – das Gluck" (we sail with a keen eye, at the wheel a strong fist and – good luck). The crew were well aware they would need all their luck to survive this night. As the *Orion* slipped away into the night towards the mainland coast, the two ships with lights ablaze continued on their way, their crews oblivious to the enemy warship nearby and the danger that lurked close beneath their keels.

Two more vessels appeared out of the darkness passing astern. Weyher's present concerns were heightened by the knowledge that HMS *Achilles* and HMS *Hector* were operating in these waters. Unbeknown to him, the port of Auckland had been closed to shipping that afternoon until 2100 hours: naval control authorities had said this was to facilitate naval exercises in local waters. Only after the war did Weyher learn that during that night's mine-laying operation, between the hours of 2100 and midnight, both *Achilles* and *Hector* returned to Auckland. The 7215-ton cruiser *Achilles*, a heavily armed cruiser capable of 32 knots, was carrying out sea trials following a major refit at Auckland. Seven months previously, she had seen action at the Battle of the River Plate in the South Atlantic, resulting in the destruction of the German pocket battleship *Admiral Graf Spee*. Against such a formidable foe, the crew of the *Orion* would have had no chance. Perhaps the *Achilles* was one of the vessels sighted by the *Orion*'s lookouts during the night – the two opposing forces each unaware of the enemy nearby.

Through the early hours of the morning the mine laying continued. Finally, exhausted from the night's physical and mental exertions, the mine crew prepared the last mine for launching. While approaching New Zealand, music broadcast from local radio stations had entertained the crew; now, as a tongue-in-cheek gesture, they inscribed messages including music requests on the last mines. At 0236 hours on 14 June the last mine plunged into the sea. In a light-hearted effort to release some of the night's tension, the crew piped the mine overboard with full naval honours. Imprisoned below, the sleepless men of the *Haxby* had counted 228 mines launched during the night.

Weyher ordered a new course and the *Orion*, now riding higher in the water, her engine generating the maximum power obtainable, departed the Gulf on a north-easterly course towards the Kermadec islands. Astern, the dawn broke across the waters of the Gulf. Beneath the surface in the silence of the depths, the mines swung on their mooring cables, passively waiting the moment to unleash their destructive forces on the unsuspecting nation. The European war had arrived at the shores of New Zealand.

2

Queen of the Pacific

Auckland, Friday 14 June 1940. The southwest wind funnelled down Queen Street swirling around the city's commercial centre, across the ships moored at downtown wharves, out across Waitemata Harbour past Rangitoto island towards the Hauraki Gulf and beyond to the Pacific Ocean. On street corners, muffled against the cold of winter, newspaper boys shouted their chorus of the day's headlines. City workers hurried past intent on catching trams and buses. Now at the end of a week's work, their minds were set on weekend leisure activities. For many, the war on the far side of the globe, although a little worrying, was not of primary interest. The weekend's activities or a beer in a pub before six o'clock closing were of more importance, unless you were of Italian origin.

Earlier in the week, Mussolini had joined Hitler and the authorities were busy rounding up Italian nationals residing in New Zealand. Even those born in the country to Italian parents were destined for internment along with German nationals and others – including Samoans with part-German ancestry from the former German colony. War affected many friendships and people with German surnames came under the scrutiny of the authorities. Even the elderly were incarcerated, enduring the hardships of camps such as Somes island in the middle of Wellington harbour. Exposed to cold winds blasting north from Antarctic regions, their internment in damp draughty huts resulted in illnesses including tuberculosis, from which many would never recover.

Nervous of possible fifth-column activities by people with alien connections now domiciled in New Zealand, the authorities instituted added security precautions. Over the weekend new regulations closed the city's wharves to the public. Access was by special permit only and the wharves, normally a popular public venue for fishing, were deserted. The *Achilles* and *Hector* had slipped into port under the cover of darkness on Friday morning. Two overseas ships at Queens Wharf were undergoing loading, their crews relaxing far from the war in the Atlantic.

Monday night's big wrestling match was a major topic that Saturday in the city pubs. A local man, Sergeant-Major Lofty Blomfield, was to take on the former US champion, Joe Corbett in an event that had been receiving a lot of promotion over the past week. The same evening, men of the New Zealand Division of the Royal Navy were to be decorated at a ceremony held in town to which the public had been invited. The sailors from HMS *Achilles*, following their victory at the battle of the River Plate, had been given a heroes' welcome home as they marched down Queen Street. During the weekend activities, with the war so far away, many gave little thought to the possibility of close threats to the security of the nation. Unknown to the unsuspecting Auckland populace, the war had arrived on their doorstep. Danger now lurked in the waters of the city's gateway.

Over the past century the nation's commerce and transport had been served by sea. The first air service to Australia had commenced the previous month with Tasman Empire Air Lines operating a Solent flying boat between Auckland and Sydney, and Pan American Airlines had been granted that week an operating licence to fly the Pacific route, San Francisco to Auckland. However, ocean liners were still the accepted prime means for transport. With the closure of the Suez Canal due to the war in Europe, the quickest means of passage to England was across the Pacific to Vancouver, followed by train across Canada then ship across the Atlantic.

Over the weekend, passengers gathered in Auckland preparing to travel on the Pacific veteran liner RMS *Niagara* operated by the Canadian Australasian Line. They would be joining the ship when she arrived from Sydney on Tuesday on her scheduled return voyage to Vancouver by way of Suva and Honolulu. The *Niagara* had now sailed the Pacific route for over 25 years, covering more sea miles than any other liner in service. She was a household name throughout the country, having survived the First World War, outrunning German raiders with her superior speed.

Now the veteran Queen of the Pacific faced the technology of a new war. No ship had yet been lost to enemy action in the Pacific, and with minimal perturbation passengers prepared to escape the New Zealand winter for an ocean voyage to Pacific destinations.

For Bill Sparrow and his mates J. Davidson, G. Hefford and W. Finn, the journey to Auckland had been the start of their adventure. The hustle and bustle of the city was a contrast to their small South Island country hometown Ashburton, now in the grips of a southern winter. The four were looking forward to escaping to the warmth for a ten-week holiday in Fiji. Their baggage included two sets of bowls and the men looked forward to relaxing in tropical sunshine, playing bowls and enjoying the social colonial life. The voyage to Fiji on the *Niagara* would be a holiday bonus, as the ship was well-known for her opulence and service, even though they would be travelling cabin class. A night at the wrestling before sailing would add to the highlights of the holiday.

John Browne eagerly awaited his sea voyage to Suva, more so as he would be travelling first-class on such a fine ship. Now 87, he had first served under sail in 1871. His years at sea followed by farming showed in his sparely built frame, which he carried in a dignified manner. The old seafarer's past experience at sea aided his preparations for the coming voyage. He would be sailing at a time of war and, although expecting little problems in this sphere of the world, he considered it prudent to prepare in case of emergency. He added a torch to his cabin baggage.

Mrs Major's visit to Auckland had been a nostalgic one. Preparing her baggage for the voyage back to Canada, her thoughts returned to earlier days of living in Auckland with her late husband. Colonel Charles Major was the founder and a former headmaster of King's College, recognised as one of the prime educational institutions in the country. Now, chattels from the estate of the late Colonel Major, including silver plate and fine furniture, had been carefully prepared for the rigours of sea freight to a new home. Travelling on the *Niagara* as a first-class passenger, Mrs Major was comforted in the knowledge that the valued family memorabilia would be treated with care.

The break in New Zealand from Fiji had been for Mrs Livingston an opportune time to visit her friends and family. Shopping in Auckland had added to her baggage, which included carefully packed family heirlooms consisting of two gold pineapple-styled gold cups and silverware. Blackball confectionery, a favourite of her husband Clive at home on their Fiji plantation, was purchased and carefully packed among her lingerie for the voyage to Suva.

Four-year-old Louis Keegan was also travelling to Suva. He had spent the weekend excitedly playing with friends and telling those grown-ups who would listen to his chatter of the adventure he was about to embark upon. His escort, Miss Charlton, was bemused by Louis' continual banter and questions as the small boy's imagination took hold. She had already experienced drama at sea since the outbreak of war. As a passenger on the *Niew Holland* she had witnessed a rescue near Singapore and now, with her young charge, she wished only for an uneventful voyage to Suva. They would be travelling first-class and she looked forward to the luxury and comfort the *Niagara* provided.

Five-year-old Jenny Chalmers was the apple of her mother's eye. At 42, after having given birth to four boys, Mrs Chalmers had rejoiced at giving birth to Jeanette. In the days preceding their departure for Suva she had given a lot of thought to shopping for the family home. Linen, towels, clothing and all kinds of essentials she knew would be hard to obtain in Fiji were purchased and carefully packed for the voyage. Travelling first-class to Suva with Jenny and her six-year-old son would be a relaxing break after the hassles of shopping in Auckland. She was looking forward to escaping winter and rejoining her husband, who had a legal practice on the Pacific Island. On the day of sailing, she decided to treat the two young children, taking them shopping with her. Jenny was excited at being spoiled by her mother when she was presented with a beautiful American china-faced, cloth-bodied doll with a wardrobe and a cream cane pram complete with linen. If that was not enough, the little girl's smiles broadened with the further gift of a little ironing board with an iron "heated" by a tiny light bulb. Her brother whooped with delight with the biggest Meccano set he had laid eyes on. The excited children hastened with their mother to board the ocean liner that waited at the bottom of Queen Street.

Other than the introduction of baggage inspection, which required baggage for consignment to the ship's hold to be delivered some hours before sailing, there was little to indicate any wartime concerns for safety in sailing the Pacific Ocean routes. The *Niagara* had sailed through the Great War unscathed: sometimes she had been pursued by raiders yet she had always outrun any danger, earning herself the title "Lucky *Niagara*". Yes, she was a fine ship with a proven record which gave confidence to passengers that they could relax on the coming voyage with little danger from sailing at a time of war in other parts of the globe.

Out on the Gulf the gannets wheeled and glided low across the foam-flecked surface, searching among the swells for signs of school fish. The waters of the channel between Moko Hinau islands and the Hen and Chickens group were a prolific hunting ground for both bird and fish. With depths exceeding 130 metres, the flow of water through the channel from changing tides provided a flow of nutrients from waters and mangroves of the inner Gulf. The birds swooped across the grey surface waters, seeking their elusive prey, oblivious to another hunter waiting in silence in the depths below, waiting to unleash destruction on a different form of ocean prey.

Tugging on their mooring cables in the ocean swell, the *Orion*'s mines hidden beneath the surface provided a refuge for schools of fish from the gannet patrols. Occasionally through the silence of the depths, propeller reverberations impinged on the steel mine casings as ships passed nearby, unaware of the fate they had narrowly avoided. On the morning of Tuesday 18 June, powerful throbbing generated by the triple screws of a large vessel pulsated down the channel. The mines swung on their mooring cables in the turbulent water column seeking their prey but no contact was made. The ship powered on through the darkness of a winter dawn towards Auckland, oblivious to the destructive forces below. The mine gyrations subsided; once more they swung quietly on their moorings, waiting. The school fish gathered again in the shelter of their shadows.

3

Auckland Arrival

The triple screws of the RMS *Niagara* churned the Gulf waters, creating a trail of phosphorescence in the pre-dawn light. The 14,000-ton mass carved through the Gulf towards the waking city of Auckland. It had passed through these waters on numerous occasions and Voyage No. 237 on which she now sailed added further to the Pacific veteran's record of having sailed more ocean miles than any other passenger liner.

Captain William Martin contemplated the coming day as he stood alongside the Auckland harbour pilot on the *Niagara*'s bridge. The city lights were visible ahead and soon they would be at their berth at Queens Wharf adjacent to the city's main street. It had been a smooth sailing across the Tasman from Sydney and the forecast predicted good conditions for their departure later that evening. Leaving the bridge to his chief officer, Frank Gibson, Martin retired to his cabin for breakfast. Below, the dining rooms were coming to life, serving breakfast to early passengers keen to go ashore once they had docked.

Bill Martin had now been with the Union Steam Ship Company for some 30 years and master of the *Niagara* for four years. She was the finest ship he had served on and his favourite. He had received his first command in 1917, the 2000-ton coastal vessel *Waipouri,* which was followed over the next nine years with the command of thirteen Union freighters. In 1926 he took over command of his first passenger ship, the *Manuka,* on the Melbourne to Wellington run. From then on through rapid promotion he commanded a number of the company's passenger vessels, including in 1931 the delivery voyage of the new steamer express *Rangitira*.

Martin enjoyed the responsibility of being in command of passenger ships and took a great interest in his passengers and their welfare. It was a far cry from the days of his youth when as a lad from Liverpool he spent seven years under sail as an apprentice seaman and second mate learning the ways of the sea. Now at 59 he prepared for the day and the voyage ahead, including the embarkation of additional passengers. He had a reputation as an amicable captain and was well liked by both passengers and crew. He would later in the morning discuss the list of boarding passengers with his purser, Brian Hurley, a practice he carried out before commencing each voyage. His endeavours to put passengers at ease early in the passage were aided through discussing the passenger list with his purser, which gave him some knowledge of the background of the people travelling on his ship. Often there were repeat passengers whom he would surprise by addressing them by name, with perhaps a comment on some aspect of their background. This approach would greatly assist to alleviate any fears or apprehensions some passengers might have. Others received the captain's comments as a recognition of their status among their fellow passengers – they weren't just a name on a passenger list. Now in time of war there was more need to give reassurance to some passengers that there was little danger from enemy attack while crossing the Pacific.

On the previous voyage from Vancouver, passengers had included Mrs Newcombe with her son and daughter. The family had already experienced the terror of war at sea. Born in Ireland, Mrs Newcombe travelled to Canada where she had met and married her New Zealand-born husband. Later the family decided to settle in New Zealand, but before joining her husband who would travel ahead to the new country, it was decided to take the family on a visit home to Ireland, where she had not returned for 20 years.

The visit was at a time in 1939 when looming war in Europe was accepted as inevitable. Many were desperate to escape Europe and cross the Atlantic to the safety of North America, and this exodus created a demand for passenger berths. The family managed to obtain berths for their return to Canada on the 13,581-ton Cunard passenger liner *Athenia*. The ship sailed with 1418 passengers and crew including evacuees from Liverpool. The large number aboard limited accommodation, so the son

John Asmussen – www.bismark-class.dk

Wissenschaftliches Institut fur Schiffaharts-und Marineschichte

Above: German raider HSK *Orion* – disguised as a freighter, a wolf in sheep's clothing.

Right: Captain Kurt Weyher – Commander of HSK *Orion*.

John Asmussen – www.bismark-class.dk

Otago Settlers Museum

Above: HSK *Orion* – the black raider at dusk.

Left: Captain Coll McDonald, USSCo.

The John Brown Archive at Glasgow University Archive Services by kind permission of the Keeper of Records of Scotland

Above: RMS *Niagara* at J. Brown & Co. shipyards – midships view.

Below: RMS *Niagara* at J. Brown & Co. shipyards – Stern view.

The John Brown Archive at Glasgow University Archive Services by kind permission of the Keeper of Records of Scotland

The John Brown Archive at Glasgow University Archive Services by kind permission of the Keeper of Records of Scotland

Museum of Wellington, City and Sea

Above: RMS *Niagara* undergoing sea trials off Scotland.

Left: RMS *Niagara*. Queen of the Pacific.

Museum of Wellington, City and Sea

Above and Below: Second-class dining saloon.

Museum of Wellington, City and Sea

Museum of Wellington, City and Sea

Museum of Wellington, City and Sea

Above: First-class library.

Left: First-class lounge.

Above: In dry dock – a tight fit.

Below: In dry dock, *Niagara*'s stern view.

Museum of Wellington, City and Sea

Above: *Niagara* farewell – departing No 5 berth Darling harbour on trans Pacific voyage Sydney to Vancouver.

Below: Manly quarantine station, reminder of the 1918 influenza epidemic.

Peter Fields

was separated from his mother and sister in a different area of the ship. On 3 September 1939, the day hostilities broke out between Britain and Germany, the German U-boat *U30* sighted the *Athenia* off the coast of Scotland. Commander Oberleutnant Fritz-Julius Lemp mistakenly identified the unarmed passenger liner as a troopship and attacked with torpedoes. The first ship to fall victim to the Second World War was soon ablaze and sinking. The Newcombe family, who were together for dinner when the torpedoes struck, were fortunate to escape. Not so lucky were 112 souls, including 28 Americans, who went down with the ship.

With memories of the outrage in the United States when US nationals were lost on the *Lusitania* torpedoed in the First World War, Hitler had issued orders for his U-boats not to attack civilian ships, fearing that Americans could be killed. He did not want a repeat performance of the 1915 sinking which brought the US into the war, resulting in the defeat of Germany. Unfortunately in the evening dusk, Lemp had mistaken the identity of the blacked-out passenger vessel and was appalled to learn of his mistake from radio signals transmitted from the stricken ship. The Germans had problems of their own during the attack, when on firing two torpedoes one stuck in the torpedo tube. In danger of the stuck torpedo exploding in its tube, the U-boat crew worked frantically to free it and it was with only seconds to spare that the torpedo was ejected to explode close-by. Captain James Cook, the veteran master of the *Athenia*, and the escaping survivors mistook the explosion for surface gunfire from the U-boat. This assumption later created outrage in the newspapers with headlines that screamed "U-boat fires its guns on defenceless civilians as they scramble into lifeboats". Reporting the incident in such a manner, the newspapers set the tone for coverage of the remainder of the war. Lemp also made a further contribution to the war's history. In command of a new U-boat in 1941, he was forced to abandon it before he could scuttle it. The British captured the vessel along with secret communications equipment that was aboard – the Enigma code machine, which gave the Allies the key to stopping the U-boat threat in the Atlantic.

The rescued Newcombe family with 600 other survivors landed in Galway, Ireland then finally arrived in Canada still wearing the clothes they were rescued in. With assistance from the Red Cross they reached Vancouver and later boarded the *Niagara* for the voyage to New Zealand. The ordeal of the *Athenia* sinking greatly affected Mrs Newcombe.

Although the war had yet to reach the Pacific, the passage on the *Niagara* was a frightening experience for her. Despite reassurances from Captain Martin that the war was far from the Pacific, she was reluctant to go below decks to her cabin. Neither realised that such assurances were to be short-lived.

For trainee seaman Ray Nelson, the approaching city of Auckland heralded a return to his native land. Having previously crossed the line on the *Niagara* to North America, Ray, at the age of 17, now considered himself to be a man of the sea. He reflected on his luck to be able to receive his training on such a fine ship. He had joined the *Niagara* under the sponsorship of Sutherland Ross, a prominent businessman from his hometown of Dunedin. From a young age, Ray had aspired to go to sea despite his mother's wishes for him to attend university. Joining the local Sea Cadet Corps, he gained some knowledge of life at sea under the tuition of naval officers, which further whetted his aspirations. However, his attempt to enlist in the navy was turned down because of his flat feet. In 1938, determined to go to sea, he listed with the local Union Steam Ship Company office. His endeavours were soon rewarded when following an urgent phone call and a fast car ride to Port Chalmers, he signed on the *Kauri* serving the Tasman run. With a young shipmate and a bottle of beer, Ray celebrated his 16th birthday 130 metres above Sydney harbour. The illicit nocturnal climb to the top span of the Harbour Bridge marked him as a lad with a sense of adventure.

For the three Belgian passengers who boarded in Sydney, New Zealand was a far distance from their homes and families. War now threatened their homeland on the far side of the globe, and for Robert Degrave and his two companions, J. Beaurang and J. Leveaux, the approaching city held little interest. The news from Europe was not good – Hitler's army was advancing eastwards across the continent – and the trio were anxious to return to help defend their country. However, travelling first-class with all the pleasures of the onboard social life assisted a little in easing their worries: shipboard incidents and gossip helped bring some humour to their days.

A topic of gossip doing the rounds of the breakfast tables that morning concerned the party held in the captain's cabin the previous evening. It had been rumoured that a fellow passenger, Air Vice-Marshal Stanley Goble from Australia who was en route to Canada to participate in the

Empire pilot training scheme, wore a corset – no doubt so he presented a trim figure in uniform in keeping with the military bearing his high rank demanded. The rumour intrigued a number of young women aboard, who contrived to discover the truth. At the captain's party, they succeeded in disrobing the jovial Air Vice-Marshal and all was revealed: he did indeed wear a corset.

The Guthrie family also enjoyed the comforts of first-class accommodation. Mr Guthrie, accompanied by his wife, daughter and son Walter, was on transfer by his employer Cable & Wireless Ltd to a two-year posting on Fanning Island in the Gilbert and Ellice Islands. Young Wally was excited to be travelling on such a magnificent ship, but the nine-year-old's thoughts often turned to his new bicycle stored with their baggage. He had yet to ride his bike and looked forward to the chance of a ride in Suva when they disembarked.

The First World War-vintage 4-inch gun mounted aft on the roof of the firemen's accommodation was a reminder that, as a British-registered ship, the *Niagara* was now at war and required to defend her passengers and crew. A rather antiquated piece of artillery, the gun had been installed during the previous visit to Sydney. A Royal Navy gunner had been attached to the ship's crew and Ray Nelson, with a limited knowledge on such ordnance from his Sea Cadet days, was assigned to the gun crew as No. 2, the gun trainer. A quick course was held for the gun crew at Rushcutters Bay Naval School: no one now questioned Ray's flat feet.

Unlike the newer quick-firing guns, the *Niagara*'s gun, most probably acquired from a war memorial site, was a breech-loader. This required the cordite charge packed in sacks to be rammed by hand into the gun. In addition to the gun, a battery of depth charges was installed as defence against submarine attack.

Although there had been no incident of enemy action in the Pacific since the beginning of hostilities, the presence of the gun was a reminder to Captain Martin of his duty to protect not only the people who sailed on his ship but also the cargo. Britain's Dominions were coming to the aid of the mother country in its hour of need, sending precious cargoes of much-needed materials and food on long voyages across the globe. Unknown to the majority of the crew, 590 boxes of gold bars weighing two and a half tons were stacked in the ship's bullion room. Loaded secretly in Sydney, the South African gold was destined to pay the US government for urgently needed war materials required by Britain to fight Hitler's advancing forces. In addition to produce, cargo to be uplifted in Auckland included a consignment of small-arms ammunition. Practically half of New Zealand's entire stock was being dispatched to aid the war effort: following the evacuation of troops from Dunkirk, England's stocks of small arms ammunition was low and the consignment would assist with the shortage.

It was the second great conflict in the life of the *Niagara* since her launching in August 1912. Once again she was being called upon to aid in the defence of the land of her birth. As she manoeuvred alongside Queens Wharf that winter's morning, the group of officials and dockworkers muffled against the cold went about their duties preparing for her departure later that evening. The *Niagara* was well-known to the Auckland wharves. In past years her arrivals and departures had been greeted with bands and crowds, and newspapers listed passengers embarking or disembarking and items of interest concerning the voyage. Now, after 25 years of service, other than shipping notices the veteran liner received little attention in the press.

4

The Perfect Ship

It was the gilded age of technological achievement. The arrival of the *Niagara* in Auckland on the morning of 8 May 1913 on her maiden voyage to Vancouver attracted profound interest from both the public and the press. Never had such a mammoth ocean liner voyaged south of the line to Australia and New Zealand. The public was captivated by media descriptions of her many features, especially the luxurious passenger accommodation and amenities.

The citizens of Auckland turned out in large numbers for the vessel's arrival. They gazed in awe at the maritime leviathan as she berthed. Standing well out of the water, the *Niagara* presented a visual impression of great bulk. The excitement of the day was further fuelled by the presence in port of HMS *New Zealand*, the largest warship to have visited. Newspapers lauded the sight of these two magnificent ships together as testimony to Britain's technological prowess.

The tragic loss of the "unsinkable" *Titanic* on her maiden voyage thirteen months previously vividly illustrated the catastrophic results when such technology failed. The Atlantic sinking was still fresh in the public's mind. During her construction on the banks of the Clyde, the *Niagara* had been described in the media as "the *Titanic* of the Pacific". The name that became a synonym for tragedy was quickly discarded after the fateful sinking.

For many of the onlookers, having endured the hardships of a long voyage from Britain and Ireland on crowded immigrant sailing ships, it was difficult to comprehend the opulence provided on such a ship as they now witnessed. The newspapers reported on the elegance of the first-class dining saloon which seated 190 passengers and was decorated in Louis XVI style. There was also a first-class lounge in Louis XVI style, a music room, a library, magnificent promenade decks and even an electric elevator to transport passengers between decks, a feature unheard of in ships serving this part of the world. The *Auckland Star* reported:

> Specially designed for the Canadian-Australian mail line, the *Niagara* is described as a handsome liner, with a remarkable turn of speed. In the planning of the mammoth vessel neither money nor effort seems to have been spared to make her in all respects equal to anything in her class afloat.
>
> Accommodation for 281 first-class passengers is provided amidships, on the main, upper, shelter and promenade decks, the staterooms being fitted for one, two, three, or four passengers, while several groups of cabins have been arranged for family parties. On the shelter and promenade decks there are a number of one and two-berth cabins fitted with bedsteads instead of the ordinary ship's berths. Two cabins deluxe, in every way worthy of the name, are situated on the shelter deck close to the main vestibule. In one of these the style adopted is Adams, with woodwork and furniture painted white, while the metal is electroplated. The other is Louis XIV style, the furniture of walnut. Each of these staterooms has a separate bath and lavatory.
>
> The first-class dining saloon, a spacious apartment, with dining accommodation for 190 passengers, is decorated in Louis XVI style, and the ceiling and walls painted in white. It is situated on the upper deck amidships, convenient to the main entrance and has a large well overhead. A feature of the saloon is that the tables are all arranged for small parties. In the first-class lounge the style adopted is also Louis XVI. It is on the promenade deck, two decks above the dining saloon, and is arranged in small bays and cosy corners. The open well over the dining saloon rises through the centre of the lounge, and is lighted by a large dome on the boat deck. The walls and ceiling are painted white, relieved in gold.
>
> The library and writing room is situated at the fore end of the first-class accommodation on the shelter-deck, and is specially designed for the comfort of passengers who desire to pass the time quietly with

> reading or writing, small tables being arranged well apart from each other. This room is finished in grey and walnut, with mouldings of white and gilt. The style is Louis XVI. The music room situated on the forward end of the promenade deck is in Adams style with white panelling and mahogany furniture. A large dome overhead adds to the splendid appearance of this spacious apartment. The smoke room is also on the promenade deck. The style adopted here is Georgian and the panelling is of polished hardwood. The arrangements of this room are according to the most up-to-date ideas.
>
> Second-class accommodation for 210 passengers is arranged aft, with dining saloon on the upper deck. This apartment, in which dining accommodation for 188 persons has been provided, is decorated in the Georgian style, the furniture being of mahogany, and the walls and ceiling painted white. The style adopted for the music and smoking rooms, which are situated above, is Louis XVI, the former being furnished in mahogany, and here again the walls and ceilings are white, while the smoking room is entirely of oak.
>
> Accommodation for 176 third-class passengers is situated forward, and good public rooms have also been provided. Visitors to the ship will be struck by the very large amount of promenade space allotted to the various classes of passengers. There is a complete system of wireless telegraphy so that the steamer can be in touch with the outside world for practically the whole of the journey.

It was not only the passenger amenities that attracted the interest of the shipping industry. Although the *Niagara* burnt coal on her maiden voyage, the ship's fuel system was to be changed over to oil fuel on her arrival at Vancouver. The *Niagara* was the first vessel burning oil to have a British Board of Trade certificate for the carriage of passengers, creating wide interest for this new technology that was expected to greatly decrease operational costs. The *Auckland Star* reported:

> For the new feature of carrying oil fuel, the ship has specially constructed bunkers of ample capacity to carry sufficient oil for the return journey, and also to carry coal should this be found necessary. The whole of the bunkers, Nos. 2 and 3 holds have been made air and oil-tight up to the main deck. Heavy fore and aft bulkheads are fitted throughout, adding strength to the ship and ensuring safety.
>
> Four electric engines are fitted to cope with the exceptionally

> complete system of lighting, etc., and, to render it unlikely that any hitch will result in a breakdown, an emergency plant for light has also been arranged on the boat deck, so that in case of accident, light will always be maintained. Altogether there are over 2000 lights throughout the ship, while an electric fan is fitted in each stateroom. The hydraulic engine installed in the engine room is capable of putting the whole of the ten hoists through a complete cycle within the space of one minute.
>
> From this feat alone it may be gathered how powerful the installation is; the engine in fact, is one of the largest and most powerful ever put into cargo-dispatching purposes. The steering gear is of the hydraulic type, embodying all the latest improvements.

The politicians and business community embraced the arrival of the new technology for different reasons, although they welcomed the luxury and comfort now offered for overseas travel. In an editorial, the *Auckland Star* extolled the patriotic and trade values the new vessel brought to the country's shores:

> The arrival of the Niagara in our harbour marks the initiation of a new epoch in the growth of New Zealand's trans-oceanic trade. It is a source of natural satisfaction to us that this great steamer, the largest and best-appointed and most up-to-date passenger boat that has yet visited Australasian ports, has been built by a New Zealand company, and once more we have to congratulate Sir John Mills upon the energy and enterprise that has become a feature of USSCo policy.
>
> The *Niagara* is a vessel that its owners and the people of New Zealand may well take pride in, and the very large complement of passengers that she is carrying on her first voyage indicates that she will do a great deal to popularise the Vancouver route as a speedy and comfortable road to England and Europe. But the *Niagara*, with her huge carrying capacity, is far more than a handsome and luxurious ocean ferryboat. She cannot fail to encourage trade between New Zealand and Canada, and we believe that there are very great possibilities of commercial expansion for us in this direction.
>
> We have frequently drawn attention to the magnitude of Canada's industrial development, and the rapidity of her progress, and it is manifestly to our interest to encourage in every way the growth of a close commercial connection between the two Dominions. The

> establishment of the Vancouver service was obviously an important step in this direction. And the *Niagara*, while promoting this closer association of material interests, will inevitably aid in the great work of consolidating the Empire, which all true Imperialists have at heart.
>
> It is no more a figure of speech to assert that the "All Red" line, so often discussed, if it were realised in fact, in the form originally suggested by Sir Wilfrid Laurier and Sir Joseph Ward, would be one of the greatest of all our Imperial assets, and the *Niagara* marks a further advance toward the point at which this "dream of Empire" will become a reality.

To commemorate the closer ties with Canada, it had been intended that the new ship would be named *Ottawa*, but when it was discovered this name was unavailable, the name *Sicamous* was chosen. Ships were often given nicknames – for example, the company ship RMS *Miowera* was known as "Weary Mary" – and when it was pointed out that the chosen name was open to misnomers such as "Sick Mouse", a name change to *Niagara* was decided at the last minute.

Captain John Gibb, commodore of the Union Company fleet and near retirement, considered command of the *Niagara* on her maiden voyage to be the culmination of his career at sea. The attention his ship received on arrival in Sydney and Auckland was most pleasing – especially the recognition he received as master of such a large vessel. He would command one return trip to Vancouver before being replaced by Captain John Rolls, who would also take over as commander of the fleet.

The delivery voyage from Clyde was not an easy one for Mary Scott. The chief stewardess recorded her feelings to Robert Noble in a series of love letters. The couple had became acquainted as shipmates while working for the Anchor Line Steamship Company of Glasgow, making runs between Glasgow, Londonderry, Ireland and New York. They fell in love, but Robert left the company to join the Panama Canal Steamship Company in late 1910. Three years later, Mary still wrote affectionate letters to him sharing her intimate plans and writing him love poems. In 1913 she decided to change companies, joining the Union Steam Ship Company and sailing for Australia on the *Niagara*'s maiden voyage. She left two sons behind after a painful parting, but was full of hope for a new future in Australia, where she had wealthy cousins in Melbourne.

In a letter written to Robert on 1 April 1913 while aboard the *Niagara* off Port Elizabeth, South Africa, she expressed her feelings on leaving her two boys behind:

> I hear it [Australia] is a lovely country. Everybody you hear speak, and they tell me I will never want to leave it. However, time will tell. Should I not like it I will stay, say, for three years and come back if God spares me, and my boys are good and steady I wont need to go to sea. It was a terrible parting with boys and, believe me, I have a good cry every day some part or other. I must work my finger ends off to get them out soon . . . Well! I cannot say yet that I rejoice at change of Company . . . However, I must make the best of it now – It was for my boys sake that I have done it & I believe it will be all right in the end . . .

Mary posted her letter from Durban when the ship made a port of call on 3 April. According to her letter she liked the ship itself, if not the workload, and Captain Gibb seemed to have plans to bring her out of the lower decks, making life a bit easier for her on the voyage:

> The ship herself is certainly a marvel. My room is just lovely and every comfort and convenience, but away from my passengers. Captain Gibb has condemned it and says a room has to be got ready on promenade deck for Sydney for 'Chief Stewardess' (That's me).

Mary struggled to keep up with her duties, having to climb several decks to service her passengers. The chief steward would not allow her to use the elevator because there were so few paying passengers; the majority were Union Steam Ship employee families. As a result, Mary was always tired and very unhappy. She missed home and she missed Robert:

> I feel very, very miserable and unhappy, Bob. Sleep and I are strangers now, and I feel just worn out. Am doing work of three stewardesses which is very hard. And the lifts are not working until we get to Sydney. Will we ever meet again Bob? I can't think that we won't.

After refuelling, the *Niagara* sailed from Durban on 6 April for Sydney via Melbourne. On arrival in Melbourne, Councillor J. Samuel Johnson, a prominent member of the community and Mayor of Footscray in 1912, came aboard to meet Mary and take her home. He assured her that he would see to the boys when they were ready to come to Australia.

On reaching Sydney and learning that the *Niagara* was to be used on the Vancouver service, Mary decided that this would be too long a run so she volunteered to serve aboard an inter-colonial run across the Tasman and on coastal routes. Now with the arrival of the *Niagara* in Auckland, Mary looked to a new future, although she was sad it would be without her beloved Bob, now working on passenger liner services between New York and Panama. She later ended a poignant letter to him expressing her sadness with a poem:

'Tis hard to say "Goodbye"
'Tis a word that causes pain,
But as the years go by,
Perhaps we'll meet again.
And if we never meet again,
I hope you won't forget
To often cast one little thought
To one who loves you yet.

Captain Coll McDonald received the accolades that were bestowed on the new vessel and read the glowing newspaper reports with satisfaction. For this was his ship, the perfect ship, the accumulation of his ship-design skills and seafarer's knowledge. A quiet, unassuming person, he had been appointed to the position of the Union Steam Ship Company's assistant marine superintendent in 1908. Born the son of crofters on the island of Mull in Scotland, he began working for a farmer at the age of nine, and never attended school during his boyhood. At the age of twelve he was working long hours for an engineering firm at Oban, followed by a period of engineering training at Glasgow. At sixteen he went to sea and later settled in Dunedin. Joining the Union Steam Ship Company in 1885, he studied hard over the years, making up for his past lack of education. Passing examinations and rising through the ranks, he finally gained his first permanent command in 1897. The following years saw McDonald command 23 Company ships, during which period he studied their good and bad design aspects. His knowledge of ship design attracted the attention of the directors at a time when the Company was entering a period of major expansion. In 1910 he was sent off to the Clyde shipyards where he was to exercise his creative flair in overseeing the construction of the *Wahine* and *Niagara*.

McDonald was aware of the important role the new passenger liner was to play in the Union Company's expansion of the All Red route (a fast steamer and train service between London, Halifax, Vancouver and Auckland), spending long hours on planning the details he required to make her the perfect ship. John Brown and Company had been contracted to build the new liner on the banks of the Clyde, the birthplace of many famous ships. During the *Niagara*'s construction, the *Titanic* was launched from Harland & Wolff shipbuilders in nearby Belfast. Then followed sea trials and her commissioning leading up to the fateful maiden voyage. Coll, who took a great interest in the safety aspects of ship design, applauded the announcement to build the unsinkable *Titanic*. The loss of the great ship on her maiden voyage four months before the *Niagara*'s launching was a disaster that remained deeply ingrained in his thoughts. He was determined that he would put his spare time to the design of an unsinkable ship and later patented a design for a "cellular" ship which entailed construction of a hull within a hull – similar to modern tanker design.

However, the *Niagara* was Coll McDonald's ship of the day and a monument to the skills of a man born in the crofts of Argyllshire who, without a formal education, went on to design the "perfect ship".

5

Pacific Service

The introduction of the *Niagara* on the Pacific service was soon gaining plaudits for a fast, efficient service. The coal-burning furnaces fitted during construction had given the ship a speed of eighteen knots during her trials on the Clyde. On arrival in Vancouver these were replaced with oil-burning furnaces, resulting in an improvement to her performance. The benefits of the change from coal to oil were demonstrated on the voyage from Vancouver in August 1913 when the new liner arrived in Auckland twelve hours ahead of schedule with only eight of the ten boilers used throughout the voyage. With fine weather forecast for the sector from Suva, Captain Morrisby decided to reach Auckland ahead of contract time and ordered full speed under eight boilers. Logging 17.5 knots for the 1140 nautical miles from Suva, the early arrival with 443 passengers on board was greeted as a milestone in the Dominion's communications with the outside world. Morrisby informed the press that had all ten boilers been used, the ship would easily have attained nineteen knots, resulting in an even earlier arrival.

Mail from Europe, America and Canada landed in Auckland, enabling express train for southern towns to reach their destination a day earlier than normal. Passengers who had experienced a smooth voyage in fine weather praised the comfort and service that set new standards for passenger travel. For the directors and accountants of the Union Steam Ship Company, the financial results of the voyage were a pleasing confirmation of the advantages of oil fuel over coal, and the accolades confirmed that they now operated the finest passenger steamer in the Pacific.

Fitted with fourteen oil reservoirs, the *Niagara* had a total fuel capacity of over 5000 tons. For this voyage she had taken on 4200 tons of oil at Vancouver, sufficient for the voyage to Sydney and return. An additional supply of 200 tons was uplifted at Honolulu on both the outward and return sectors. Her oil consumption was around 90 tons every 24 hours, compared with around 160 tons of coal for the same duration. With the cost of oil at 19 shillings per ton, and coal at 16 shillings per ton in Vancouver, the direct saving in the cost of fuel for the voyage was approximately 27 per cent.

The engineers accepted the change to oil as a definite improvement to their working conditions. Charlie McLean, an engineer from Glasgow who joined the *Niagara* for her maiden voyage, found the transition from working in the grime of coal-fired engine rooms a blessing. The stokehold was now one of the cleanest parts of the ship and wonderfully cool.

For the merchants, the inaugural service heralded new prospects for trade. The *Niagara* left Vancouver with full cargo holds containing some 3600 tons of produce, the largest cargo ever to have left that port by steamer. Included were 3600 cases of apples; agriculture machinery; motor-cars; 5000 bundles of laths; drugs; dental supplies; organs; cash registers; and other sundries including 1000 bunches of bananas from Fiji. Some 1000 tons destined for the markets of a growing nation were unloaded in Auckland, and a further 2600 tons for Australian distribution remained on board for the final sector across the Tasman.

Coll McDonald remained on in Glasgow to oversee the planning of a second *Niagara*, named *Aotearoa*. The Company board was most gratified with the service and performance of their new vessels *Niagara* and *Wahine*, the latter having also been introduced into service at this time. Coll received acknowledgment from the directors of their recognition of his valuable work in the design and construction of these fine ships. It was intimated, along with a commendatory resolution from the board, that he would be awarded a substantial bonus for his efforts.

On the outbreak of World War One in 1914, the *Aotearoa* was still in the builder's yard undergoing fitting out, which curtailed any plans for the new ship to joining *Niagara* on the Pacific service. When she was launched, she was requisitioned by the Admiralty, armed and renamed HMS *Avenger*. But her life ended when a German torpedo sank her in 1917.

One reported incident involved the *Avenger*. When on patrol, a disguised German raider, the *Wolf*, came under her guns for two days. The raider, armed with one 6-inch gun, two other large guns, four 4.7-inch guns, an anti-aircraft gun, two large and two small torpedo tubes and a seaplane, completely hoodwinked the unsuspecting British. Allowed to proceed into the Atlantic, the *Wolf* slipped around the Cape of Good Hope into the Indian Ocean where she sank several vessels before reaching the South Pacific mid-1917.

The *Wolf* became a threat to Pacific shipping, laying at least two minefields off the coast of New Zealand. The *Port Kembla*, en route from Melbourne to Wellington, sailed into one minefield positioned off Farewell Spit, the northern tip of the South Island. A mine explosion ripped through the forward hold, sinking the ship within half an hour. Nine months later, the *Wimmera*, bound for Sydney, struck a mine eighteen miles north of Cape Maria Van Diemen sinking the ship with a loss of 26 lives. Using the Kermadec islands as a base, the *Wolf* with her crew of 400 prowled the Pacific shipping lanes north of New Zealand seeking prey. The German raider sought the *Niagara* with the aid of her seaplane. The patrolling aircraft on one occasion did sight the elusive prey, but the *Wolf*, capable of only 10 knots, was easily outrun by the *Niagara*.

Even the centre propeller failures experienced during 1915 would not hinder the liner from outrunning the Germans. Crossing the Tasman from Sydney in March, a blade from the three-bladed centre propeller failed and was lost. It was a tight squeeze with only inches to spare to fit the ship into Auckland's Calliope dry dock for replacement of the damaged propeller. In May, two days after leaving Auckland for Suva, the replacement propeller, having completed little more than one round trip, also shed a blade. The blade loss caused severe vibration for some seconds until the engineers shut down the low-pressure turbine driving the centre propeller. Operating with only the two wing propellers, the ship continued on to Vancouver, maintaining an average speed of 16 knots even with the drag from the now-stationary propeller. On arrival, divers unfastened the defective propeller and hoisted it aboard for the return trip. The removal did not improve the speed on the southbound voyage, but the ship, more deeply laden with cargo and fuel, still maintained the timetable for the trip.

It was discovered that the three-bladed centre propeller set up excessive vibrations which caused stresses on the stern and rudder posts, shell riveting and other components, resulting in costly repairs when in dock. Replacement with a four-bladed propeller greatly reduced these costs and also overcame excessive pitting of the centre tail-shaft liner. Fitting the replacement propeller reduced turbine revolutions by 15 rpm.

With the ending of hostilities in 1918, large numbers of military personnel were returning to Australia and New Zealand, some on troopships, others as passengers on regular steamship services. At the time of the *Niagara*'s departure from Vancouver in September, North America was in the grip of an outbreak of influenza that was sweeping through Europe. This deadly virus, named "Spanish Flu" by the media, was ultimately the cause of some fifteen million people worldwide losing their lives. Transported across the Atlantic by troops returning from the battlefields of Europe, the disease, one of the worst outbreaks for centuries, killed half a million people in the United States.

Within three days of the *Niagara* departing Vancouver, passengers and crew reported sick with fever and accompanying headaches. First a bellboy succumbed, then the illness quickly struck others aboard. By the time of arrival at Suva on 9 October, 83 were sick. The ship's doctor, Arthur Latchmore, realised he had a major problem on his hands and not just an outbreak of dengue fever as he had first thought. The Fiji authorities refused to allow any disembarkation, except for two persons only, and placed the ship under quarantine until departure.

Approaching New Zealand, the *Niagara* signalled the USSCo office about the influenza outbreak onboard. The office in turn, notifying the Naval Intelligence Office in Wellington, requested urgent medical assistance and hospital accommodation for the ship's arrival.

Among the *Niagara*'s passengers arriving in Auckland on 12 October were William Massey, Prime Minister of New Zealand, and his Minister of Finance, Sir Joseph Ward. Returning from an Imperial conference in London, both prominent passengers had symptoms of the influenza outbreak and were keen to disembark. With pressure not to delay the Ministers, a decision was made not to place the ship under quarantine restrictions.

The Minister of Health was advised that there were 101 sick passengers and crew on board, 26 of whom would require hospitalisation. He therefore instructed the port authority that clearance of the ship was not permitted until he gave instructions to do so. A telegram sent to the ship requested confirmation of the number of deaths onboard, if any, since the ship had left Vancouver and, whether the epidemic was, or was not pure influenza. In answer, the Minister received a reply that one death had occurred from bronchial pneumonia and only two passengers for New Zealand were down with the influenza.

Whether the Minister's account of what transpired was factual, or if indeed the *Niagara* was instrumental in introducing a deadly epidemic into New Zealand, has never been proven. The authorities, acting under the pressure of having important personages aboard, would have been influenced not to place the ship under quarantine. In fact, due to the large number of sick people aboard, the entire ship's complement should have been placed under strict quarantine. The Minister later stated that he had informed the Governor-General of the situation, and that quarantine of the ship and her entire complement was discussed. Consideration of the repercussions resulting from such action indicated there would be great difficulty in preventing the Australian authorities from declaring New Zealand an infected country. This would then result in all ships sailing from New Zealand being declared infected. With the danger of such a declaration causing all shipping to cease, quarantine measures were not imposed.

History has often blamed the *Niagara* for the introduction of Spanish flu into New Zealand. With a large proportion of the country's doctors and nurses still overseas, compounded by the low resistance of servicemen returning from the war, the influenza epidemic swept rapidly throughout the country at an alarming rate. In only eight weeks, 1860 people died.

More than 6500 people are recorded to have succumbed from the disease or its complications; Auckland alone had 2000 deaths recorded. Massey and Ward were openly accused of allowing the spread of the disease from the *Niagara*. However it is debatable if the ship did play such a major role as her accusers implied. The politicians and passengers landed in mid-October, and reports in a medical journal for that month stated there was evidence the disease had been in the country for at least two months before that. Before disembarking in Auckland, the *Niagara* passengers had treatment in a chamber for the inhalation of various antiseptics. Further, as the disease had been present since August, Massey and Ward could not be justly accused as being responsible for the introduction in October.

The Union Steam Ship Company vessel *Tulane*, which sailed the Pacific Islands route, was also in Auckland and tied up alongside the *Niagara* on 21 October, the day after the liner's arrival. On the 22nd, the *Tulane* sailed for the South Island port of Lyttelton, then returned to Auckland before departing on 30 October for Fiji and Samoa. On the voyage south there was sickness among the crew, and on return, before leaving Auckland, two crew members diagnosed as having flue symptoms were replaced. On arrival at Suva, there were further cases of influenza among the crew and passengers; the vessel was placed under quarantine restrictions while Fijians unloaded cargo.

The vessel sailed for the Fiji port of Levuka where it was not quarantined, then departed with a clean bill of health for Samoa on 5 November. At the time influenza was not a notifiable disease and when the ship arrived in Apia, the unsuspecting New Zealand administration permitted crew and passengers ashore, even though some were suffering from sickness. The epidemic that followed swept through the Western Samoan islands causing a large death toll. This tragedy was to have repercussions for years to come with relationships between Samoa and New Zealand. It was not until 2002 that the New Zealand Prime Minister, Helen Clark, made an official apology to the Samoan people for the administration not placing the *Tulane* under quarantine on her arrival at Apia. Some have laid the blame for the Samoan epidemic on the *Niagara*, but as the sickness was in New Zealand before her October arrival, and also in Fiji when the *Tulane* transited en route to Samoa, this accusation is incorrect.

One voice at the time refuting reports blaming the *Niagara* for the outbreak of the disease in New Zealand was that of Dr Metcalfe Sharp, who had been placed in charge of the stricken vessel after her arrival in Auckland and had then travelled with the ship to Sydney. Upon the vessel's arrival, the Australian authorities had no hesitation with placing both passengers and crew in quarantine at the Manly quarantine station. The trans-Tasman crossing and subsequent incarceration with the ship's complement presented Sharp with an exceptional opportunity to study the sickness. In an interview with the *Evening Star*, Sharp stated that it was beyond doubt there were severe cases of the influenza in Auckland before the *Niagara* docked from North America. Having been placed in charge after the arrival, he instigated drastic measures to fight the disease on board – including strict isolation and fumigation procedures. These actions prevented the further spread of the epidemic during the ten days while the ship was in port. Asked what he considered the most effective method of preventing the disease to be, Sharp replied that pending the discovery of an antitoxin, he thought that two per cent of sulphate of zinc in a steam inhalation was the best, followed by the moderate use of proof spirit as a gargle. He added that he personally considered alcohol as a powerful antiseptic: when exposed to infection in the confines of ships' cabins, he took no other precautions than the use of spirits and declared he had been immune to the disease. He admitted, however, that the habitual heavy drinker was the more serious case when stricken by the disease than the abstainer or teetotaller, but in his opinion and from experience, the abstainer was more readily susceptible to the disease.

It is not recorded if the consumption of alcohol increased for the Auckland return voyage to Sydney or while the ship was under quarantine there. But no doubt the good Dr Sharp with his theory would have been instrumental in ensuring that it was well above the norm for crossing the Tasman. It is recorded that the *Niagara* returned to Auckland free of the virus, a "clean ship."

A record of this sombre episode in the *Niagara*'s long history of serving the Dominion remains visible to this day. Carved in a rock face near the wharf at Manly where the ship was held in quarantine is a ship's flag with the inscription, *R.M.S. Niagara, Influenza Oct.1918*.

Isolated by oceans, both Australia and New Zealand were susceptible to the outbreak of epidemics introduced by crew and passengers on ships arriving from afar. Unless strict quarantine measures were taken on the arrival of ships with sickness aboard, an epidemic could quickly spread to the local populace, often with devastating results. The *Niagara* was again caught up with the imposition of quarantine measures in 1921. This time smallpox was the culprit and once more crew and passengers found themselves the guests of Sydney's Manly quarantine station.

The 1920s and 30s were for many a time for travel. The attraction of a sea voyage on the new passenger ships attracted the adventurous to set out from the Antipodes and explore the world. Travel by sea was an enjoyable leisurely experience for passengers and a major feature of their travels abroad. The Pacific voyage to North America was a popular route and the *Niagara* was favoured for her elegance and service. The emancipation of women was now well established in Britain's former colonies of Australia and New Zealand and many young ladies travelled on the ocean liners in search of adventure and romance. It was also an era of opulent travel for the rich. Travelling in first-class splendour, they were feted by captain and crew with social events, champagne, sumptuous banquets and continuous entertainment. Chaperoned young ladies danced the Charleston to the lively ship's orchestras while their dashing young escorts lived the post-war years travelling the world in style.

The times were also an era of immigration where numerous young people left the harshness of industrial cities travelling third-class to seek a better life in the Dominions. In her youthful years the *Niagara* became known as the Queen of the Pacific and her regular sailings were always heavily booked. For a period of over thirteen years, the liner operated without an overhaul, maintaining regular on-time sailing schedules. In 1925 the newly launched 17,491-ton liner *Aorangi* joined the *Niagara* on the Pacific service. In 1931, to counter competition from the American owned Matson Line, the Union Steam Ship Company joined the Canadian Pacific Railway Company in a joint venture to form the Canadian Australasian Line. The *Niagara* and *Aorangi* were transferred to sail under the flag of the new operation.

Occasional incidents on the Pacific crossings created diversions both pleasant and unpleasant for crew and passengers. On the evening of 17 July 1935, the *Niagara* departed Victoria under the command of Captain T. E. Hill. Sailing in a heavy fog, the ship proceeded cautiously down the Straits of Juan de Fuca towards the Pacific Ocean. The passengers, including Joe Lyons, the Prime Minister of Australia, settled down for a relaxing evening. With the damp foggy conditions the decks were deserted, and many passengers were seated enjoying a movie.

Soon after 8pm, when approximately 40 miles off Victoria, the startled bridge watch stared in horror as a vessel emerged out of the fog on a collision course with their own ship. There was no time for either crew to take avoiding action and the two vessels struck bow-on. The sudden jolt, accompanied by the sound of tearing metal, brought passengers and crew rushing onto the fog shrouded decks.

The 4535-ton King Line motor vessel *King Egbert* had sliced into the *Niagara*'s port bow. Forty feet of the C-deck port bow railing and ten feet of superstructure on B-deck had been shorn away. An inspection revealed that only three hull plates had buckled above the water line, far less damage than at first feared. Designer Coll McDonald's "perfect ship" had survived the collision in far better shape than the *King Egbert*. The bow of the motor ship had smashed inwards. Shell plating from the forefoot to the main deck was crushed and distorted back to the collision bulkhead. The hawser pipes and anchors were gone, carried away in the wreckage from the demolished forecastle. With his ship in danger of settling by the head, Captain Paul Graine ordered ballast water pumped aft.

On the *Niagara*, Captain Hill and his crew calmed the shaken passengers crowding the misty decks. Reassured there was no danger from sinking, they returned to resume watching the movie. A dance followed, hastily organised to keep the passengers occupied as the ship slowly returned through the fog to port. The hearing on the cause of the accident was held in private and found that the collision was unavoidable with neither captain to blame.

In 1937 the *Niagara* diverted from her route to accomplish two missions of mercy. Sailing north to America, a radio call received from the steam yacht *Viking* requested medical assistance. The two vessels rendezvoused to enable the transfer of a nurse and a Melbourne eye specialist to assist the American millionaire, George Baker, who had been suddenly stricken with peritonitis. A few weeks later on her return passage south, she was called upon to rescue a shipwrecked crew from an island in the Phoenix group. Passengers accepted such diversions as part of the adventure of sailing the Pacific.

Voyages across the Pacific are not always the smooth crossings the ocean's name belies. Powerful storms generated in the North Pacific and cyclones in the tropic regions have caused the demise of many ships. The *Niagara* ran into such a storm in January 1936 while en route from Vancouver to Honolulu with Captain Martin in command.

The storm was one of the worst experiences in the steamer's history, causing anxiety to both crew and passengers. For two days the ship battered terrific seas whipped up by 80 mph gale winds. Seas swept the ship from stem to stern, smashing two lifeboats which had to be dumped at sea. The tempest twisted railings like rope, snapped forward ventilators and even a hydraulic winch from their mountings. With the seas sweeping over her, the ship hove to for twelve hours. All vestibule doors were locked and passengers were ordered to keep below decks. In an effort to break the force of the sea, the crew poured a mixture of crude and fish oils through the Third Class bathrooms and crew forward lavatories on D-deck; and Captain Martin ordered the forward tanks to be pumped dry to provide additional forward buoyancy. These actions had an appreciable effect in lessening the force of the storm's onslaught.

Around mid-afternoon, the bridge crew was startled to see a wall of water, rising higher than an imaginary horizontal line from the upper portion of the crow's-nest, racing towards them. They braced for the impact as the liquid wall towered above, its apex crowned by a curling white crest. The monstrous wave swept across the vessel with a force that smashed in doors and windows. A considerable volume of water poured down the passageways and into cabins. The old ship, in a very heavy state, shuddered with the impact and sluggishly climbed the mountain of water to face the next onslaught. The *Niagara* survived the tempest in what was later described as "a splendid manner" to finally arrive at Auckland with gaps in her railings and davits empty of lifeboats – a testimony to the battle she had fought with the forces of nature.

By 1939 the veteran liner was beginning to show signs of her age and the storms she had endured. Five return voyages a year from Sydney to Vancouver, each a distance of some 16,000 miles, had taken their toll.

Fresh off diesel-engine ships, 29-year-old Robert Birks noted the signs of wear and tear when he signed on as the ship's fourth engineer. He had qualified for a steam endorsement on his engineer's ticket and was in the process of obtaining a full steam engineer's qualification. Eventually he would become the youngest company engineer with a "double header" qualification on both external and internal combustion engines. He found a cool welcome from the other engineering officers. The older steam engineers resented the intrusion of diesel men into what they regarded as their exclusive domain. The end of the steam engine era was evident and the steam men were fighting the inevitable. It was difficult for them to tolerate the arrival of the diesel man and they showed this by treating Bob with disdain, speaking to him only when required.

As fourth engineer he was responsible for the port engine. He was appalled by the state of the machinery placed under his care. The lack of maintenance was evident to Bob, who considered the condition of the machinery an absolute disgrace. Part of the problem was soon obvious.

The Chief Engineer had been nicknamed "Whiskey Nose" by the crew. The man had a permanent pink nose caused by the booze he consumed. This drinking problem in turn contributed to the poor state of the ship's engines.

The triple-expansion engines, known as four-legged triples, were configured with two small low-pressure cylinders at each end rather then the usual single large low-pressure cylinder. Steam, fed from the high-pressure cylinder through the intermediate pressure cylinder, was directed into the low-pressure cylinders at a pressure of 27 psi (pounds per square inch). This steam pressure, when exhausted from the low-pressure cylinders, was directed through a change valve where it was relieved to a reduced pressure of 9 psi. This reduced steam pressure powered the Parsons steam turbine engine driving the smaller central propeller. The *Titanic*, built in the same era, had a similar engine configuration, only much larger.

To the engineers, steam engines with the noise of their valve gear operating on the Stevenson link-motion principle were known as "clinkers". They are relatively quiet in operation – producing a constant "thumpity-thumpity" noise. However, Bob discovered that the *Niagara*'s engines instead produced a constant "bang-bang" noise with each of the four reciprocating strokes. It was clear to him that there was a problem with the engine eccentrics being excessively loaded under high pressure. Removing the cover from the change valve, he discovered that the packing on the slide valve, sealing the higher steam pressure, had practically disappeared. This allowed the full pressure force to act on the machinery instead of the intended lower steam pressure.

The old steam hands, annoyed at a diesel man poking his nose into what they considered their domain, told Bob to mind his own business. Concerned about the constant load on his engine, he warned Whiskey Nose that something would eventually fail. His warning was ignored.

The ship continued her Pacific crossing, the thousands of engine revolutions creating a constant hammering protest. Finally, under the constant abuse the operating rod to the change valve tore apart, the result of both negligence and poor maintenance.

It was to be engineer Birks' last trip on the ship. In Vancouver, a fortune-teller informed him that he would not return to that city on the *Niagara*. At the time Bob was not to know that upon his arrival back in Sydney in February 1940 he would be transferred to another ship. Nor did the fortune-teller predict that the ship he was leaving would make only one more visit to the Canadian port.

The following month an astrologer predicted events that would befall the Canada-Australia shipping service. In a letter to a Canadian newspaper, a Mr F. Hathaway, through what he termed his researches in "astro-cosmic sciences", predicted that "Another disaster at sea is shown in the Pacific . . . This aspect falls on the Canadian-Australian shipping lane and threatens a British vessel trading between Australia and Canada . . . This will most likely be the first major Pacific sinking." Both predictions were soon to come true.

6

Midnight Departure

Darkness enveloped the Auckland waterfront early on the winter's evening. Lights reflected down from the ocean liner and danced across the harbour's oily surface, throwing patterns of moving light across the *Niagara*'s dark green hull. Lights shone down on the foredeck illuminating the activity associated with final preparations before releasing the ship from her day's bondage.

Since her arrival in the early hours of that morning, loading of cargo and passengers' effects had continued throughout the day. The large consignment of small-arms ammunition was loaded into the holds. The Germans had occupied Paris and Allied troops were undergoing evacuation from the beaches of Dunkirk. Britain was on her own and the Dominions were rallying to the aid of the motherland. Answering the call to arms, others from New Zealand were joining those from Sydney en route to the conflict. A Canadian, Mr E. Campbell, had enjoyed his ten months working in New Zealand as a painter but was now returning to Vancouver to farewell his family and betrothed before joining the Canadian forces.

James Daly from Sydney, assigned to the position of gunner on the *Niagara*, had already had his share of action in this war. He had been the gunner on the *Tairoa*, a merchant ship sunk in the Atlantic by the German battleship *Admiral Graf Spee*. Then followed seven weeks as a prisoner on the German prison ship *Altmark* before being rescued. Now in charge of the *Niagara*'s gun and crew, Daly was looking forward to the relative peace of sailing the trans-Pacific route.

Unknown to the passengers and majority of the crew, the *Niagara* carried another consignment to support Britain's fight for survival. On D-deck, packed into the strongroom alongside the Chief Purser's office, were 295 wooden boxes. Each box contained two bars of gold, each weighing some 400 ounces (12.44 kilograms), a total consignment of over eight tons of gold bullion.

In time of war, gold assumes a greater importance than in peacetime. As an accepted means for payment of debts and with a high value in relation to mass and weight, gold provides a relatively easy transferable means for payment between countries for war materials. With the outbreak of hostilities with Germany, the Commonwealth Bank of Australia controlled all gold resources in that country. Such controls required individuals in possession of the metal to deliver it to the Bank. In return, the Bank paid at a fixed price based on the London and US value, less shipping and insurance costs. This price was in the region of ten pounds ten shillings an ounce.

The USA, although it had not yet entered the war, supplied the majority of war material requirements for the British Empire. To support Britain's payments for these materials, the Commonwealth Bank shipped gold across the Pacific to America: the lend-lease arrangement between the United States and Britain had not yet been established. Gold shipments were made every four weeks on average and, with the constraints on wartime shipping, consignments were larger than the normal peacetime shipments. The gold shipment on this voyage, valued at £2.5 million sterling, had originated from South Africa. The *Niagara* had previously played a wartime role in moving gold to North America. On two previous voyages, the Commonwealth Bank consigned two shipments on behalf of the Bank of England, each valued at £2 million.

With the late-evening departure, many of the 136 passengers, including a number of young children, retired to their cabins following dinner. Others enjoyed an after-dinner drink and the camaraderie of fellow passengers in the well-appointed passenger lounges. Music from the ship's four-man band led by Patrick Watters provided the evening entertainment. Pat and pianist Denis Morgan had been with the band for two years. It was a good job for the young musicians with plenty of free time in the ports they visited while voyaging across the Pacific.

They needed to be versatile and played more than one instrument – Pat played both the clarinet and saxophone. Music ranged from classical at mealtimes to dance and jazz in the evening. Most passengers loved to dance, which helped in contributing to a relaxed and pleasant voyage.

With the small number of passengers on this voyage (the ship could accommodate 590 passengers), many of the 202 crew were either not required or on light duties. For the three stewardesses, the main priority was attending to the needs of the women and children aboard. Miss Herring had now served on the *Niagara* for fifteen years and Mrs McMahon for fourteen. To these women, the ship was another home and, unlike the homesick stewardess Mary Scott on the 1913 delivery voyage, one to which they had become attached.

For another member of the crew, the ship was a permanent home. The sea was in his blood. His mother had lived on the *Niagara* before him and his father, an aristocratic Persian, was owned by a waterfront police officer at Vancouver. Aussie the ship's cat was born at Suva and knew all the ports on the Sydney to Vancouver run. He had explored the Sydney waterfront during his five years as a member of the ship's crew and on two occasions might have missed sailing time had he not been found by his shipmates. On one occasion, crew picked Aussie up on the steps of the Chief Post Office, and on the other they found him ambling along one of the main streets.

Passengers considered Aussie a little standoffish, as his high-strung temperament did not always endear him to them. However, the crew recognised his worth as a rat-catcher, and he fully earned his regular meals of milk and rabbits' legs in the morning and steak in the afternoon. His owner Robby Burns, the providore-storekeeper on the ship, ensured Aussie, who turned up regularly for his meals, was supplied with his daily rations.

Passengers joining the *Niagara* in Auckland spent the afternoon farewelling family and friends or settling into accommodation and exploring the ship. To four-year-old Master Keegan, it was an awesome experience. He sat spellbound in their first-class cabin as Miss Charlton arranged farewell flowers into a vase. She had noticed a number of young children on board and was confident that Louis would soon be occupied with newfound friends.

Further forward, in the more pretentious surroundings of a third-class cabin, Mr Lum Ah Wing tried to settle his four young boys down for the next stage of their journey from Sydney to Suva. Although adequate, a third-class cabin was hardly the place to confine four young boys for any length of time and their mother, Choy Lim, would be happy when they finally reached their destination.

The Poll Tax introduced by the New Zealand government in 1881 was still in place and reflected the attitudes that the Chinese still had to face. The tax, requiring each Chinese immigrant to pay £100, had been legislated to make it as difficult as possible for Chinese to come to New Zealand. Attitudes to the Chinese had slowly changed, but the tax had caused past hardships for many Chinese families trying to settle in the country. With such European attitudes, to be Chinese travelling in these times on a passenger liner catering for European tastes and culture did not make for a pleasurable voyage. Choy Lim was grateful to have the company of three other Chinese female passengers in third class.

At the scheduled departure time of 2330 hours, the liner slipped her moorings. Absent was the fanfare of early years when her arrivals and departures were greeted by excited crowds and brass bands. With the exception of essential duty crew and a few remaining late-night revellers, the decks and lounges were practically deserted. The majority of passengers, having dined and enjoyed the evening entertainment, had now retired to their cabins for the night.

Mrs Chalmers settled her young children early, the results of the day's shopping finally separated from the youngsters. Jenny tucked her precious new doll into the pram for the night and with her brother scampered off to their beds. Relaxing in their first-class cabin after the busy day, Mrs Chalmers herself prepared for an early night with the children. She carefully stowed their possessions, including a number of very fine pieces of jewellery. One piece, a large black pearl dress ring, especially meant a lot to her. The pearl had been a rare find made by her husband when diving off a reef near their home some years earlier. She admired the glistening pearl, a reminder of their home in Fiji to which they were returning.

Mrs Wise, wife of the Honourable Wilfred Wise, Director of Public Works for the Fiji government, was concerned about her husband's health. She arranged the flowers delivered earlier to their stateroom into a vase, and then ordered chicken sandwiches for delivery by steward to their stateroom at midnight. Returning to Suva with her was the car in which she had travelled some 4000 miles around New Zealand. The vehicle was now securely tied down onto the hatch cover of No. 2 hold.

A low rumble from the engines signalled the ship's departure from Queen's wharf. The *Niagara* slipped away into the Auckland harbour channel leading out into the waters of the Hauraki Gulf. The steady vibration transmitted through the quietness of the darkened stateroom soon lulled the Wises to sleep, providing some relief to Mr Wise from his bronchial attack.

On the bridge, the glow of the dimmed night lighting reflected off the faces of the evening watch. Following the disembarkation of the Auckland pilot Burgess, the officer on watch, Third Officer Ron Beeby, gave the helmsman course headings to take the ship out into the Pacific. The bridge telegraph rang "half engine power" to the engineers below.

At 2350 hours, with Rangitoto island abeam, the course set for the Tiri Tiri light was altered to 356 degrees to pass Moko Hinau light. The calm waters of the Gulf stretched ahead reflecting the light of the overhead moon. In the distance, beams from the Gulf islands' lighthouses flashed their distant message, providing a reassurance for the *Niagara*'s crew as they had done for mariners over years' past. Unknown to the crew, only a few days previously, these same lights had aided an enemy in setting a barrier of destruction across the waters they were now sailing.

The lights of Auckland disappeared astern into the night, beyond their phosphorescent wake. The ship approached the channel between the Moko Hinau light to starboard and the Maro Tiri light on the Hen and Chicken islands six miles to the west. On the bridge, Beeby noted the bearings of the lights. At 0334 hours he informed Captain Martin, now resting in his cabin, of the ship's position. Receiving the order to change course to 009 degrees, Beeby in turn relayed the order to Bill Hart, the quartermaster, now at the ship's wheel.

Above in the crow's-nest, Reg Kerr noted the flashing lights, one on each bow. Protected against the winter's night, he was grateful for the fine clear weather and a smooth sea. With his isolated duty soon to finish, he thought of the hot cup of tea now brewing below. After the cold, a hot drink would be welcome before turning in for the night.

7

Death Knell

In the cold darkness of the depths, the *Orion*'s mines swung silently on their moorings to the movements of the ocean. Travelling through the liquid void, the sonic vibrations steadily grew in strength, heralding the approaching mass from the south. Protruding mine horns captured the pulsations through their soft metal covers encasing the glass tubes of sulphuric acid. The fluid shimmered in anticipation as the shock waves increased. In the core of the mine, the highly explosive charge of Amatol (a compound of TNT and ammonium nitrate) remained dormant, waiting the surge of electrons to release the destructive force the charge contained. The German Y-type mine was so designed that when it was struck by a vessel, the impact would bend the protruding horns, breaking the glass tubes. The released acid ran down to the bottom of the tube to envelop small plates of carbon and zinc, thereupon producing an electrolytic battery cell action with a current of 1.8 volts. This electrical current, conducted through a thin platinum wire to the Amatol charge, triggered the mine's explosive force. This was designed to occur approximately one to two seconds after striking the mine, ensuring maximum impact of the explosion along a ship's hull.

After a long day and late night departure, Ray Nelson was glad to finally get to his bunk. Sleeping for'ard in the crew's quarters adjacent to the third-class accommodation, Ray, clad only in his singlet, collapsed onto his top bunk and was soon asleep. Able Seaman Harris, also tired, looked forward to the end of his four-hour watch at 0400 hours. Switching on the water urn, he prepared the cups for tea at the end of watch.

The full-away signal from the bridge had been received around midnight. In the engine room, Third Engineer Fred Hughes stood on the starboard engine middle platform maintaining the engines at full speed. Each boiler, oil-fired by four furnaces working under Howden's forced-draft system, produced steam at a pressure of 220 psi to power the reciprocating engines. The Parsons low-pressure turbine engine further converted this steam by expanding the vapour through low-pressure turbines. The resultant energy, released through the vessel's triple propellers, churned the Gulf waters driving the *Niagara* on through the night at seventeen knots towards the Pacific ocean.

The engine room clock indicated 0340 hours. To Bates, a member of the engine room watch, it was immaterial whether it was night or day. His duties as a greaser required him to work hidden from the outside world, surrounded by massive machinery and plumbing, the pulsating heart and arteries of the ship.

The vibrations passed into the mine, their intensity increasing. Amplified by the ocean, the waves of sound scattered a shoal of fish from their night shelter beneath the sphere. Fifteen thousand tons of steel mass hurtled from the night striking the tethered mine.

The spherical mine, ripped from its seabed mooring, glanced off the steel hull, the protruding horns bending under the sudden impact. In an instant, the released acid triggered the electrical reaction. The Amatol detonated with a massive force that slammed into the hull under the No. 2 hold.

0343 hours. Harris reached for the hot-water urn preparing to pour hot water into the teapot. Suddenly, the urn tore from the startled seaman's hand, flying with teapot and cups across the room. The concussion from the blast tore upwards through the ship's structure, lifting Harris four feet in the air before flinging him on his back to the floor. Thankful for the bulkhead protecting him from the full force of the blast, he scrambled to his feet. His eyes seared by the explosion, Harris stumbled his way onto the foredeck into smoke billowing from No. 2 hold.

High in his crow's-nest perch, Reg Kerr was jolted by the shock of the blast beneath him. Clutching the platform he gazed down upon a scene of destruction. All the hatches and beams from No. 2 hold were blown away. A cloud of grey smoke billowed from the hold and a pungent smell of cordite reached his nostrils. Quickly abandoning his perch, he descended through smoke to the security of the deck.

Upon altering course soon after seven bells, Ron Berry prepared to check the compasses. Moving out onto the bridge, he grasped for the compass binnacle as the shock of the explosion tore through the hull below. The explosive flash erupted thirty feet above the startled bridge watch into the night. A large cloud of sawdust thrown upwards swirled onto the deck. The bridge windows exploded inwards onto the shocked crew with a crash of breaking glass. Bill Hart, flung back from the wheel, struck his head against a cabinet door. Picking himself up off the floor, he clung to the wheel, dazed. The helm seemed to be inoperative with no response to his inputs from the wheel. Telegraphs immediately signalled "close watertight doors"; the whistle sounded action stations. Electric alarm bells set to ring in emergency failed to operate – their batteries had become dislodged by the explosion.

Jolted from his slumber, Bill Martin felt as if the explosion was almost beneath his wrecked quarters. Quickly the captain donned his trousers then an overcoat before rushing out onto the bridge. The starboard bridge wing was gone. The wheelhouse had been reduced to a shambles. Observing smoke billowing from No. 2 hold and noting the ship's list, he issued orders for crew to muster passengers at boat stations.

Standing on the engine platform, Fred Hughes felt a terrific vibration as if the engines were going to pieces. Investigation indicated they were still operating, but engine speed had decreased considerably. Further aft in the engine room, Bates was concentrating on his oiling duties when, without warning, an adjacent seawater pipe burst outwards, drenching him. Accompanied by Sixth Engineer Allen, Bates scrambled through the cascading seawater in search of the cause. Water continued to pour into the engine room at a rapid rate. Discovering the water service pipes on the port side of the engine room torn apart, Allen hastened to report the situation to Hughes. With increasing concern, the engineers wrestled with the onslaught of water as off-duty engineers arrived at their stations. A few minutes passed, then suddenly the telegraph rang. "Stop engines!"

The explosion had destroyed the forward lighting system. With the aid of a torch, Harris stumbled across the deck to No. 2 hold. The beam

Museum of Wellington, City and Sea

Museum of Wellington, City and Sea

Above: MV *King Egbert* – showing 1935 Vancouver collision damage.

Right: *Niagara* – damage from *King Egbert* collision.

Museum of Wellington, City and Sea

Above: Collision damage forward of *Niagara*'s bridge.

Below: *Niagara* in dock – repairs of the *King Egbert* collision damage.

Museum of Wellington, City and Sea

Museum of Wellington, City and Sea

Museum of Wellington, City and Sea

Above: *Niagara* port and centre propellers.

Right: *Niagara* rudder assembly.

Museum of Wellington, City and Sea

Left: Captain William Martin, USSCo.

Below: *Niagara* lifeboat drill.

Museum of Wellington, City and Sea

THE NORTHERN ADVOCATE

JEFF MAYNARD

Above: Lifeboat with survivors of the 1940 *Niagara* sinking.

Right: John E. (Johnno) Johnstone – Diver.

George Ellis

Left: Johnno testing the Austox oxy-hydrogen underwater cutting equipment.

Below: Salvage vessel *Claymore* moored over the *Niagara* – 1941.

New Zealand National Maritime Museum

Ray Nelson

Jeff Maynard

Above: Johnno gives Ray Nelson instruction on helmet diving.

Right: Diving bell suspended from the *Claymore*.

Jeff Maynard

Left: Ray Nelson prepares the diving bell for lifting.

Below: Recovering the bell.

Jeff Maynard

cut through the darkness reflecting back to Harris from a liquid surface. Seeing cargo already floating in rising water he rushed to the bridge to warn Captain Martin, who realised they might be in the imminent danger of sinking.

Ray Nelson woke suddenly as he crashed to the floor with his top bunk toppling on top of him. Groping in the darkness he found a pair of trousers, restoring some dignity before exiting the cabin in haste. Emerging into the chaos of the forward crew quarters he scrambled past the debris to emerge onto the forward deck. A scene of destruction greeted him. The upward force of the blast through No. 2 hold had blown the hatch covers off – the car lashed to them was gone. Twisted and torn deck beams protruded through splintered decking. Window and skylight glass was shattered and doors had been blown from their frames. Immediate thoughts of an attack from a submarine or raider sent Ray racing aft to his post at the gun station.

On the gun platform, Jim Daly and his gun crew established there was no danger from an enemy attack. However, the now-evident list signified there was perhaps a danger of the ship sinking. Making his way back for'ard, Ray noted that the inclined slope down towards the bow had increased significantly. Reporting to the bridge for duty as a captain's messenger, he received instructions to find the ship's carpenter, Spence, and sound the depth of water in No. 2 hold. It was a normal duty for the carpenter to maintain regular checks on water levels in the bilges. Ray found Spence between decks close to No. 2 hold preparing to check the level of the rising water. Deploying the sounding rod, the two sought the bottom of the hold. To their astonishment, the sounding rod did not stop but dropped straight down through the bottom of the ship. The mine blast had torn open the bottom of the hold.

Reporting the situation to Captain Martin, Ray was ordered to ensure the portholes were secured in the for'ard crew and third-class accommodation areas. The ship was now listing over to port. Halfway down the forward companionway, Ray discovered he was up to knees in water. It was obvious the ship was taking water on at a fast rate. He hastily retreated to inform the captain.

Nobody had been seriously injured. It was amazing that the blast had not caused more serious injury or loss of life. There was little panic among the passengers who were now assembling on the boat deck in various states of dress. Many were still in night attire. A number of men missing their trousers used blankets to wrap around their lower bodies.

Wilfred Wise awoke to the sound of crockery and glasses shattering. The flowers his wife had attended to only a short time before were thrown to the floor to join the remains of their chicken sandwich supper. A momentarily silence was broken by the slamming of cabin doors and raised voices in the passageway. A steward knocked on the door and advised the couple they were required to assemble on the boat deck. There did not appear to be any danger of sinking and the Wises, puzzled by the instruction, joined the exodus to the outer deck. Their demeanour soon changed when instructed to don lifejackets that were being handed out. Wearing a coat over his pyjamas, Wilfred sent his wife back to the stateroom to slip a dress on over her nightgown. She returned clad not only in a dress but also her furs.

Air Vice-Marshal Goble, woken by the explosion, had no time to don his corset. Determined to maintain a military bearing among the chaos around him, he squared his shoulders and attempted to calm the ladies with words of authority. In such dignified company, Mrs Wise stood clutching her furs admiring the manner in which the officers and crew were conducting themselves. Calmly going about their duties, they assembled the passengers and prepared the lifeboats for launching. To her this was the phlegmatic British spirit that would surely win through in the end. Her only regret was for the personal belongings that remained in her cabin, especially her jewellery and passport. She clutched the furs closer to her body.

The loud explosion had woken the Guthrie family. Young Wally wanted to go to the bathroom, partly to go to the toilet but also because he was curious to see what had happened. His father led him down the passageway now full of hazy smoke. Very few people were about, there was an absence of noise, and an eerie calm had settled over the ship. In the bathroom the wall mirror had shattered and the glass lay about the floor. Sensing something serious had occurred, Wally became concerned for their well-being. His father, now aware a major problem had occurred, quickly ushered the lad back to their cabin then hastened off to investigate. Returning almost immediately, he ordered the family to quickly evacuate the cabin. Mrs Guthrie told the children to gather their personal effects as she commenced looking for her handbag. With some urgency in his voice her husband interrupted their actions with the stern command, "Let's go!" Still in their pyjamas, the family grabbed their coats to join other passengers making a hurried exit up the central staircase to the boat deck.

Mrs Chalmers scrambled from the floor. She and the children had been tossed from their beds by the force of the explosion. Frightened but keeping a cool head, she quickly donned her dressing gown and slippers before attending to the bewildered children. They stood rubbing the sleep from their eyes, not comprehending what had awakened them. They watched their mother hasten to the cabin door where she frantically pulled at the handle. The door would not budge: it was jammed shut, defying her efforts to open it. Jenny and her brother clutched at their mother's dressing gown as she frantically pounded at the door shouting for help. Unfortunately she had a quiet voice and her muffled cries for help went unheeded. The only sounds entering the cabin were creaking and groaning from the tormented hull accompanied by the hissing of escaping steam. A gaping hole in the buckled and torn hull plates alongside their cabin exposed the heaving ocean surface. With increasing terror, the frightened children gazed out the jagged opening. They clutched tighter to their mother who was doing her best to reassure them although she herself was beginning to think they would all die trapped in their cabin.

Accommodated in the for'ard section, the third-class passengers were close to the mine's impact. The Canadian Campbell was thrown from his bunk by the explosion, receiving a premature baptism of enemy action before he had got the chance to join up. In adjoining cabins, bunks collapsed under the powerful shock, dumping their occupants onto the cabin floor.

The Reverend and Mrs C.E. Rowley awoke to find themselves on the floor in a tangle of sheets and blankets. Their first concern was for their four-month-old baby daughter. Born in Sydney, her first months of life had been full of incident. Both parents were citizens of the United States to where they were travelling from Sydney. The Reverend intended to join the US forces as a chaplain and had been the first American clergyman to serve on circuit with the Presbyterian Church of Australia. Before their departure, local newspapers had taken up the issue of whether baby Rowley was a citizen of Australia or the US. This created some debate in the newspapers, but it was finally decided she was a citizen of both countries. Now once again she would become an item of news, this time as a shipwrecked baby. For Mrs Rowley the main issue for the present was the survival of her baby. Not knowing what fated awaited them during the next few hours, she had the presence of mind to quickly pack the baby's needs into a bag including, milk with warm water mixed in a thermos flask.

Also a minister of the Presbyterian Church, Dr J.G. Inkster of Ottawa observed the arrival of the sudden disaster like a clap of thunder from out of the night and a further hindrance to his departure from New Zealand. During his visit, Dr Inkster had created considerable criticism with what was termed his outspoken references to Communistic tendencies. He considered his statements had been misconstrued, however, and with his departure from Auckland he had thought the controversy would be behind him. Now fate had brought his journey away from the controversy to an abrupt halt. As he prepared his wife to embark into a lifeboat with the other wives, he gave thanks to God for the beautiful moonlight night, fine weather and a placid sea. Perhaps this was pre-ordained fate and he might still have another opportunity to correct the wrong impressions he had created with his contentious dialogue.

Conscious of the ship's increasing list to port, Mrs Chalmers called frantically for help as she pounded on the jammed door. The frightened children could hear the public-address system above the creaking and groaning of the ship summoning the passengers to muster on deck. Finally, to the relief of the trapped trio, a voice on the other side of the door answered their frantic cries. Ordered to stand back they waited while a steward heaved at the jammed door. Eventually it gave. There was no time to lose as the list had now become more pronounced, so the steward shepherded the children towards the door. Suddenly little Jenny spotted her doll's pram with her precious dolly slowly trundling across the sloping cabin floor towards the breach in the hull. She turned, wanting to rescue her treasures, but the quick-thinking steward scooped the frightened girl into his arms and ushered the family out into the passageway. Over his shoulder Jenny saw her pram and dolly floating slowly out through the opening into the darkness beyond.

Standing among the shattered remnants of the bridge, Captain Martin noted his ship had taken on a decidedly head-down attitude with a pronounced list to port. All pumps were selected to No. 2 hold but their combined efforts could not stem the onrush of water as the ship settled by the bow. Where possible, bulkhead doors had been closed to maintain the ship afloat as long as possible, but it was obvious to the captain that little time remained. Conscious of the gold bullion locked in the strongroom below, he asked his Chief Engineer, Ken Sinclair, if the engines could still operate for an attempt to beach the sinking ship. Receiving an affirmative, he issued orders for "slow ahead engines".

For five minutes the ship moved slowly towards shallow water, but with the inability of the pumps to stem the flow into No. 2 hold there could be little time left afloat. With the propellers now rising above water, Martin reluctantly gave up all hope of saving his ship. He signalled the engine-room crew to stop engines and abandon ship. Chief Sinclair ordered the engine oil-fuel pumps shut off and engine-room staff to their lifeboat stations. Preparing to depart, he observed that water was now coming through the for'ard stokehold high up on the port side, an indication the No. 3 bulkhead had collapsed. Lifeboats were swung from their cradles and lowered to B-deck where passengers were assembling. With the list to port, boats on that side of the ship were considerably closer to the surface than the starboard boats.

Chief Radio Officer Gordon Power had commenced his duty in the Marconi room at midnight. Feeling the shock of the explosion he immediately switched the transmitter on before pressing a bell to summon his two assistants. Upon receiving orders from the Captain, the radio operators maintained a constant transmission of distress signals. The SOS and auto alarm signals were immediately answered by Auckland Radio ZLD and were later reported to have been received in San Francisco.

A growing crowd of passengers milled about on B-deck searching for their allocated lifeboat stations. Calm prevailed with little panic among the passengers as they followed orders from officers and crew. The Guthrie family were frightened. Within a few minutes of arriving on starboard B-deck, the women and children of their group were being assisted into a lifeboat. To the youngster the boat seemed to be very full – perhaps there would be no room for him and his father. It was a relief when he was hoisted aboard and he spotted his mother and sister seated at the other end of the boat.

Choy Lim quickly gathered the four children and aided by her husband joined the other Chinese third-class passengers stumbling through the darkness to B-deck. With her family she huddled barefoot, dressed only in her silk pyjamas, waiting their turn to board a lifeboat. For the for'ard third-class passengers there had been no time to gather any clothing. First and second-class passengers some distance from the explosion had more time to dress before vacating their cabins. As Choy Lim shivered in the winter's night, a woman nearby was sobbing. Clad in a fur coat over her negligee, she lamented the loss of everything with the ship.

The increasing list to port began to cause problems with launching the starboard boats. The angled hull now required the craft to be slid down the hull-plates into the sea. No. 1 lifeboat, in the starboard forward position, was allocated for the captain and crew and so was designated to be the last boat launched.

In the engine room, water steadily rose above the floor plates. The remaining engine-room crew, aware of the increasing descent of the bow and knowing they were exposed to some danger, continued working. They toiled in the knowledge that time was running out, but before abandoning their stations they needed to cool the boilers. Filling them with cold water would prevent an explosion when they came in sudden contact with cold seawater. Fireman Murray, absorbed with his duties, did not hear the final orders to cease work and abandon ship. He was soon alone among the machinery now silent amid the sounds of water cascading from burst piping.

Above on B-deck the evacuation proceeded. The numbers of passengers and crew at the boarding stations diminished as the boats were launched and pulled into the night away from the stricken vessel.

Having been escorted safely to their port lifeboat station, the Chalmers family awaited instructions. For those who had joined the ship in Auckland there had been no time for lifeboat drill and they waited in small groups while the boats were prepared for launching. A lifejacket was placed over Jenny's shoulders, but as with the other children it was far too large. She was placed along with other children into the rear compartment of the lifeboat, where the lifejackets had been stowed. It was a nerve-racking experience for the children sitting squeezed together in a knees-up position. Jenny clung to her brother as the lifeboats were lowered towards the water. Lurching downwards in a series of staggered drops, the falls squealing noisily as they passed through the davits, the boat with its complement of passengers and crew safely reached the calm ocean.

Aussie darted from the arms of the crewman attempting to place the terrified cat into a lifeboat. He had been seen up and around before the explosion as though he had sensed some danger. Incidents of ships' cats sensing impending danger have often been reported, including the disaster that had befallen the *Titanic*. Only one cat had been aboard that ill-fated ship, and before departing Southampton she had been observed by her minder, a stoker, carrying her four kittens, born en route to that port, ashore one by one. The stoker signed off from the crew, remarking that the cat knew something. Aussie, on the other hand, would have no part of joining the lifeboat passengers despite the efforts of several members to rescue him. When the last lifeboat departed, Aussie was still aboard.

As the starboard No. 3 boat descended towards the ocean, it suddenly lurched to a halt. Tilting sharply at one end, it swung on the falls. Young Wally clung to his father. Shouting erupted from the deck above as the lifeboat hung precariously over the oily surface.

Ray Nelson had taken up his position in the No. 1 boat and awaited Captain Martin who, with the radio operator, would be the last to leave. Behind, he noted that the No. 3 boat seemed to be having some difficulties with launching. The lifeboat crew had joined the ship in Sydney and were relatively inexperienced with launching the ship's lifeboats. When part-way down the ship's sloping side, the aft block had jammed, causing the boat to tilt with a bow-down angle.

It was an anxious moment, especially for the women and children who were the majority aboard the boat. First Officer Beeby, seeing their predicament, ordered Ray to go and help.

To get to No. 3, Ray discovered he would have to leap some distance out into the darkness to grab the boat falls. If he missed, he would plunge some 60 feet into the ocean. The lifeboat was now suspended with its bow in the water with the stern, held by the jammed falls, some six feet higher. The young seaman leapt outwards grasping for the stretched cable. Grabbing the fall he clung momentarily, allowing the rush of adrenalin to subside before clambering down to the anxious occupants. Young Walter Guthrie sat wide-eyed clutching his father as the seaman dropped into the boat. He was fearful they would all end up tossed into the sea. The jammed falls would not release under the weight of the boat with its occupants, so Ray grabbed the boat's axe and severed the rope fall. The released boat hit the surface with a splash.

Nearby the No. 1 boat skidded down the inclined side of the listing ship. On receiving Ray's assurances that he was freeing the jammed block, Captain Martin ordered the No. 1 crew to pull away. No. 3 soon followed, the last boat to leave the doomed vessel. (Pulling away from the ship's side, Ray felt the shock of a further explosion reverberating from the depths. At the subsequent inquiry into the sinking he reported this observation, but was not believed. Later, he would be proved correct: the shock was certainly a second mine exploding beneath the *Niagara*'s hull as the ship settled.)

The overhead moon cast its light across the calm waters of the Gulf as the dying ship sank lower into the darkened depths. Across the liquid silver stage the shadows of lifeboats gathered like the cast in the final act of a tragic opera, their occupants silent as they waited the death of the star.

Suddenly from the rear deck, a beam of light flashed across the water. Alone in the bowels of the engine room, with water rapidly rising around him, fireman Murray had suddenly realised his predicament. Quickly making his way to an upper deck he confirmed he was alone on the sinking ship. No. 3 boat crew, sighting the frantic flashlight signals, returned to his rescue.

The sounds of the condemned vessel crossed the silence of the waters to the lifeboats. Passengers and crew huddled together in the cold predawn hours, fascinated by the scene before them. The *Niagara*'s generators, left running, pulsed their energy into electrical circuits illuminating cabin and deck lights, a final signal of farewell. The list to port increased and the bow settled deeper as the invading ocean slowly swallowed the dying ship. Across the water, the sounds of internal structure collapsing under the hydraulic forces reached the audience as cries of pain.

8

Victims of War

Within the bowels of the stricken liner, a wall of water surged upwards engulfing the lower deck levels. Reaching the grand staircase it forced onwards through passageways, sweeping the opulence of a former era under a swirling liquid mass. Into the saloons and grand dinning room the invading ocean came, hurling furnishings across the floors where a few hours earlier passengers danced to music from the ship's band. Now the musicians' instruments tumbled in the swirling waters as the sea roared across the dance floor in a foaming onslaught. Onwards down deserted passageways, smashing into cabins where two hours previously occupants had slept oblivious of the approaching danger, the wall of water gained force. As *Niagara* slipped deeper into the ocean, the roar of escaping air compressed by the rising waters added to the crescendo of sound. Unsecured portholes and windows were punched open by the increasing internal pressure, accelerating the torrents of water invading the ship. The angle of descent increased. Crockery, glassware, ornaments, and furnishings crashed from their stowage, joining the avalanche of loose items propelled forward as the stern lifted higher into the night.

The survivors waited for the final curtain call. Lights, the final beacons of life remaining, were snuffed out as rising waters choked the generator diesels. A crew member, hoping the overhead moon would provide sufficient illumination for colour film, attempted to record the ships final moments with his movie camera. The low surface mist, forming a burial shroud around her hull suddenly parted revealing the *Niagara*'s stern rearing from the ocean, her triple screws gleamed momentarily in the moon-light and then she was gone.

For many witnessing her plunge into the depths, it was similar to the sorrow associated with attending the funeral of an old friend. Charlie McLean had been crew on *Niagara*'s maiden voyage; now, witnessing her demise, his memories returned to past voyages they had shared sailing the Pacific. Only deckchairs and flotsam afloat in the increasing stain of surface oil marked the ship's former existence.

In the safety of their lifeboats, the thoughts of many crew and passengers turned to their personal loses. Mrs Major, still in distress from the ordeal of the sinking, mourned the loss of all her possessions she was transporting to Canada. Gone were the valuable family plate and estate furniture, reminders of her late husband and their years together.

Seventy-year old Mrs Williams sat huddled under a blanket, thinking sadly of the presents she and her husband had been taking to Suva to celebrate their golden wedding with family. Now they were at the bottom of the sea.

Mrs Clive Livingston, likewise travelling to Suva, was also saddened over the loss of gold. The heirlooms she had carefully packed into her baggage, including the gold cups and silver, were now gone. Thinking of her lost effects, she laughed at the thought of the blackball confectionery she purchased for her husband. Now at the bottom of the sea, the bags of sweets would be slowly dissolving among her lingerie.

For young Louis Keegan the adventure continued. He had woken Miss Charlton shouting that the windows had broken. In fact, it was the vase of flowers she had carefully arranged earlier crashing to the floor. Now Louis sat in the lifeboat clutching Miss Charlton. Bewildered by the events of the evening he asked her why the ship had gone away taking their suitcases.

Wally Guthrie felt the cold but it was bearable. Next to him, his father, feeling an object in his coat pocket, discovered his Kodak folding camera, still there from the previous day's departure. Later in daylight he photographed the lifeboats scattered around on the clam sea. Wally's thoughts turned to his new bike he had never ridden, now at the bottom of the sea. He sobbed quietly as he mourned his loss.

Members of the ship's band mourned the loss of their instruments: Pat Watters had lost his saxophone and two clarinets, while Jack McIntyre regretted bringing a new bass fiddle rather than the old one on this trip.

Denis Morgan thought of the fine ship's piano he had played for the past two years, lost along with his music.

Crew sports committee members commiserated on the loss of the entire fine sporting gear on board. Equipment donated in 1938 by millionaire English philanthropist Sir Jullien Cahn was lost, plus a handsome silver boxing cup presented by the late Sir James Murdock of Sydney. Over 2000 books in the ship's library were also gone.

Passenger Davidson had been in such a hurry after the explosion to don a lifejacket and reach the deck that he left his teeth behind. Unable to chew on the ship's biscuit from lifeboat rations, he sucked the hard square object while commiserating with his Ashburton mates on the Fijian holiday they would now miss. Bill Sparrow, still in his pyjamas, commented on their lost holiday clothes and sets of bowls now in the deep. Davidson, thinking of the bowls lying in their last ditch, decided that as he could not eat the hard biscuit, he would take it home as a souvenir of the trip.

Jenny Chalmers nibbled at the ship's biscuit she had been given. Like her brother she could make no impression on the hard tack. A crew member, seeing their predicament, rested his oar to pass the grateful children each a piece of chewing gum. Watching her children abandon their efforts to chew the hard biscuits, Mrs Chalmers gave thanks that they had all come through their ordeal safely. Her precious pearl ring, other jewellery and the Auckland shopping including the children's toys were now all at the bottom of the sea – but they were all safe.

Sitting in the lifeboat, 87-year-old John Browne congratulated himself on his fortitude in preparing for such an emergency. Sitting unruffled, he took a professional interest in the predicament they were now experiencing, his trim white imperial beard bristled in traditional British seafaring fashion. Before retiring he had prepared his clothing and effects on a chair by his bedside. Awakened by the explosion, he had taken his time dressing and preparing for the expected ordeal in an open boat. He had heard of situations where cabin doors would jam shut on sinking ships causing the occupants to be trapped and drown. With this in mind, he threw a pillow to stop the door from closing while he continued with his preparations. From previous experience and with the possibility of having to eat hard emergency biscuits, his false teeth were a priority. Collecting his dentures together with his torch, glasses, overcoat, a rug, and a waterproof, he donned a lifejacket and departed the cabin. Not wanting to be the subject of amusement however, he decided to leave his stick behind. Now, aboard the lifeboat observing the dress of fellow occupants, it was apparent that others had ignored such preparations. Many were missing their false teeth; some men were wrapped in blankets in place of trousers left behind and a few women wore fur coats over their night attire. Although personal losses were on many minds, all were thankful no lives had been lost and only a few had minor injuries. More passengers, bad weather and rough seas would have resulted in a different story with lives lost.

The majority afloat that morning were unaware of a greater loss among the cargo and effects. Five hundred and ninety bars of gold, over eight imperial tons of the precious metal stacked in the strong room, had gone down with the ship. Valued at close to £2.5 million sterling, the bullion was desperately needed by an Empire fighting for its existence. Captain Martin, aware of the gold's importance, had made desperate efforts to bring the stricken ship closer to shore but she was unable to survive the increasing flow of ocean pouring through the breached hull. His efforts were thwarted and now the vessel lay 66 fathoms deep.

As dawn broke, aircraft appeared flying low over the scattered lifeboats. Rescue ships, not sure what had sunk the *Niagara*, cautiously approached the scene. Boarding passengers and crew off the stricken ship, the rescue vessels with lifeboats in tow sailed for Auckland, where the citizens were just awakening to radio news announcing the sinking. They were not yet aware that the war in faraway Europe had arrived on New Zealand's shores.

The heavy fuel oil spread out over the ocean, calming the wind-ruffled surface, its oily sheen reflected the morning sun in bands of colour. Bleeding from ruptured fuel tanks adjacent to the mine strike on No. 2 hold, the liquid rose from the depths. Among the flotsam, little blue penguins struggled in the water as the sticky fluid matted their feathers, robbing them of the ability to move with ease through their environment or the buoyancy to survive. The dead birds added to the mass of ship's debris drifting westwards towards the distant shoreline. Clinging to a floating water tank, Aussie, his fur caked in the sticky substance, gazed at the lifeless forms that floated nearby.

The Northland beaches became littered with the lifeless forms of little blue penguins and other seabirds. Their bodies lay engulfed in the sticky mass of fuel oil, some three inches deep, spreading 25 feet up the sands to the high water mark. The last victim of the sinking arrived ashore among the carnage on the beach at Hora Hora, north of Whangarei, some days later. The water tank on which Aussie had clung rode through the surf depositing the cat among the flotsam and oil from the wreck. Discovered later asleep in a nearby shed by a farmer, the exhausted shipwrecked moggie quickly regained his normal temperament when stuffed ignominiously into a sack. For a worldly travelled feline, the farmer's sack was only a temporary setback. Aussie escaped and was no doubt soon spreading the genes of his Canadian forefathers among the feline population of Northland.

To the north, close to the Kermadec islands, Captain Kurt Weyher cursed his luck. About to give chase when the lights of a ship were sighted, he was informed the *Orion*'s engine was again experiencing problems. Slowing to five knots to facilitate repairs, Weyher was desperate to keep the lights of the ship ahead in sight. His engineers advised that they should be back up to speed by midnight. Hopefully they would catch up to the unsuspecting ship by daylight.

Nicknamed "The Singing Captain" by his cadets when he was commander of the naval training sail ship *Gorch Fock*, Weyher was in no mood for singing. For the past four days since departing New Zealand waters and heading north, the *Orion*'s crew maintained a close listening watch to New Zealand radio frequencies. The continued silence on any action in the Gulf raised doubts whether the mines were positioned at the correct depth or even if they were alive.

Full engine power was restored soon after midnight and Weyher pushed the *Orion* at full speed in pursuit of his prey. With dawn beginning to brighten the eastern horizon, the ocean dash of the past hours had succeeded in placing the German raider in a position ahead of the unsuspecting steamer. Weyher could now plan his attack at leisure.

A radio officer appeared on the bridge. Hurrying to Weyher he excitedly reported receiving SOS distress signals from the *Niagara* in the Gulf close to Auckland. With a growing sense of relief the German officers scanned Lloyd's Register for details of the *Niagara*. Yes! The mines were set correctly; the *Niagara*'s draft was recorded as 26 feet. *Orion* had struck her first blow in the Pacific; the first maritime victim of the war in the Pacific had fallen.

For a moment Weyher, a man of the sea, reflected on the loss of the veteran Queen of the Pacific. It was sad for a ship to be lost in such a manner and no doubt many more would follow her to the bottom of the Pacific before this war was over. Returning his attention to the present task, Weyher ordered his gun crews to battle stations as the unsuspecting quarry approached. This was no time for a naval commander to reflect on the loss of a veteran ocean liner. He raised his binoculars and focused on his next victim.

PART TWO

The Salvors

9

Gold from the Sea

The little ship rolled in the ocean swell, fighting the moorings that held her from heading into the deep swells rolling from the south. Held fast in the centre of a catenary of six mooring cables, the *Claymore* shook and bucked like a horse being broken in as the swells swept past her rusted hull.

Exposed to the October equinox winds, the open waters of Hauraki Gulf could quickly become a maelstrom of white water. In these conditions a prudent skipper would seek shelter in the lee of the Gulf islands or the protection of nearby Whangarei harbour. The ever-changing moods of the Gulf were now familiar to Captain John Williams. Except for the harshest weather he was reluctant to slip moorings and run for shelter. To the crew, Williams was often a difficult person to get on with. They now accepted his pig-headed approach, which in the past had seen them in danger from being blown sky-high by a German mine or sent to the bottom of the sea in the tempest of a storm.

Exposed to the storms that swept the Gulf, the crew cursed the madness that captured their souls. They cursed their stupidity for staying on in a rust-bucket of a vessel moored out in storms where cables parted, but they all knew if they were to succeed they needed such a leader. For over eight months the *Claymore* and her crew had battled the tormented ocean to maintain station over the sleeping Queen. Time was of the essence as they peeled away her hull plates to reach the golden reward she held.

Williams spoke briefly into the mouthpiece of the telephone strapped below his chin, straining to hear the reply from the deep. Some 360 feet below, the diving chamber swung from its cable. Inside, diver John Johnstone pressed his face against the glass porthole endeavouring to identify shapes of objects diffused in the shadow light of depth. Like a puppet on a string, the mechanical grab jerked in time with the motions of the dive chamber (bell) as they danced to the *Claymore*'s surface gyrations. Visibility was hampered by the lack of light, creating problems for Johnstone in locating the opening that led down through the twisted steel into the bullion room.

Although the October sea temperature at the depth of the bell was cold, the gas Johnstone breathed through the rubber mask enclosing his lower face was warm and dry. His exhaled breath passed through a canister of soda-lime granules, scrubbing the carbon dioxide generated by his body's metabolism. Oxygen from a high-pressure storage cylinder in the bell replenished the gas mixture maintaining the life-sustaining process. Wiping the condensation off the port before him, he ordered the bell to descend deeper into the darkness. Johnstone was conscious a wrong move could snag the bell in the mass of torn steel that now surrounded his tiny habitat.

On deck, Williams relayed the order from below, "Down the bell!" The winch-man, conscious of the need for caution, gripped the winch lever tightly as he gently applied power to the winch drum. The *Claymore* heeled over from the weight of both the chamber and the grapnel. Their cables stretched tight disappeared into the depths.

"Hold the bell!" Williams' tone belied the tension that prevailed over the deck crew as they waited the next order.

Johnstone issued instructions from the depths, directing the grab into the mass of debris below. Over the past weeks the grasping claw had produced only mud and debris as they had burrowed into the body of the sunken liner in search of the elusive gold. This time Johnstone noted that the grab did not cause the usual sound of metal against metal but rather more of a dull thump as it struck into the darkness of the bullion room.

Johnstone spoke into the mouthpiece. "Up the grab but slowly this time." Then, "Hold the grab!" as it appeared from the shadows. The clamshell jaws revolved slowly, maintaining their grip on the object extracted from the maw-like opening. Through the dark water, Johnstone strained to focus his eyes on the suspended grab swaying in time with the bell from the transmitted motion of the ship above.

On board, the change in Johnstone's tone of voice caused Williams to tense as a shiver of excitement ran through his body. The change in the captain's demeanour, not missed by the nearby winch crew, caused growing excitement to spread among the men on deck. Shouting into the mouthpiece, Williams transmitted the excitement to Johnstone in the depths below. "Johnno, what the hell is it?" he demanded.

Through the port window, a square box shape materialised clasped in the jaws. Despite the warm regenerated gas that passed through his body, a chill came over Johnstone as it dawned on him what he was looking at. He stared hard at the object, confirming to himself it definitely was a box in the grab. But did it contain gold bars? Should he announce to the excited Williams they had gold, when on bringing the box to the surface they might find it contained something else? But he needed to give Williams some indication of what was in the grab rather than returning to the surface with no warning. Trying to maintain a steady voice Johnstone said, "There's something in the grab and I think it's worth looking at. Better take it up and see for yourself."

For the past ten months Captain Williams and his salvage crew had battled the open waters of the Hauraki Gulf, striving to get into the *Niagara*'s bullion room. Now thoughts of past hardships over the months were quickly cast aside as gold fever took hold. "Up the bell!" Williams' command resounded across the deck. Winches engaged, winding in cable. Crew not involved with the recovery of the bell gathered at the side rails, waiting for the bell to surface.

Inside the bell Johnstone watched the grab disappear as he ascended through the twilight of the depths to the surface daylight. Quickly, Ray Nelson leapt onto the hatch of the bell as it broke the surface. Clutching the cable for support he spun the bell with nimble footwork that would make an Irish dancer proud, and unwound the cable twist, oblivious to the ducking he received from plunging with the bell into sea up to his waist. Inside the bell, Johnstone blew water ballast to lighten the load in preparation for hoisting aboard.

Fifteen months had passed since Ray, sitting in the lifeboat, had witnessed the *Niagara*'s plunge into the depths. Little did he then realise he would soon return as a member of a salvage team to challenge the ocean depths for a fortune beyond his imagination. With the excitement building around him, Ray's feet spun the bell with more vigour than normal. Inside, Johnstone clung to the interior of the spinning bell, excitement overcoming the build up of nausea.

Lifted aboard, the bell hatch was quickly removed to allow Johnstone, flushed from breathing oxygen, to emerge from the bell. The excited deck crew surrounding the bell watched Johnstone's expression for a hint as to what lay clutched in the jaws of the grab swinging in the depths below. Their excitement became contagious, spreading through the ship. Orders were issued to the winch operator for a careful retrieval of the grab, though he was well aware of the importance of the moment and the damage that would result from any wrong action. Eager hands carefully guided the grab as it emerged, water and silt streaming from the clamshell buckets.

The smell of the decaying wreck below invaded the men's nostrils as they manhandled the wooden box from the grab onto the deck. Swift hammer blows broke the box apart. A silence descended on the men as they gazed with reverence upon the two objects lying on the deck in a bed of sodden sawdust. Only noise from the *Claymore*'s generators and the screech of a gull searching for jettisoned food scraps broke the silence. The sun reflected from the golden surface creating a memorising effect on the salvors, as gold has done to man down through the ages.

The spell finally broken, feverish hands swept the 400-ounce gold bars from the deck. The cold of the depths from where they had been plucked entered the flesh of stroking hands feeling the touch of gold. Slowly realisation penetrated the minds of the dazed men, absorbed in their first sight and touch of a bar of gold. They had finally recovered gold from the *Niagara*. And more gold waited in the depths below their feet. It was a time for celebration.

10

The Challenge

Gold at the bottom of the sea has through the ages challenged man to penetrate the ocean depths in search of lost fortunes. Covering over 87 per cent of our planet, the ocean depths increase in pressure by one atmosphere (14.7 psi) for every 33 feet (10 metres) of depth, presenting a formidable challenge to the would-be salvor.

To the directors of the Bank of England, closeted in their sandbag-protected London head office in Threadneedle Street, the news of the loss of the *Niagara* on the other side of the world was received with dismay. The loss of £2.5 million of the Empire's monetary reserves would be a blow at any time, but was more so now when gold was needed to purchase war supplies from the USA. Cable messages from the Commonwealth Bank of Australia indicated the *Niagara* was lying in a depth of some 60 fathoms (110 metres) at pressures exceeding 175 psi. What to do? The diving technology of the day was confined to divers wearing helmets and rubberised canvas suits, with the divers exposed to surrounding water pressure. Dives to 200 feet were possible but for only ten minutes to prevent decompression sickness, more commonly known as the bends. The *Niagara* was reported to lie at least some 160 feet deeper, presenting a challenge for salvors to survive and work under the pressure of this depth. Only the Italians had experience in working in such depths. In 1931 the Italian salvage company Sorima, using an observer encapsulated in a diving bell at atmospheric pressure directing a surface-operated grab, had been successful in recovering £1 million of gold specie from the wreck of the *Egypt* lying in 396 feet in the Bay of Biscay. Now that Britain was at war with Italy, the expertise of Italian salvors was unavailable.

Nevertheless the gentlemen of the Bank of England were not prepared to lose their gold and issued instructions to their colonial bank counterparts to inquire if equipment and expertise was available to carry out salvage in such depths. The Commonwealth Bank immediately consulted naval authorities in Melbourne to determine if there was a salvage concern in Australia with the required skills and equipment to carry out the recovery of the lost bullion. One man was suggested, although the authorities were not hopeful that he would be successful with such a task. His name was Captain John P. Williams.

Managing director of the United Salvage Propriety of Melbourne, John Williams was initially cautious when approached by the Bank but soon became enthusiastic with the thought that here was the opportunity to accomplish a record salvage feat. His decision to accept the challenge was further fuelled by the notion that he would strike a blow against the enemy if the gold was recovered and he would be doing his duty for the Empire in its time of need.

A syndicate of Australian partners was formed under the name of the United Salvage Syndicate and a contract was negotiated with the Commonwealth Bank: its terms required the bank to pay the syndicate the bulk of the expenses, and there was provision for a bank representative to attend the salvage operation and take custody of any bullion salvaged from the shipwreck.

In accepting the contract, Williams was not aware that the Bank of England directors had agonised over the amount they were prepared to pay as a reward for the gold's recovery. They were well aware that the Italians and their partners had been paid 70 per cent of the bullion value recovered from the *Egypt*. A secret exchange of telegrams between England and the Commonwealth Bank in Australia expressed the English directors' horror at the prospect of having to pay a similar amount: 50 per cent was the absolute maximum they would be prepared to pay, and ten to 20 per cent would be more acceptable.

Williams and fellow directors of the United Salvage Company, consumed by the patriotic fervour of the day to support the mother country, and unaware of the limit the English bankers were prepared to go to, agreed to the amount of £28,000 plus 2.5 per cent of the value of any gold they recovered. The 45-year-old Williams was also aware of the *Egypt* salvage eight years previously and was keen to prove that Britishers could match the Italian feat and, if necessary, better it. He signed the contract to recover the gold bullion in October 1940.

Diver John Johnstone had previously worked with Williams on salvage projects and was appointed to the position of chief diver of United Salvage. Experienced in salvage work, Johnstone had been instrumental in the recovery of cargo from sunken wrecks around Australia. His deeds and daring diving exploits were well known to the public, having been publicised in the press.

One incident recorded in 1929 went under the heading, "Seconds from Death – A Diver's Bravery". Johnstone had been employed diving in the Yarra River, Melbourne where an old quarry had been flooded to form an island in the river; the work required the diver to place blasting charges. Blasting had been going on for several weeks when Johnstone laid 100 plugs of blasting gelignite under a rocky shelf in ten feet of water. A 20-foot length of fuse fabricated from a gunpowder train encased in a strong-tarred fabric especially made to burn underwater was attached to the charge. Johnstone was hauled back into a boat containing four others and the powder monkey lit the fuse, casting it into the water. Aware they had twelve minutes to reach safety, the men pulled vigorously on a rope attached to a post on shore. Despite arduous pulling on the rope, progress to shore 130 feet away was slow and after several minutes the boat came to a standstill. All five men now pulled desperately but they were stuck fast. Suddenly Johnstone noted smoke bubbles which, instead of going straight up were trailing back towards the boat. A quick glance over the stern revealed a heavy wharf plank was jammed against the boat bottom making the boat immovable. To the occupants' horror they also discovered the tough fuse entangled around a keel bolt, resulting in the charge being still under the boat having been dragged along with it for about 20 feet.

Two courses of action were open – go down and put the fuse out or cut the boat free, dislodge the heavy plank and try to reach safety in the time remaining. Johnstone realised that the first course was their only means of escaping death. Donning helmet and weights, which occupied more time, he descended into the water knowing they were only seconds from death.

The river was muddy and in the blackness underwater it was only with difficulty that he found the fuse. Running his hands along it until the sting of hot tar indicated he had reached the burning portion, he slashed at the fuse with his knife. Then picking up the whole ten pounds of charge, Johnstone, in a state of collapse, hauled it onto the boat. The remaining length of fuse between the cut end and the detonators was only eight inches.

Tests the following day showed the fire would have covered the short length of fuse to reach the explosives in 25 seconds. Within one and a half hours of their escape Johnstone relaid the charge and it was fired, this time from a safe distance. The resulting column of rock and water rose 150 feet into the air. This was the man chosen to descend to the *Niagara*.

Johnstone and Williams realised that to salvage the gold from the *Niagara* in the depths the ship was reported to be lying would require them to use technology similar to that used on the *Egypt* salvage. Consultations with engineers David Issacs and George Ellis of Melbourne resulted in a design for an underwater observation chamber able to withstand the pressure down to 600 feet. "Johnno" Johnstone had previously used George Ellis' expertise to overcome problems with working underwater and they had become good friends. George was employed at that time as a manager with Austox, the firm that later became CIG and is now BOC Australia. He had a reputation for getting things done. He was a skilled welder and was also Senior Welding Examiner for the Victorian technical schools. Both men had previously featured in the newspapers when Johnstone successfully carried out a salvage of 92 tons of cobalt from the 30-year-old wreck of the *Joliette* at Thio, New Caledonia. Using an underwater oxygen-hydrogen cutting torch invented by George and an associate, Stan Green, Johnno, in what the newspapers reported as a world record, cut 3400 feet of steel plating from the wreck.

The underwater observation chamber the salvors planned is often termed a "diving bell" but differs from the apparatus similarly named that has been in use since the 1700s. Whereas the traditional diving bell is normally open at the bottom and requires internal air pressure to be equal to the surrounding water pressure, the observation chamber is sealed off from water pressure and is constructed to withstand the differential pressure between the water pressure at operational depth and the internal atmospheric pressure. The occupant, breathing a gas at atmospheric pressure, is therefore not exposed to the dangers of decompression sickness that comes with breathing a higher pressure than surface atmospheric pressure.

Thompsons Engineering and Pipe, a firm in the northern Victorian town of Castlemaine, fabricated the main chamber components. The upper section of the chamber, comprising observation windows and the access hatch, was cast from manganese bronze for a wall thickness of five eighths of an inch. This was then bolted to the lower housing, a 52-inch long tube of half-inch thick mild steel rolled to form a 36-inch diameter. From Castlemaine, the chamber was transported south to the Austox facility in Melbourne where, under the supervision of George Ellis, it was fitted out and prepared for diving operations. Integral tests were carried out by submerging the chamber in a flooded brick-making clay quarry known as the "Surrey Dive" near Box Hill, Melbourne. This "Dive" was used as a swimming hole by the public and rumoured to be bottomless but obviously it was not.

So sure was George of the chamber's ability to submerge safely that he allowed his six-year-old son Russell to accompany him on a test. The lad stood on a box to enable him to peer through a porthole into the murk of the quarry water. All these activities were required to be hush-hush and the curious onlookers watching the strange goings-on in the quarry were oblivious to the true purpose of this strange contraption.

After some searching in New Zealand, a ship for the salvage operation was located in Auckland. The war had caused a shortage of suitable vessels and Williams, with limited funds, had to settle on the *Claymore*, a derelict steamer he found lying in Auckland harbour. A considerable amount of work was required to prepare the dilapidated vessel for the salvage challenge that lay ahead.

Others were also showing interest in the sunken liner. Despite the fact that the gold on board the *Niagara* had supposedly been a secret, rumours were circulating that the ship had been carrying a valuable cargo. By November 1940 the USSCo was receiving inquiries from would-be salvage exponents.

Nicolas Jdanoff had arrived in Fiji from Hong Kong ostensibly to explore the possibilities of growing tea and coffee in the colony and was reportedly interested in a rubber plantation on the coast. Contacting the USSCo manager in Suva, Jdanoff expressed his intent to carry out salvage on the *Niagara*. He asked if a special permit was required and what terms would be demanded by the concerns in question for salvage of the steamer and her cargo. He said he knew the ship was carrying a valuable cargo and that he had experience with salvage in depths of 45 fathoms.

The Suva manager referred the request to J. Greenland, the general manager in Wellington, advising that Jdanoff said he had a salvage company based in Hong Kong called the Russian Salvage Company. According to Jdanoff it had successfully carried out salvage operations on two cruisers sunk during the Russo-Japanese War, a destroyer sunk in the Philippines and a vessel belonging to Moller and Company. Equipment for the *Niagara* salvage would be supplied from Shanghai. The Suva manager made enquiries locally about Jdanoff and was informed by the Fiji police that he was Russian-Chinese but naturalised British. At one time, according to the Hong Kong police, he had been engaged in buying scrap metal that he then shipped to Japan. It was understood he had been involved with salvage work for the President Line but had been dropped for reasons unknown: the police described him as a "slippery character", and it was of some concern to learn that he was aware the *Niagara* had been carrying a valuable cargo.

It is possible that with his Japanese associations and Pacific activities, Jdanoff was using the *Niagara* salvage possibilities as a front for Japanese interests in the Pacific. A salvage operation on the sunken vessel would have enabled access to the waters of the gateway to Auckland without raising any suspicion. It would be interesting to know what happened to Mr Jdanoff following the outbreak of war with Japan thirteen months later.

Another salvage scheme Greenland received the same month through the company office in Sydney was from a Mr B. Roberts who had recently arrived there from New Zealand. In referring the inquiry to Greenland, the Sydney manager remarked that Roberts was a rough-looking person but the fact he had a room on the fifth floor of 90 Pitt Street gave him some credibility. He had reportedly carried out a few small salvage jobs in the past and had been referred to the company by Lloyds and local insurance companies. Roberts' plan was to raise the *Niagara*, tow it into shallow water, pump out the water and salvage the cargo. To accomplish this, twelve airtight tanks were to be constructed of which several would be submerged and attached to the vessel's bow. Water would then be pumped from the tanks, raising the bow until the vessel was standing on her stern with the bow now at a depth of 260 feet. Additional tanks were then to be attached and pumped until the hull floated free of the bottom enabling the submerged vessel to be towed to shallow water. Roberts said he had seen a similar method used to raise German battleships at Scapa Flow and in addition to the divers whom he had available, he planned to use diving bells of an American design fitted with mechanical arms and powerful lights. Greenland was concerned that Roberts also knew of the gold on board and that a party of divers was planning to recover the bullion. He commented he did not give them much chance of success in the reported depth of 60 fathoms.

Roberts' rough hand-written proposal and sketch of the salvage scheme did not impress Greenland, and the would-be salvor was informed that arrangements had already been made to salvage part of the vessel's cargo. Roberts' reported knowledge of the gold on board would no doubt have added to the concerns of the London bankers. It would seem it was difficult to keep such knowledge a secret in the South Pacific.

11

Men and Mere Boys

The supposedly secret venture was soon the subject of numerous rumours doing the rounds of bars on Auckland waterfront. Ray Nelson, now sailing as crew on a coaster, heard of Captain Williams' arrival from Australia and the plans to salvage the *Niagara*'s gold. Keen to join the salvage crew, he sought out the captain and told him of his aspirations to revisit the ship he had abandoned some four months earlier. He was accepted and reported to the Irish-born bosun Danny Scott, who had worked for Williams at his Melbourne company Fleet Forge making hard-to-find metal ship fittings. Ray warmed to the tattooed, hard-drinking tobacco-chewing sailor and in the coming months would admire his many talents for improvisation.

On 9 December 1940 the *Claymore* sailed from Auckland to commence the search for the wreck 100 miles to the north. It was less than six months since the night the *Niagara* had struck the mine that sent her to her grave. Williams decided to search for the lost liner using a circular sweep, whereby an anchor held one end of the sweep wire while the *Claymore* dragged the anchored end of the other end in a circular sweep. This method was against the advice of the first mate, Doug Munro, who as a local trawler-man preferred to use a sweep wire strung between two otter boards. However, Williams with his stubbornness would not accept Munro's advice or his estimated position where the wreck might lie.

This attitude prolonged the search, and the crew, subjected to the long hours of hauling on sweep cables, lost enthusiasm for the project. Williams added to their ordeal by ignoring navy orders against venturing out into the Gulf until minesweepers had completed a full sweep of the area. He was frustrated by the navy's apparent lack of interest and confidence in the salvage operation. For its part, the navy described the operation as a lost cause with a rust-bucket salvage vessel crewed by misfits and commanded by a captain who ignored the dangers of a minefield.

Weyher's remaining mines hidden in the Gulf waters caused anxious moments for the crew. Although the New Zealand Navy had commenced mine clearance operations, a number of mines remained in the area of the *Claymore*'s operations. On more than one occasion entanglements with mine cables endangered the vessel and her crew, with narrow escapes from destruction.

The arrival of Captain James Herd to assist Williams brought a change to the crew's morale. Here was a man with a wealth of knowledge and experience in working at sea on salvage operations. Taking over the task of resolving many of the operational problems, he amazed the crew with his ability to overcome equipment problems that had been a major cause of concern. Herd's arrival enabled Williams to focus his attention on neglected management issues.

Herd soon realised that the circular sweep method was time-consuming and subjected the crew to additional cable-handling hardships. He convinced Williams that trailing a sweep strung between otter boards would be a better method. Resuming the search using the new method was to prove successful. In a short time, almost by accident while trailing the sweep through an area outside Williams' target area, the sweep cable caught on a large object. Using a shot-line with a sounding lead weight, the crew probed the depths seeking to identify what had snagged the sweep cable. Examining the greased base of the retrieved weight they discovered traces of green paint. Ray confirmed the colour was the same as the green hull of the *Niagara*.

With mounting excitement the diving bell with Johnstone as diver was hoisted over the side. Encapsulated in the chamber, plunging up and down with the rolling of the *Claymore*, Johnstone was lowered into the ocean. In addition to the wild heaving of the chamber, a spinning motion caused by the lay of the cable contributed to his feeling the onslaught of seasickness. The nausea soon dissipated when his attention focused out the portholes to the submarine world into which he now descended. On the bottom, the effects of a current dragged the chamber sideways. A debris field of various items including suitcases and boxes passed beneath the bell, grabbing the diver's full attention. Suddenly, the shock of impact jolted through the chamber. The bell had swung into something solid. Johnstone issued urgent instructions to raise the chamber. Through the portholes he glimpsed the shadowy structure of a ship's davits as the bell was hauled to the surface. They had found the *Niagara*.

Further dives revealed that the ocean liner was lying on her port side at an angle of approximately 70 degrees. Her bow pointed in the direction of Auckland, a testimony to Bill Martin's desperate last-minute attempts to get the sinking ship into shallower water. From the confines of his chamber Johnstone observed the fractured hull plates below No. 2 hold where the mine blast had torn the hull structure apart. Further aft below the engine room, a large hole extended aft some 230 feet, proving that Ray Nelson did hear the sound of a second mine as he pulled away from the sinking ship. Such damage would have dispatched the *Niagara* quickly to the depths, allowing little time for passenger and crew to escape in the lifeboats.

With the starboard side of the wreck uppermost, the salvors needed to remove hull plates and structure to gain access to the bullion room 30 feet below. This was accomplished with the use of explosives and the mechanical grab tearing away the steel plating and beams. A large opening was slowly made in the ship's side. Taking turns in the observation chamber, Johnno and his brother Bill, a Navy diver on loan, directed the placement of blasting charges and operations of the grab. The explosive charges ripped through the surrounding structure, sending railings and wooden deck cabin partitions to the surface. There they floated in a large surface layer of oil released from the fuel tanks.

Moorings consisting of six concrete blocks, each five tons in weight, were laid out around the wreck. Mooring wires from the blocks were led up to kauri log buoys from which mooring pennants, 120 feet long, were attached to white-painted buoys to facilitate tying up. The salvage vessel would lie in the centre of the six mooring buoys where, by using the winches, the ship could be manoeuvred to position the bell or grab over any position on the wreck.

Initial problems were experienced with the rolling and pitching of the *Claymore* on her moorings, which made the bell bump against the wreck or seabed. The problem was rectified by Herd devising a "monkey" – a heavy weight travelling up and down the stay to counteract the jerking of the bell. To overcome the spinning of the bell and grab, Herd had the crew plait together three 1.5-inch flexible steel wire ropes. Both fixes were a success.

Referring to the plans of the *Niagara,* a system was devised where each porthole, davit, entry port or recognisable feature was given a letter or number. Both Williams and the divers then studied and committed this reference plan to memory. On reaching the wreck, the diver would convey to Williams an accurate location, enabling the grab to be accurately positioned. Three types of grab were used depending on the requirement, the largest weighing 25 cwt.

Throughout May the blasting continued and finally the chamber could be lowered inside the wreck. The diver could see the white bulkhead of the passage leading down to the bullion room, but debris and torn steel now covered access to the gold beyond. The grab began clearing away the debris, dumping it down the *Niagara*'s side where it came to rest or slid further down onto the seabed.

The *Orion*'s mines were now breaking free from their moorings, presenting a new danger to the *Claymore* and other vessels that sailed the Gulf. The crew narrowly escaped further close encounters with the deadly mines. Once, when the chamber was being recovered, a mine tangled in the mooring line, so Johnstone in helmet diving gear had to descend to attach a line to the mine to pull it free. In so doing, his lifeline snagged the horns of the mine and, when released, the mine shot towards the surface dragging the unfortunate diver with it. Johnstone found him-self clutching the mine horns as he was pushed upwards with his helmet pressed against the bottom of the *Claymore*. After a heart-stopping period the crew managed to pass a line to a navy minesweeper. As the mine was pulled from Johnstone under the *Claymore* it suddenly broke free, surfacing close to the vessel's bow. It had been a close call and without Johnno's intervention between mine and hull, it would certainly have exploded. Others were not so lucky.

On the morning of 14 May 1941, HMS *Puriri,* a near-new coastal merchant ship commissioned into naval service as a minesweeper less than a month before, sailed off the entrance to Whangarei Harbour seeking a mine that had been down-buoyed and marked the previous day by the naval patrol launch *Rawea*. Constructed in 1938 for the Anchor Shipping and Foundry Company of Nelson, she had been used to carry general cargo around the New Zealand coast before entering service with the New Zealand Division of the Royal Navy (it was not until September 1941 that the King gave approval to the proposal that the Division should be known as the Royal New Zealand Navy).

The minesweeper HMS *Gale* had fixed the position of the buoy the previous evening but owing to the approaching darkness, the *Gale*'s commander decided to delay sweeping the mine until the following morning, when the two minesweepers searched a rough sea in poor visibility and were unable to locate the mine at the position of the previous night.

Lieutenant Douglas Blacklaws had been given command of HMS *Puriri* for this sweep operation as the regular commanding officer had been taken ashore ill with appendicitis. Blacklaws originally hailed from Aberdeen and served as a master mariner with the USSCo from 1925 to 1939. He had practically no experience with mine-sweeping operations – this perhaps resulted in the fatal outcome to the deployment. Rather than approaching the mine area in the accepted formation for such an operation, where each minesweeper deploys a paravane (a knife-bearing torpedo-like device with fins or vanes, towed from the bow) to sweep the water on each side thus providing the following vessel clear water to work in, the two commanders abandoned this practice, thinking they would have no problem sighting the buoyed mine. The mine, however, had originally been discovered when it was hauled to the surface in the nets of the fishing boat *Pearline* and when investigated by the *Rawea* crew it was found after hauling in 30 feet of line that the mine remained about six feet below the surface. There it was left, marked with a buoy, but in the interim the weight of fishing net had possibly pulled the buoy below the surface.

Blacklaws, directing search operations from the top of the wheelhouse as the *Puriri* followed astern of the *Gale*, was becoming concerned they had not yet sighted the mine buoy. Taking bearings on nearby Maro Tiri island, he noted they were about one and a half miles west of the mine's reported position. He decided to order a change of course to starboard to follow in the *Gale*'s wake. Leaving seaman Duncan Stewart with the warning, "Keep a close lookout, the mine should be around here somewhere!", Blacklaws commenced climbing down the ladder to the wheelhouse. Suddenly a violent explosion shook the minesweeper and Stewart found himself in the midst of flying rocks as tons of rock ballast erupted skywards. The startled seaman ducked behind the large compass

New Zealand National Maritime Museum

The Northern Advocate

Above: Arthur Bryant packing underwater explosives.

Right: The clamshell grab tears into the *Niagara*.

New Zealand National Maritime Museum

Above: The bullion room door comes aboard the *Claymore*.

Below: Waiting for gold. Captain Williams seated on the right.

New Zealand National Maritime Museum

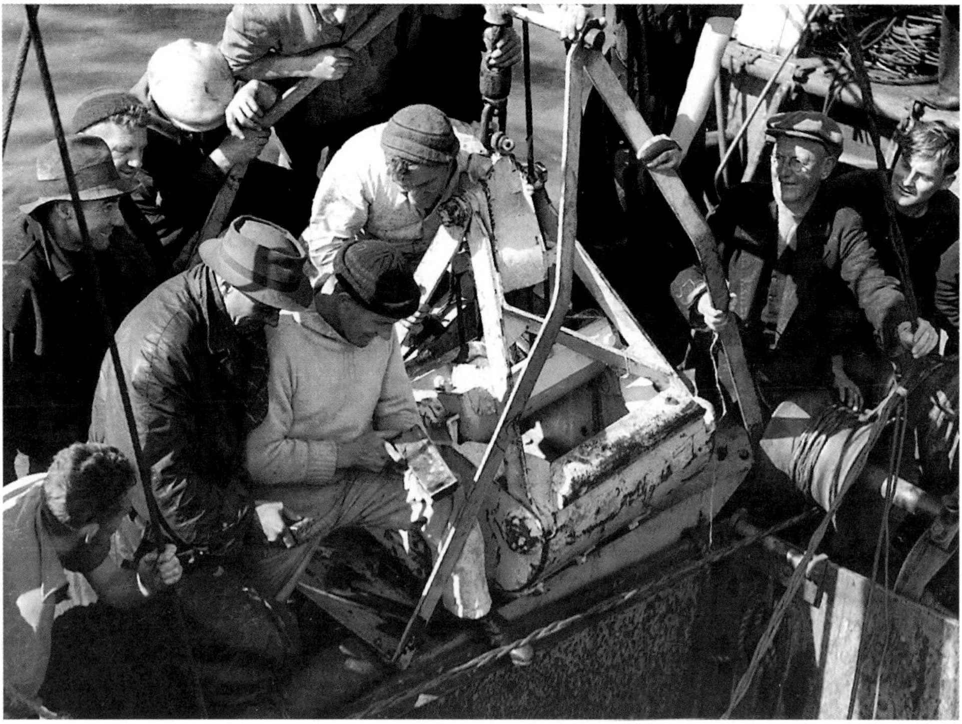

New Zealand National Maritime Museum

Above: The first gold bar is recovered. Johnno feels gold as Williams and the crew look on.

Below: *Claymore* crew surround a stack of *Niagara* gold bars.

Ray Nelson

New Zealand National Maritime Museum

Above: *Niagara* gold. One week's work. A stack of gold bars deposited at the Bank of New Zealand, Whangarei.

Below: Minesweeper HMS *Puriri*. A victim of *Orion*'s mines.

The *New Zealand Herald*

ALAN MARTIN

ALAN MARTIN

Above: Risdon Beasley salvage vessel *Foremost 17*. On the slip at Eden, preparations before crossing the Tasman.

Right: *Foremost 17* crew prepare mooring gear for the *Niagara* gold salvage – 1953.

ALAN MARTIN

Left: Risdon Beasley mechanical salvage grab.

Below: Risdon Beasley Galleazi diving bell on the deck of *Foremost 17*.

ALAN MARTIN

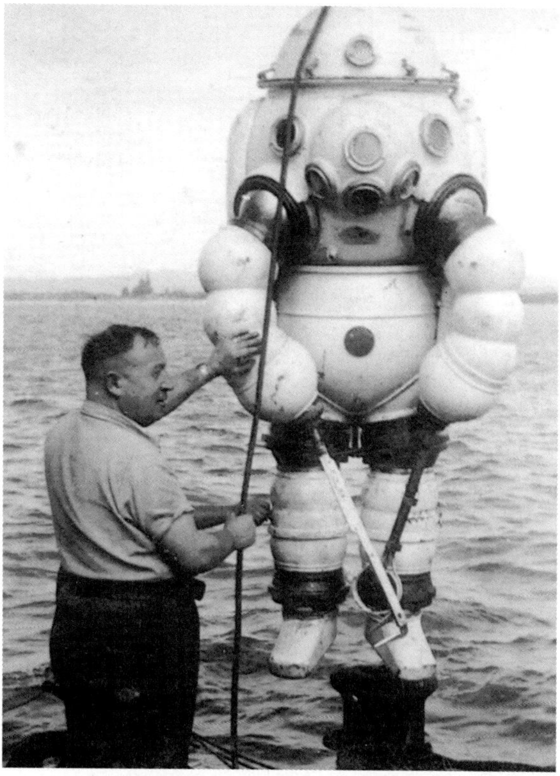

Alan Martin

Jeff Maynard

Above: Harold Chadwick prepares the iron man for a dive.

Right: Deploying the iron man atmospheric diving system.

Ray Nelson

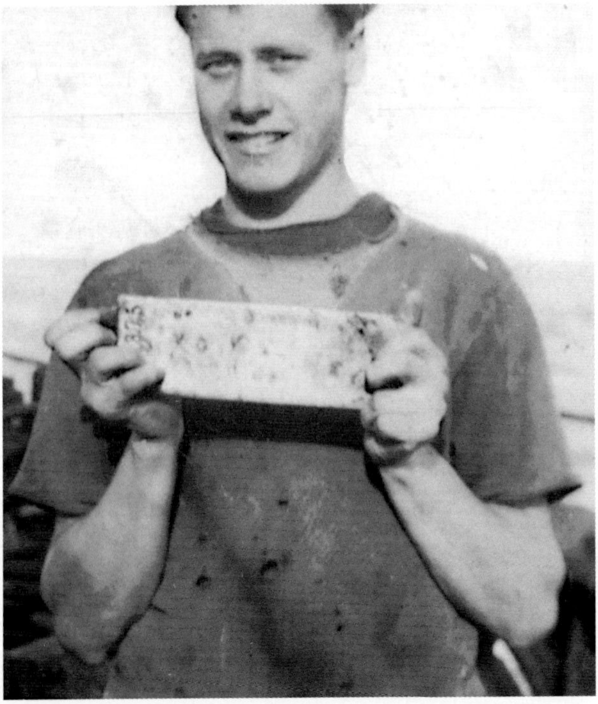

Alan Martin

Above: Ray Nelson wearing the CO2 scrubber unit used in the bell.

Left: Alan Martin with a 400 ounce gold bar recovered from the *Niagara* – 2005 value US$176,000.

casing to avoid the missiles as they flew about him. A sharp pain erupted through his leg as a rock slammed above his knee. Struggling upright, he searched around for Blacklaws, but he had disappeared. It was later reported the he had been seen falling into the sea among stone ballast and debris.

Dudley McNabb was working in the close confines of the paint locker when the ship struck the unseen mine. He felt the 188-foot vessel lift from the water as the mine struck and knew immediately what had happened. Momentarily disorientated in the darkness of the locker, he struggled to open the jammed door. There was little time if he was to save himself from a watery grave as the sudden explosion had torn the *Puriri* in two and she was quickly sinking.

Stewart struggled down the ladder dragging his injured leg and found the bridge covered by fallen ballast rocks. Both steel lifeboats had been pierced by the rock shower and were useless. He joined the rest of the crew as they struggled towards the stern to abandon the sinking ship; among them was McNabb who was lucky to escape entombment in the paint locker. Discarding their boots the surviving crew leapt into the sea and swam clear of the *Puriri* as she disappeared below the surface within three minutes. Five injured, including Stewart, and 24 other seamen suddenly found themselves alone as they struggled to remain afloat on the Gulf waters. They were the lucky ones. Lieutenant Blacklaws and four crew members had gone down with their ship. HMS *Gale* arrived 40 minutes later to rescue the survivors.

At the subsequent naval inquiry, the blame for the vessel's loss was attributed to the commander, who was held to have failed to carry out an organised search and to take proper charge of HMS *Puriri*. That seems a little unfair as Blacklaws had received little training or experience in mine clearance and the command had been thrust upon him when the regular commander had taken ill.

By early July, Johnstone was able to discern the white bulkhead of the strongroom but the chamber, now inside the liner, was in danger from the possible collapse of A-deck, which overhung the access opening. Operations were now directed to clearing away the danger from A-deck. The maw of the grab crunched onto bathroom and cabin fittings, adding to the growing pile of debris on the sea floor. To remove an obstructing beam required placing a three-inch tube blasting charge on a ten-inch surface. The surface crew completed the delicate manoeuvre following instructions from the diver some 360 feet below. At last – the bullion room door was in sight. Great care was now required to remove the door. Too much explosive could cause the walls, now acting as the floor supporting over two tons of gold, to collapse. The gold would then disappear into the bowels of the ship, making recovery impossible.

The services of Lieutenant Haynes, R.N. (Rtd) were called upon for advice on the size and design of the explosive charge needed. The war caused difficulties with obtaining shaped charges designed to direct the explosive force in a controlled manner. This shortage required the salvage team to design their own underwater charges by sealing the explosive charge inside three-inch diameter iron tubes some three feet in length. Suspended end-on from a gantry, the tube charges were lowered through tidal waters to the wreck. Following a practice period the crew gained confidence where, under directions from the bell, they were able to place the charge on a spot six inches in diameter. A great deal of experiment was required to gain some control over the explosive force released by the charges placed on the wreck. Test charges were used on the bow section of the sunken vessel, some distance from the bullion room, to develop charges that would give a clean cut of the steel hull plates. The door of the bullion room required a different approach, otherwise all could be lost.

Haynes arrived on board the *Claymore* during unfavourable weather. Williams, not wanting to delay until calmer conditions, sent the retired naval lieutenant down with Johnstone to survey the wreck and the salvage work that had so far been accomplished. Haynes described his dive and findings to the Navy as follows:

> Accompanied by the chief diver, John E. Johnstone, I descended to the wreck at 0930 and carried out an extensive survey of the progress of the salvage and also toured the starboard side of the Niagara, noting the position and, as far as visibility permitted, the extent of the damage caused by enemy mines. From my observations I am of the opinion, the reasons for which will be stated later, that the ship was struck by two or more mines, the second a considerable time after the first.
>
> The Observation Chamber (bell for short), lowered at the rate of 60 feet per minute, was placed on the wreck on A-deck where,

when one's eyes became accustomed to the conditions, visibility of about fifteen feet was possible. By bad luck the bell landed on the edge of a large hole in A-deck plating, overbalanced and I found myself sitting on top of the chief diver. I was not perturbed, being under the impression that anything might be expected to happen at such a depth under conditions where every piece of twisted plate, stanchion, girder or davit is reaching to hold and keep. The bell was hove clear and after a survey of this portion of the structure, I was lowered into the wreck to a point on D-deck shown in the *Niagara*'s plan as the Chief Steward's room, now demolished by explosives and grab. On this deck a considerable pile of fractured plate, angles and girders, the result of demolition, remain to be removed by the grab. The wood decks, under pressure of depth, remain loose and scattered.

The Chief Steward's room referred to extended athwartships from the starboard side of the ship. A line drawn vertically from a pair of boat's davits on boat deck a little before the foremost funnel cuts the porthole of this room on D-deck. The door of the room opened on to a passageway toward amidships, and directly opposite is the bullion room intact. It will therefore be seen that when the debris referred to on D-deck has been cleared, a matter of about three days with the grabs, the way is clear for the more delicate operation of opening the bullion room, which, so far as the Salvage Company is concerned, is the chief reason for my visit to the wreck.

I have given my opinion that a small charge placed at the forward upper corner, close to and under C-deck joining the vertical forward side of the bullion room, should effect a fracture, and on the supposition that there is a certain amount of pressure remaining in this sealed room, the additional pressure of the explosion will force the door outward. This danger of using heavy charges at this stage was emphasised. The charges and method recommended by the Naval Authorities for this particular work have proved to be of tremendous power. Plates and girders are cut clean as by knife and in many instances not one rivet remains at a distance of from 15 to 20 feet from the detonation. In order to provide space for work and also visibility, the outside plating and decks have been blasted and removed around the goal aimed at to a length of approximately 65 feet and 30-foot height. Plates up to a weight of nearly 3 tons have been blasted by explosion, torn out by grab and dumped clear or on the wreck.

Having completed my survey of the actual scene of salvage operations, I proceeded on a tour of inspection of the exterior of the wreck. I estimated the ship to be resting on her port side at an angle of about 70 degrees. From a vertical line just abaft the foremast to a vertical line just before the bridge superstructure, the bottom of the ship appears to be entirely blown in, a huge gaping hole extending in height of about 18ft. There is then a clean run of shell plating extending about 10 feet forward followed by another hole approximately 22 feet by 18 feet.

I then went to the bridge superstructure and moved along aft. The forward funnel has gone by the board owing, I imagine, to the cutting of the funnel guys by explosions. The bell was lowered to the bilge keel to a position roughly 100 feet aft of the forward damage described earlier, and between the forward and after funnels. Here the shell plating has been blown in revealing a hole about 45 feet in length by 8 feet high at its greatest width. At this point there is no doubt that the ship's back is broken. The bilge keel departing from the horizontal describes the arc of a circle between the forward and after damage. Fractured shell plates star out in various directions.

I cannot connect this damage with anything done by the first mine forward, for the reason that had it occurred simultaneously, the boiler room staff could hardly have escaped.

The bell returned to the surface at 1056 and after a further hour's work with bell and grab the wind freshened and operations were abandoned for the day. From my survey of the progress of the work to date I am of the opinion that a fortnight's actual work on the wreck will, with average luck, bring success. There are about three days grabbing and possibly a little more blasting required to clear away the debris on D-deck immediately in front of the bullion room, after which the salvage party will begin the final operation.

Haynes commented on his dive in the bell:

Conditions inside the bell are not uncomfortable. Breathing was normal, and it is considered that any discomfort such as palpitation or rapid breathing in the average healthy person could be ascribed to apprehension which at great depths and under conditions such

> as are being experienced in the present salvage operations will be understood. In short, it is a job for experienced divers temperamentally fitted for it.

The brothers John and Bill Johnstone were such divers. With great care Bill set about directing the placement of small charges along the hinges of the door. With careful stage detonations the door finally gave way, falling into the bullion room. The door aperture was widened using the grab and finally, the grab was lowered into the debris covering the gold below.

It was now October, well beyond the time frame predicted by Haynes, some ten months since the *Niagara* had been found and over six months since the salvors began to blast their way to riches. Williams and his salvage crew now forgot the hardships and dangers of the past months as every bite of the grab reached closer to their goal. With growing expectations they inspected each deposit of debris dumped onto the *Claymore*'s deck. Finally, on 13 October, the grab emerged from the depths with the box clenched in its maw, the box contained two bars of gold. In his report to the navy, Haynes stated that on his first acquaintance with the *Claymore* and her crew, the whole position had struck him as ludicrous: "An old, ill-equipped vessel with a total complement of fifteen men, only ten of whom are actually engaged on the wreck including two divers, and many of them mere boys, were tackling the most difficult salvage job yet attempted. Unlike the *Egypt* they were working throughout the winter in a greater depth of water and pestered by enemy mines."

Over the next eight weeks this team of "men and mere boys on an old ill-equipped vessel" recovered a further 533 gold bars. When salvage operations ceased on 7 December, 35 bars remained in the strongroom or rested nearby where they had dropped from the grab.

Due to wartime censorship the story of the salvage, although known to the press, was not released for publication until salvage operations had ceased and the government had cleared publication. However, before release of the story in New Zealand, the Bank of England gave approval to the Commonwealth Bank of Australia for release of the story for propaganda purposes to the Australian media. The Australian Prime Minister, John Curtin, released details of the gold salvage to the Australian press. This created uproar from the New Zealand press, including complaints to the Prime Minister, Peter Fraser, who at the time also had not been officially informed of the success of the salvage operation. Fraser in turn wrote a strongly worded telegram to the directors of the Bank of England complaining that they had not informed the government, who read the report in an Australian newspaper.

The salvage was proclaimed a world record for deepwater salvage. The London *Daily Telegraph* published the story of the salvage on 23 February 1942, hailing the gold recovery as "the greatest feat in the history of deep-sea salvage". In reporting the depth of recovery as 438 feet, the newspaper commented, "By their courage, patience and perfect team work, the members of the party wrested from Italy the palm won by salving the *Egypt*'s gold and silver at a depth of 396 feet in the Bay of Biscay." Although eclipsing the Italian salvage by only 42 feet, this was grasped upon by the embattled British as a victory to be proud of.

The foreward of a book published in 1942, *Gold From The Sea* by James Taylor, a journalist who had joined the *Claymore*'s crew, extols the achievement as having "established a diving record of which the Empire might well be proud". Further in the narrative, the author related how Williams' greatest joy was that he had shared in depriving Italy of the honour and prestige of holding the deep-sea salvage record. It was wartime and the Italians were the enemy: proclamations of this kind were regular issue from the government propaganda machine.

In London, politicians seized upon the news to support their own agendas. During the March sitting of the House of Commons, Alfred Edwards, the Labour member for Middlesbrough East, asked Sir Kingsley Wood, the Chancellor of the Exchequer, "Is the Chancellor serious in telling us that shipping space is being used to convey gold to pay the Dominions? Wouldn't the gold be safer at the bottom of the sea than in New Zealand?" Then he asked if the Prime Minister, Winston Churchill, was "aware that £30,000 worth of British labour has recently been used in salvaging gold alleged to be worth £2 million, but which is useless for the war effort; and if he will take steps to prohibit the use of labour and materials on any kind of gold production operations, seeing that the Allies already have larger stocks than can be usefully utilised".

March 1942 was a grim period for Churchill and the British Empire. With the disastrous recent losses of the battleships *Prince of Wales* and *Repulse*, the surrender of Singapore and loses in North Africa, Churchill was in no mood to be questioned on a triumph such as the record gold salvage. No doubt fortified by his pre-breakfast whisky and daily intake of wine, he rose to the Opposition question. In reply, Churchill stated he was aware of the gold salvage and it was certainly not useless for the war effort. He made the point that Britain had to pay for those essential imports which were not covered by Lend-Lease, or the generous financial arrangement made by the government of Canada. For this purpose exports had to be maintained, and gold was from many points of view a very advantageous export. He concluded with a comment added at the request of the Bank: "And I regard this salvage operation as having rendered a valuable service."

Churchill informed the House that the salvage operation referred to was that of the gold on the *Niagara* which went down in June 1940 and that the whole of the gold, valued at £1.75 million, was salvaged at a cost of about £70,000. Erroneously stating the value of the recovery and that the scene of the wreck had been in the Tasman Sea, he continued, "Mr Curtin recently gave details to the press, much to the indignation both of the New Zealand government and of ourselves, as we thought it a grave mistake to publish anything, at any rate until the gold had safely been moved away from Australia where it now is."

Commenting on the Opposition statement referring to the stock of gold held by the Allies, Churchill informed the House, "The statement that the Allies already have larger gold stocks than can be usefully utilised is beside the point, since the United States who hold immense stocks of gold had not offered to lend-lease it to us, and are not likely to do so. This country needs to maintain an adequate gold stock in view of our larger liabilities to other countries both inside the sterling area and outside it. This is a very explosive topic and no doubt the less said about it the better."

The crew of the *Claymore* disbanded in Auckland and the ship returned to the mudflats of Auckland harbour, her moment of glory passed. Except for their memories, the crew had little to show for their heroic efforts: no rewards or decorations were bestowed upon them. They accepted it was their duty, for King and Empire, to challenge the ocean depths during this time of conflict.

The salvage contract granted United Salvage Company an initial payment of £25,000 Australian for costs based on £10 per week for the ship plus wages for the crew of fourteen at an average of £8 each per week. A total of £19,597 was claimed for these charges. United Salvage paid approximately £5000 for costs of the salvage equipment including mooring gear and the bell. The contract awarded the salvage company 2.5 per cent of the value of the gold recovered, resulting in a payment of £59,266 Australian. The contract document had not arrived until well after operations had commenced. Now, with the job completed, both Williams and Herd felt bitter about the final award to the salvors. Nonetheless, as the Empire was at war, they decided not to make an issue of it.

However boys will be boys. To Ray Nelson, so much gold presented a challenge for his youthful skills. Given the task with one of his young mates of scrubbing the gold bars clean, the resourceful lads would occasionally drop a bar on a steel deck beam. The lads pocketed the resultant gold chips. The Commonwealth Bank of Australia representative, charged with recording the recovered gold bars, was none the wiser. Ray eventually had his particles of gold made into a ring, a fitting souvenir of his participation in the gold salvage. Later the ring was stolen, causing him to reflect that in the end, crime does not pay.

The Bank representatives reweighed each gold bar and found the total weight to be light by 9.099 ounces. Perhaps more than one ring was made from *Niagara* gold.

12

Unfinished Business

The thought of the remaining 35 gold bars lying in the *Niagara* was constantly on John Johnstone's mind during the remaining war years. To Johnno it was unfinished business – a challenge to a diver of his reputation, which in some quarters was being questioned. Over the years since the 1941 salvage, continuing rumours alleged that the salvage crew had recovered more gold bars from the *Niagara* than had been accounted for. Such rumours were strongly denied, but could be disproved only by recovery of the remaining gold.

With the ending of hostilities in 1945 and a return to civilian diving, Johnstone was now free to pursue salvage opportunities, including the many Japanese war wrecks in the waters around New Guinea. But with the advances in diving technology and the knowledge he gained from the 1941 salvage, Johnno considered that before tackling the Japanese wrecks he needed to attend to the unfinished business of the remaining *Niagara* gold.

To carry out such a salvage project, he was aware he would require the financial backing of investors to form another salvage syndicate. The value of the remaining gold at the time was in the region of £175,000 sterling; surely this would be an attraction for local Melbourne investors. Johnstone reportedly secured an agreement in 1942 from the bank granting him rights over future salvage attempts for the remaining gold. In so doing, he alienated his standing with John Williams, who considered that Johnstone had gone behind his back in securing the new salvage agreement.

Johnstone soon discovered the folly of his actions when prospective local investors, who had expressed strong interest in the venture, withdrew their support almost overnight. He got word that reports were circulating among the local business community stating any involvement with Johnstone's venture would only end in financial loss. Also that the man was crazy to contemplate chasing the lost gold. Johnno blamed Williams for spreading these stories, realising that he had upset his former boss.

On the other hand, Williams, who had terminated the salvage operation on Johnstone's advice that the remaining gold was inaccessible, was later astounded to learn his former chief diver had informed the Bank of England to the contrary. During a visit to London after the war, Williams was invited to meet with a bank representative who asked if he was interested in returning to the wreck to recover the remaining gold. Williams was informed that Johnstone had told the bank he knew where the remaining gold was and could recover it. Williams refused the invitation, even though the value of gold had increased and the bank offered to pay costs with a 50 per cent share to Williams. Johnstone and Williams, who had accomplished so much in 1941, were never to speak to each other again.

In April 1948, following his unsuccessful attempts to raise capital in Melbourne, Johnstone travelled to New Zealand seeking to attract investors and to gain the backing of the government. The media took great interest in Johnstone's proposals and reports of his plans featured in local newspapers. He proposed that the new salvage venture be combined with a scientific expedition to study marine life at depths previously unexplored off New Zealand coasts. Staff of the Department of Scientific and Industrial Research would be invited to accompany the salvage team. A new diving bell capable of depths to 1000 feet was to be constructed to Johnstone's design for use on the *Niagara* and to prove that salvage was possible in far greater depths than had been achieved before. With the bell used in 1941, Johnstone reported it was not possible to reach all the gold and many boxes in inaccessible parts of the debris remained: with other bars irretrievably lost in the mud, the value of the remaining salvageable gold would be around £100,000. The new salvage agreement signed with the Bank of England reportedly awarded the salvage group 50 per cent of the gold recovered, rather than the 2.5 per cent paid to the previous salvors. However, New Zealand income tax would claim a considerable amount of profits after salvage expenses.

An Australian company agreed to build the new diving bell at a cost of around £850. It would be smaller than the previous bell, but would have a grab operated by the diver from inside the chamber. This grab would dispense with the former laborious system of juggling with a separate grab from the ship, with the diver giving telephone directions to the winch-man. The steel telescopic grab arm working on a ball socket would have a six-foot radius of action with the ability to extend ten feet. Using the analogy of a mechanical robot, Johnstone informed the press that the new grab would have controllable pincers to close over any bullion. The operator would then place the gold into a special tray lowered from the salvage vessel. Accommodation in the new bell would be for only one person rather than two observers as in the previous bell. The new smaller bell, manoeuvrable in confined spaces, could search among previously inaccessible twisted hull structure. Weighing 35 cwt, it would be constructed of 3/4-inch welded steel, seven feet high, three feet in diameter at the base and five feet at the top. A battery-powered spotlight was to aid the search and the diver would have a telephone for communication with topside. A steel cable with a breaking strain of seventeen tons would suspend the bell for its excursions in the depths.

With his previous experiences of working on the *Niagara* in winter conditions, Johnstone planned to commence the new salvage operation in November when conditions would be more conducive to a successful recovery. Confident of raising the gold in three months, he hoped to have a meeting with the Minister of Finance to discuss the possibility of tax relief for the salvage operation. Although the salvors would be working on a 50/50 basis with the government and bank, unless the government offered tax relief, the cost of operations together with the heavy taxation would not make the operation a viable proposition. New Zealand at that time was experiencing a financial crisis and as the salvage operator would be paid in paper money, the recovered gold would be invaluable to the country. In fact, Johnstone found the government most willing to assist with the proposed venture. The Leader of the Opposition, Sid Holland, arranged for his meeting with the First Naval Member, Commodore Simpson, who offered to supply a 600-ton minesweeper as the salvage vessel at a charter rate of £500 per month. However, despite exposure of the proposed salvage in the press, Johnstone was unable to raise the capital he required for the second attempt. He left New Zealand determined to find the necessary finance for the salvage of the remaining gold. He decided to travel to London to seek investors.

The large number of wartime shipwrecks, especially those with valuable cargoes, were the catalyst for attracting investment in salvage companies. Over 10,000 merchant ships had been lost during the Second World War. The successful pre-war salvage methods developed by the Italian company Sorima for salvage of bullion from the *Egypt* and the 1941 *Niagara* salvage had proven the feasibility of cargo recovery from deepwater wrecks.

In 1926 Risdon Beasley formed his Southampton-based marine service company Risdon Beasley Ltd (RBL). With the outbreak of war, having had some experience in marine salvage, the company was contracted by the Admiralty to manage a fleet of salvage vessels. At the end of hostilities, having enjoyed some success with naval salvage contracts, RBL was aware that a large number of vessels lost during the war carried valuable cargoes, which now awaited salvage. The British government, under the War Risks Insurance Scheme, insured the majority of these valuable wartime cargoes and title now lay with the Department of Transport (DOT). The Salvage Association, incorporated by Royal Charter in 1867, acted as agents for the DOT and administered salvage agreements between the government and salvors. The Association has overseen thousands of sunken cargo recovery attempts: some have been successful but many have ended in failure.

RBL realised that as a British company it was in a good position to contract for the recovery of these valuable cargoes, and set about expanding their capabilities to work on wrecks in greater depths. Sorima was slow to get back into the salvage business after the war. As an Italian company there were naturally problems with obtaining British government salvage contracts. Before the war, deepwater salvage had been the preserve of Sorima. RBL capitalised on the situation and, blending Sorima's proven methods with the skills they had learned in the war, the British dominated salvage in the deep. Sorima's last successful venture was the recovery in 1953 of $61,000 in bank notes from an American ship before the company finally ceased operations in 1960.

In 1951 RBL recovered tin ore from the *Oronsa* at a depth of 290 feet in the Irish Sea. However, Beasley recognised that working in shallow waters around the United Kingdom did not give him an advantage over smaller salvage groups. In 1952 the company commissioned the first ship specifically built for deepwater cargo recovery, expanding operations for shipwrecks worldwide. By the mid 1950s, with Sorima now out of the picture, Beasley established a world monopoly for all cargo recovery below 180 feet, a depth then recognised as the limits for salvage divers. Using smash-and-grab techniques, observation chambers and grabs, the salvage group tore and blasted its way into the lost ships, searching for the riches they contained.

The five-week sea voyage from Australia to England gave Johnstone ample time to prepare a prospectus to present to London investors. In the event his endeavours came to naught, he considered that the time involved would be looked upon as a holiday. Arriving in London, his first priority was to visit the Bank of England to confirm that the salvage agreement of 1942 was still valid. He reported that he was told the agreement was "good for the next hundred years", adding that he had received a letter to support this. The visit also revealed that two other salvage interests had made approaches to the bank concerning the *Niagara*. To Johnstone, this interest indicated he was in the right town to find his investors. Eventually, he arrived at the doors of Risdon Beasley.

He had several meetings with the salvage company, which was well-versed in his exploits on the 1941 salvage. They listened with interest to his proposals to recover the remaining gold bars. The wreck lay on the other side of the world, a far distance from RBL's normal theatre of operations. It would be a costly venture to take a salvage ship, crew and equipment to New Zealand for the chance recovery of 35 bars of gold bullion, which may not now be accessible. The Williams 1941 salvage venture had failed to recover the remaining gold and it was only the word of the visiting diver that supported a further search. Johnstone left England feeling content that RBL was interested and would give consideration to his salvage proposal. He was told he would be informed of a decision in due course. He was to wait another two years.

Back in Australia Johnstone, now joined by his brother Bill, continued his endeavours to form a salvage syndicate. In February 1950, Bill wrote to the Governor of the Bank of England with new proposals to salvage the remaining gold. The bank's reply the following month confirmed acceptance of the proposals. The syndicate could proceed with preparations pending the finalisation of an agreement and establishing with the Commonwealth Bank of Australia, procedures for certifying costs for the venture.

The new proposal required the total cost of the venture to be to the salvors' account and no financial assistance would be given by the bank, even if no gold or insufficient gold was recovered to meet the costs. All gold recovered was to be delivered to the Commonwealth Bank of Australia for the account of the Bank of England, which would then purchase the gold at the current buying price (which at the time was 248 pence per fine ounce). The proceeds from the gold recovered would then be used to pay the costs of salvage, and the remainder was to be divided 60 per cent to the salvors and 40 per cent to the Bank of England.

Armed with the bank's consent, Johnno set about attempting to attract investors to the new syndicate. Bill travelled to New Zealand in search of a suitable vessel and equipment that would be required, including mooring ropes, derricks and winches. In an effort to eliminate the cost of bringing a vessel with crew from Australia, Johnno was determined to avoid the demands the Seaman's Union of Australia would place on the venture. He had previously experienced such demands on earlier salvage operations with the Union being awarded £14,000 for the refloating of the 10,000-ton *Manganella* and £41,000 for refloating the *Reynella* in New Guinea.

While Bill was in New Zealand, Johnno received a letter from Risdon Beasley requesting further information on the *Niagara* and conditions for salvage of the gold. He immediately sent a reply with information that investors, interested in the formation of the new syndicate, were awaiting Bill's return with his report before determining if the syndicate would proceed or not. In answer to questions raised in the letter, Johnno offered his opinions. To overcome the Australian union type of problem, he suggested he would arrange a crew where each member would take one share in the venture. In answer for the estimated costs for RBL to bring a salvage vessel, he advised that using a New Zealand vessel could reduce costs. He gave assurances that, unlike his 1948 visit when Labour was the government, now that Holland was Prime Minister, the government would give every assistance. However, taxation was still an issue and was the principal reason why in 1948 the attempt did not proceed. Johnno suggested that Risdon Beasley write to Holland to clarify the situation of taxation on the recovered gold, as this could take a considerable amount from the profit.

Referring to the letter Bill received from the bank, Johnno informed Beasley he was not agreeable to the 60/40 split even though both his brother and the syndicate members were. He considered that a 75/25 split would be required. His reason was that the bank was over-optimistic in thinking that all of the remaining 35 gold bars would be recovered: with an improved grab, it might be possible to recover 30 bars but even that may be optimistic. If only twelve or fifteen bars were recovered, the salvage expenses and initial outlay would remain the same, so the bank should give consideration to a 75/25 agreement.

Another question raised was that as 35 gold bars remained from the 1941 salvage, why had the bars not been recovered at that time? Johnstone replied that he considered the problem was due to the design of the grab used on the previous salvage. A type normally used for loading coal onto ships, the grab design was unsuitable for dislodging bullion boxes from the corners of the bullion room. He considered their efforts had been a trial-and-error exercise. At the time, they had no technical data to refer to. His thoughts now were that the bulk of the gold not recovered still remained in the room. He recalled five bars he could see but could not recover. Four were in the room out of reach of the grab due to the grab cable fouling on plating above. The other was lying in a depression on a hull side plate where the grab was unable to grasp it.

Risdon Beasley suggested that Johnstone should make another visit to England to discuss the situation. He replied that until there was a definite decision from the present syndicate on whether to proceed, he must support them. If upon Bill's return from New Zealand the syndicate decided not to proceed, then RBL would be free to approach the bank and negotiate a new agreement. If this eventuated, Johnstone said he would support their recovery effort including flying to England for discussions if so required.

The Melbourne syndicate eventually decided not to proceed with the proposed salvage venture. Another two years were to pass before John Johnstone returned to the *Niagara*.

13

Smash and Grab

With RBL's expansion into worldwide salvage operations, the *Cumberland*, with a cargo of 1850 tons of lead and copper sunk off the coast of Australia at a depth of 325 feet, was an attractive proposition for their new deepwater capabilities. In 1952 the company salvage vessel *Foremost 17*, whose design was not suited to long sea voyages, was towed to Australia for the recovery of the *Cumberland*'s cargo. To save on crewing costs, a salvage crew of 32 was later flown to Australia where they joined the ship, now based at the coastal town of Eden, for the cargo recovery operation.

As with young Ray Nelson nearly a decade earlier, the excitement of challenging the ocean to wrestle riches from her depths had captured another seventeen-year-old. Alan Martin, a member of the crew joining the *Foremost 17*, was the product of English seafarers and proud of the polar explorations of his grandfather, who sailed to both the Arctic and Antarctic in the nineteenth century and was with Shackleton on the *Pandora*.

Cargo vessels, although not the treasure galleons of old, provided rich pickings for those who dared. With the post-war shortages there was a demand for metals. Divers wearing traditional helmets and soft-suit dress worked the coastal waters – often pushing the limits of human exposure to the pressures of depth. There were numerous incidents, some fatal, of divers stricken with decompression illness. Alan had witnessed the results of this ever-present danger to those who plied their trade in the ocean depths. Divers and crew were not deterred by such dangers in their quest to recover the many sunken cargoes that littered the seas off Great Britain. A sense of achievement consumed all involved when, emerging from the depths with water and debris cascading from its jaws, the grab was swung aboard clutching cargo torn from the lost ships. Recovering large quantities of metals also had other rewards for the young salvor. For metals such as copper and tin, Alan would receive a bonus of two shillings and sixpence for each ton recovered, a tidy supplement to the wages paid to a young lad in those days. And there was no shortage of wrecks around the coast. On one location in the Irish Sea, RBL discovered three shipwrecks together, stacked one on top of the other.

With their experience working the shipwrecks around Britain, the crew of the *Foremost 17* tore into the wreck of the *Cumberland* nearly 50 fathoms deep. Sunk in 1917 after striking a German mine, it was a refrigerated ship carrying a combined cargo of frozen meat carcases and tons of copper, lead and zinc. Divers Frank Higgins and Dick Young were lowered in an atmospheric diving chamber to direct operations for placing the explosives and directing the grab in tearing through the deck structure to get the cargo. Alan and his fellow deckhands were startled on one occasion when the grab emptied its contents, a large quantity of bones, onto the deck. Initial thoughts that they had scooped up the remains of a dead crew member turned to relief when they realised the bones were the remains of the cargo of frozen carcases.

Finally in March 1953, after working eighteen months, the *Cumberland* salvage was completed. The salvors recovered 1825 tons of valuable metals. Comprising nearly 95 per cent of the metal cargo, the result was celebrated as an excellent return. During the operation, the salvage vessel made frequent trips back into Eden, a fishing port from which a number of trawlers operated, where the recovered ingots were unloaded into a compound near the wharf. It was later discovered that a large number of the lead ingots had gone missing. Having been originally lost to the ocean depths then recovered by deepwater salvage, most of the missing lead no doubt returned to the ocean depths as components of lost trawl nets.

The *Niagara* lay nearby, across the Tasman Sea off the northern coast of New Zealand. To take the salvage vessel to the wreck site would not be a major cost and a search for the remaining gold could be a worthwhile fill-in job while waiting for the next major salvage venture. RBL had by now negotiated a salvage agreement with the Bank of England. It was time to attend to John Johnstone's unfinished business.

Johnstone returned to England at Beasley's invitation, this time by air, and spent some seven weeks there attending weekly meetings. In return for giving the salvage company the benefit of his experience and vast knowledge of the complexities of diving on the *Niagara*, he received an agreement from Beasley to protect his interest and involvement with any future RBL salvage operation on the wreck. Staying at an old English inn, the Australian diver was somewhat intrigued by the old-world atmosphere including the date AD1140 carved in stone above the main entrance. Surrounded by such British tradition and impressed by his host's business acumen in marine salvage, Johnstone felt at last he was making progress in reaching his goal – to recover the remaining gold from the *Niagara*.

The question now arose as to what active role Johnstone would play in the salvage. Johnno, now nearly 60, assured Beasley he had no doubts about RBL honouring their agreement: he had nothing to hide and all he really wanted was to see the company divers recover the remainder of the gold. It had taken him a long time and a lot of patience to get down to the bullion and in doing so he considered he had come to know every torn plate and twisted beam around the bullion room. He was prepared to offer every assistance if Beasley required him to go to New Zealand, he said, but if the company divers did not want him on the scene, he would accept this: "I have had all the 'Honour and Glory' I ever want, but I want to see that bullion on top."

On returning to Australia, Johnno received a letter from Beasley confirming the arrangements they had agreed to. The rate of remuneration to be paid to him would be £21 10s sterling per week from the time he left Melbourne until his return. In addition it was agreed that he would receive a bonus on the gold bars recovered on the basis of:

> In respect of the first eight bars recovered – Nil
>
> In respect of each bar recovered above eight bars – 200 pounds sterling per bar.

In addition he would receive expenses for travel and the cost of his subsistence while on board the salvage vessel. In the event that his services were found not satisfactory and he was required to leave the ship, he would receive only the bonus for the number of bars exceeding eight recovered up to the date he left the ship. The payments would be full and final settlement of all claims that he or his brother Bill might have in connection with the operation including any advice or assistance already given.

With the completion of the *Cumberland* salvage, the *Foremost 17* sailed for New Zealand, arriving in Auckland early in April 1953. Johnstone located the salvage vessel berthed at a city wharf. It was with some feeling that he boarded her to join the salvage crew.

The proclaimed world-record feat of recovering gold from the *Niagara* at a depth of 438 feet was well known to the salvage world. The men of the *Foremost 17* studied the newcomer with interest. Here was the man who had reportedly dived deeper than the Italian divers of Sorima and who knew first-hand the conditions of diving for gold on the *Niagara*.

Johnstone was impressed with the salvage vessel and equipment; this was certainly going to be a more professional operation than his previous experience. Low in the water, equipped with four hefty derricks with a lifting capacity of 20 tons, a powerful windlass and four deck winches, the *Foremost 17* was certainly a different prospect than the *Claymore*, once described as "a floating junk heap of bits 'n' pieces with a cargo of nightmares".

Meeting Rodney Paul, the salvage officer in charge of the operation, Johnstone was introduced to the diving team. Frank Higgins and Dick Young had been the divers on the *Cumberland* while Harold Chadwick was joining the team in Auckland as diver for the "iron man" articulated diving suit. A former lieutenant in the Royal Navy, Chadwick (Chads) had once held the world depth record for diving in standard flexible diving dress. Contracted for deployment in the iron man, he would often say, "If the dive was under 180 feet, you have only been paddling!"

The iron man was an atmospheric diving system of the German Neufeldt and Kuehnke Articulated Shell design, manufactured in Italy by Roberto Galeazzi. Like the divers using the diving bell, a Galeazzi observation chamber also on board, Chads would be encapsulated within the steel shell under atmospheric pressure, thus avoiding the danger of the bends. Unlike a diver in the bell, the diver in the iron man, with his arms and legs enclosed inside articulated limbs, was able to move around, rather like a knight in a suit of armour. The articulated joints used a system of seals and lubricant to exclude the external water pressure while allowing limited movement. The system was lowered, aided by water ballast, on the end of a cable with the diver breathing on-board oxygen. Sorima had used a similar system with limited success on the *Egypt* salvage.

Another piece of technology on board was a suction device. Untried as yet, it was intended to assist the recovery by sucking gold bars from the bullion room. However the grab, directed by an observer in the diving bell, was the system that would be the mainstay of the salvage operation. A smaller, lighter chamber than that used by Johnstone on the earlier salvage, it was designed to carry only one diver. It had been used with success on the *Cumberland* by Young and Higgins, and Paul considered that this proven method would be more successful than the other untried systems.

RBL had earlier obtained charts from both John Williams and Johnstone indicating the *Niagara*'s position. Johnstone also reported in a 1950 letter that the wreck lay at a depth of 73 fathoms. He had earlier forwarded a sketch of landmarks on the surrounding islands, including a prominent tree on the mainland used to align the position of the wreck. During a 1947 visit to Auckland he had met again with Doug Munroe, the one-time crew member of the *Claymore*, who had more accurately calculated the wreck position than had Williams. Doug was then a trawler skipper and reported that the *Niagara* was a curse for trawlers fishing the area, snagging their trawl nets. Williams had also written to Risdon Beasley in 1952 with position details. With such information available, Paul considered that relocating the wreck would not present a major problem for the salvors.

Under Johnstone's guidance, the *Foremost 17* commenced the search to relocate the wreck. However, as with the initial search, the lost liner proved to be an elusive target, even with the aid of the salvage vessel's Asdic sonar system. Johnstone insisted that the search continue sweeping depths in excess of 400 feet in accordance with the reported depth of the previous world record salvage. He was adamant that the wreck would be found at a depth of 75 fathoms. Williams' reports also supported this. Paul, now becoming frustrated with the delay in finding the wreck, began to have doubts about the information supplied by Johnstone and Williams. Johnstone considered Paul a man of few words, a bank manager type of person, and later reported he never really had got to know him. He named him "Mr Gloom".

With the delay, young Alan Martin and his crewmates noted that Johnstone appeared worried with his failure to quickly put them over the bullion wreck and that his demeanour had become quieter. This phase of the operation lacked the excitement of the *Cumberland* and the constant activity of tearing into a shipwreck in the ocean depths. As the search continued, an atmosphere of boredom settled over Alan and his mates.

One day a fishing boat approached the salvage vessel, its skipper hailing, "You guys searching for the *Niagara*?" On receiving the affirmative, a reply came back across the water, "Well, you are in the wrong bloody place. Follow us, mate, we'll take you to her."

The little fishing boat set off, her crew joking about "bloody lost Poms, couldn't organise a party in a brewery if they tried!"

Arriving at the indicated position, the Asdic operator soon reported they were over a large wreck. Local fishing knowledge had surpassed the endeavours of Risdon Beasley's salvage technology. As a reward, the grateful salvors passed bottles of whisky down to the fishermen who went happily on their way. To Paul's chagrin, he discovered that the wreck lay nearly three miles away from the position indicated on Williams' chart, and the depth of the seabed was not the reported 75 fathoms but rather a shallower 66 fathoms.

14

Vindicated

With the discovery of this anomaly in position and depth, Johnstone felt his integrity with the salvage crew was now in question. His mana would be restored only with the recovery of gold from the depths beneath their keel. How would he find the *Niagara* after the twelve years since he last saw her? Would they be able to reach the remaining 35 gold bars or had the upper steel decks collapsed, taking the gold into the bowels of the wreck never to be recovered? These questions could be answered only by descending through the depths for a reunion with the lost liner. The boredom of the search over, Alan and his crewmates set about with a will laying the six giant mooring anchors and cables that would hold the *Foremost 17* in position over the wreck. It was now April and the southern winter would soon arrive.

Initial shallow-water tests of the iron man had revealed problems of water leakage through the articulated limb joints. On one test dive a frantic Chadwick shouted to the topside crew to haul him back to the surface. Water was leaking at a fast rate into the shell and the crew, hearing the anxiety in the diver's voice, wasted no time hauling the dive system back aboard the ship. The communications cable strapped to the main lifting cable would normally be separated as the diver was winched to the surface, preventing it from being wound around the winch drum with the main cable. But with the urgency now required, both cables were fed onto the winch at maximum speed. They were just in time. Water had risen to the hapless diver's chin by the time he was swung back aboard ship.

The problem lay with the articulated joints. These were packed with shims of varying thickness, providing a selection according to the depth at which the diver was to work. If the joint shims were too thick, there were problems with the joint seizing solid; if they were too loose, water under pressure of the depths would enter the suit – often at a fast rate. In an attempt to overcome leakage problems, Chadwick and his fellow divers wound bands of rubber sheet over the joints. A lot of faith had been placed in Chadwick using the iron man to recover much of the remaining gold from the bullion room. Now they were finally over the *Niagara*, Paul was beginning to have doubts.

It was decided to send Johnstone down first in the bell to establish the present condition of the wreck. He did not like the way Paul ordered him to be ready to dive the next morning. There seemed to be an implication that a lot of time had been wasted and that Paul considered Johnstone partially responsible for this. He did not sleep well that night, tossing and turning as he wondered what he would find.

With the top entrance cover bolted down, the encapsulated diver sat astride a motorbike seat mounted on a central swivel support enabling him to look out in any direction from the twelve circumferential ports. In rough seas the ship's wallowing and rolling would cause the hapless diver, subjected to minimal body clearance, to slam against the inside of the bell. In such situations the diver would wind a towel around his head turban-style to act as a protective fender. Johnstone admired the compactness of the Risdon Beasley bell and thought they would be able to get further into the bullion room than with the previous larger bell. He was keen to meet once again with his old adversary of the deep and eagerly prepared for the dive.

Descending into the depths, the bell's ports reflected flashes of surface light into the water column, attracting schools of fish to the intruder. Johnstone gazed out at the shoal of kingfish swarming around the chamber, marvelling at their beautiful streamlined shapes. The wreck below had become the focal point for a large community of marine life that now paraded around the excited diver. Visibility was excellent and the bell was held at 300 feet while Johnstone peered out of each port in an attempt to locate the wreck. Unable to discern the shape he was seeking, he called for another 30 feet depth.

Shadows materialised from the darkness and the barrel of the 4-inch stern gun came into focus – the bell was suspended too far astern. Johnno called for it to be repositioned 300 feet forward. The topside crew operated the winches hauling in and releasing cables to the six anchors as they manoeuvred the vessel with the bell swinging on the cable below. The wreck passed slowly and although Johnno could discern lifeboat davits he became confused about his location. After an hour he asked to be hauled to the surface. He reported that the wreck was covered by a vast forest of kelp, so he was unable to find his way to the bullion room. In order to proceed, he said, they needed to remove the kelp forest by using the grab aided by explosives. In his later account of this first dive he left open a question as to what actually transpired on his dive. Vast forests of kelp do not grow in the depths of the *Niagara* and later explorations have revealed only sponges, coral and encrusting growth on the wreck.

According to Paul, Johnstone, Chadwick and the other two divers got on well together, but they were unaware that Johnstone was unwell and at times in some pain until later when his condition deteriorated. In addition to overcoming the leakage problem and preparing the iron man to work in deeper water, Chadwick also made descents in the bell to the wreck to familiarise himself with the area he would later be deployed in. However it was Frank Higgins and Dick Young who carried out all the actual salvage diving work directing the grab and placing of explosives.

All aboard were encouraged when on the second and third days of grabbing in the debris outside the bullion room, two gold bars were recovered. It was a great relief to Johnstone that finally gold had been recovered – he had been vindicated. He felt as if great weight had been lifted from his shoulders, even to the point of forgiving comments about his integrity when he had set out to promote another attempt to salvage the gold – some from those he once considered as friends. He had proved them all wrong – including the Bank of England which Williams had told that the remaining gold was beyond recovery. In a letter to a friend in Whangarei Johnstone wrote, "I feel very happy about it all as I have lived for this day and now say – I am not mercenary but it's that certain something in me that is difficult to explain. I first want to see the job through. Please God be with us."

The divers had succeeded in getting into the bullion room in the bell but were unable to see any of the remaining bars. They suspected that one bar was lodged on an angle beam, and the bottom of the room appeared to hold something more than the blanket of silt they could see. Johnstone and the two divers were confident that gold bars lay beneath the silt. However, as in the case of the grab used by the Williams salvage, it was clear that the grab now being used would be prevented in reaching into all areas of the room by the overhanging part of C-deck.

It was now early May and Chadwick was still having problems with the sealing of the iron man. After a lot of work and improvisation, he managed a dive to the seabed at 382 feet, remaining for only three minutes before being hauled back to the surface. On deck, it was discovered that water had filled both legs. Chadwick remained optimistic he would be able to get the articulated joints sufficiently tight to enable him to remain below long enough to perform useful work in the bullion room.

Much to Paul's consternation, the press by now was reporting the latest *Niagara* salvage venture as major national news. Reporters were everywhere, even chartering aircraft to fly overhead while they were engaged in diving activities. Every little movement of the salvage vessel or its crew was news. Paul became resigned to the fact that it was better to make regular statements to the media rather than to have reporters digging up information he did not want published. News reports had even implied that the salvage team would be going after the *General Grant* gold off the Auckland Islands to the south of New Zealand.

The *General Grant* had been lost in 1866 while on passage from Melbourne to London. Of the 83 persons on board, only fifteen survived the sinking. The manifest recorded that the ship was carrying 2576 ounces of gold, but it was rumoured there was also a great deal more gold aboard – including the personal holdings of a number of goldminers travelling on the vessel following successful pickings in the goldfields of Australia. Legends of a vast amount of gold aboard the ship spawned a number of attempts over the years to discover the lost treasure. Many expeditions resulted in the loss of life of participants and all ended in failure. However, the name *General Grant* still conjured the romance of seeking sunken treasure and always attracted stories in the press. How such treasure fever can afflict people is illustrated by the tragedy of Eugene May.

May died in 1926 at the age of 68 from self-inflicted wounds. A graduate of three universities, an expert chemist and a soldier of fortune, he had been informed of the treasure by a survivor who showed him where the *General Grant* had sunk in a few fathoms of water. The survivor fired May's fervour by telling him there had been $US10 million in bullion and gold dust in the vessel's strongbox. In 1912, May fitted out an expedition in Australia and was ready to sail to the Auckland Islands when the *Titanic* went down. There followed a hue and cry for safer ships' equipment, which May was unable to afford. He had to abandon the venture losing $60,000. A subsequent attempt he promoted in California failed to eventuate. Further ventures to search for the legendary treasure ship also failed. Finally, despondent over his failure to reach the treasure, while staying in a cheap Oakland lodging house he took a knife and slashed his wrists. He died soon after in hospital. A friend informed the press that he intended to take May's ashes to the Auckland Islands and spread them over the ocean above the place where the *General Grant* had gone down.

Johnstone had earlier discussed the *General Grant* with Risdon Beasley as a possible target for salvage. An old gentleman, a Mr Sheehy, who had also written to Risdon Beasley, had approached him in Melbourne. In Johnstone's mind the wreck had become an obsession with the old man. Despite being informed by the diver that to go down to the Auckland Islands to carry out a survey would cost a lot of money, he was not deterred, replying, "All right, just say how soon you will be ready to leave." However, Johnstone would not be attracted by what he considered to be a "wild goose chase" and for Risdon Beasley such ventures were for dreamers and not for a professional salvage company. Besides, the 35 gold bars remaining in the *Niagara* totalled over 14,000 ounces. Why then spend a lot of money to go to the isolated southern islands on the off-chance there maybe more than the 2576 ounces of manifested gold?

A constant ocean swell on the beam accompanied the persistent easterly winds of May. As the salvage vessel needed to moor up approximately fore and aft above the wreck – laying in a north-to-south direction – the swell presented problems for the divers directing the grab. The rolling surface ship made it impracticable to direct the grab in the confines of the bullion room and work was delayed for periods until surface conditions became calmer.

As with the Williams salvage, the overhanging part of C-deck also prevented the grab reaching all parts of the room. This obstruction to the grab cable required further blasting by the divers but was kept to a minimum for fear the blast shocks may disturb the bullion room and the gold would be lost. The RBL team considered that the previous work carried out by Williams was a hindrance to their operation and not the way they would have approached the initial job. Their method would have been to cut the section with the bullion room intact from the hull and raise it to the surface. Williams and his team in 1941 did not have the advantage of the salvage equipment now available to the English company.

Finally the salvors' efforts produced results and further gold was recovered. Young and Higgins carried out all the diving, with Johnstone, now in a passive role, giving the pair all credit for their efforts. He enjoyed the camaraderie with the two divers, especially their evening chats discussing the day's diving operations. However, his health deteriorated and he reluctantly left the ship in June, returning to Melbourne where his doctor placed him under the care of a specialist. Paul was sorry to see Johnstone leave. He had been unaware of the old diver's deteriorating health and the pain he was suffering. At the time of Johnno's departure, eighteen gold bars had been recovered and he told Paul he thought it possible they would get a final recovery of 23 or even 24 bars.

Chadwick also departed the salvage, returning to England. The iron man had been a failure. Paul would have liked to have given the system a better test, but when they did get periods of fine weather all their efforts needed to be focused on the speedy recovery of the gold. For this the grabs were adequate and the practicalities for using the iron man on this job were limited. In zero visibility Chadwick would never have succeeded in picking up the gold bars.

The limitations of the suction device they had brought along were also obvious. The equipment was so big and weighty that if lowered down onto the wreck, under the constant movement of the *Foremost 17* it would have certainly caused damage to the bullion room. To have been able to pick up any gold, the suction mouth would need to be placed directly over the bar. Even if the ungainly system could be manoeuvred into such a position, it would be far easier and take less time to use the grab.

The salvors gained a wealth of knowledge about using the grabs that would be beneficial to RBL on salvage ventures for years to come. The plate grab they had obtained from Auckland and fitted with serrated teeth had proved very successful in picking up individual gold bars from flat surfaces, whereas the smaller cactus grab missed the bar on closing nine times out of ten.

By the beginning of July, 29 bars had been recovered, surpassing Johnstone's predictions. Despite Paul's reservations about recovering the remaining six, one further bar was retrieved before the salvage came to a close on 22 July. Of the five remaining bars, Johnstone knew of one box containing two bars that had dropped with wreckage down into the machinery space, and at least one he had seen fall from the grab that was lost in an unknown location. The bar he had reported lying in the shell-plate depression had apparently dropped through one of the many holes and gaps that had appeared in the plating since the previous salvage.

And so ended the 1953 *Niagara* salvage. The 30 bars recovered totalled over 12,000 ounces, a value at the time exceeding £164,000 sterling and a worthwhile return on the cost of the salvage. A newspaper reported the conclusion of the RBL salvage with the comment, "Now thanks to their skill in their unusual occupation, the *Niagara* has yielded up the last of her treasure and is never likely to be viewed again by man." In appreciation for their fine effort, the crew were flown back to England rather than to undergo the lengthy sea voyage; three of the crew including young Alan decided to settle in Australia.

John Johnstone had now put his critics to rest and with pride in his *Niagara* achievements gave live commentary with the films he had taken of the two salvage projects to numerous groups and schools. In a letter written to a friend in 1972 he noted, "I haven't seen John Williams for nigh on 15 years. To have gone back and got the rest was a body blow to him and he's never forgotten or forgiven me." Johnno died in 1976 while resident of a Melbourne nursing home. His diving feats are still the subject of television documentaries, books and articles – many continue to record the 1941 salvage as a world record in a depth of 438 feet.

Risdon Beasley continued with the recovery of sunken cargoes, becoming the largest cargo recovery salvor in the world. In the 30 years from 1947 to 1977, it recovered 51,194 tonnes of sunken cargo from 77 ships. The company finally ceased operations in 1981, as practically all feasible recoverable cargoes of value had been worked out. With the departure of the *Foremost 17*, the *Niagara* was left once more to lie in peace in the depths of the Hauraki Gulf.

The mid-1950s saw the arrival of recreational diving where humans, with the aid of underwater breathing apparatus, were returning to the ocean depths from where life on earth had originated. The demand breathing-pressure regulator, commonly known as the aqualung, co-invented in the 1940s by Frenchmen Emile Gagnan and Jacques Cousteau, had opened the doors to underwater exploration. Free-swimming divers, unrestricted by cumbersome dive dress and surface tethers, discovered an enchanting, fascinating world. As the sport grew, New Zealand divers were attracted to the romance and adventure of exploring sunken ships. Hidden in the seas around New Zealand coasts, these time capsules and the possible riches they contained were an attraction for exponents of the new submarine sport.

One wreck remained beyond the reach of these ambient pressure divers, an unreachable goal lying in the pressures of deep water. The *Niagara* remained hidden in the depths – an unseen spectre of a dream world, inaccessible with the limitations of diving technology of the day. This was to change with the race to the Moon. In the 1980s, developments in microchip technology created by man's thrust to escape Earth's gravity into space opened the doors to the deep ocean. Once more the sunken liner was to become a goal for human intervention.

PART THREE

The Explorers

AUTHOR'S COLLECTION

AUTHOR'S COLLECTION

Above: Author spearfishing, Banks Peninsular 1953. Jerseys gave some protection against cold water.

Right: Jaan Voot, Keith Gordon and Wade Doak clad in home-made rubber dry suits. Banks Peninsular 1955.

Jim White

Above: The author pool tests his home-made Jim White design aqualung, 1956.

Below Left: Jim White prepares a home-made aqualung regulator for a dive. Christchurch 1956.

Below Right: Kelly Tarlton, wreck diver, treasure hunter. 1937–1985.

Jim White

Rosemary Tarlton

Australian Natural Maritime Museum Collection
Reproduced courtesy of the Museum

Above: A painting of the *Niagara* by E.B. Norton.

Below: Tutukaka Marina – dive expedition base.

Author's Collection

Dr Mark Spencer

Above: Diver swimming at 92 metres inspects the results of Risdon Beasley's 1952 smash and grab salvage on the *Cumberland*.

Bottom Left: *Niagara* wreck highest point, the stern docking bridge railing at 328 feet. (ROV Image)

Bottom Right: ROV image of *Niagara* third-class saloon skylight twisted from mine blast.

Author's Collection

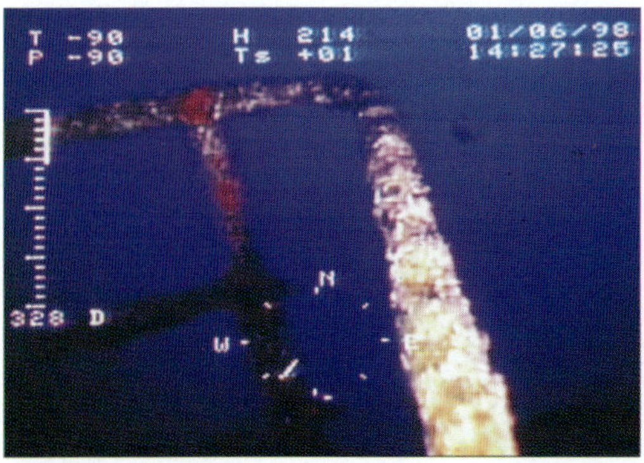

Author's Collection

15

From Snorkel to Robot

The sudden appearance of shoals of fish heralded the shipwreck we were seeking. Shining scales reflected our lights, the iridescent hue exploding suddenly from the darkness of the depths we were probing. The school of golden snapper provided a focal point and as they parted, distant shadows materialised to capture our full attention. Our eyes strained to discern the sunken liner lying in her grave at the bottom of the sea.

The small team of veteran divers crowded into the close confines of the cabin gazed transfixed as the shadows ghosted onto the monitor screen. I slowly eased the control stick forward and the shadows came closer, taking on form.

Below at a depth of 320 feet, the little robot obeyed the signal transmitted down into the depths. A constant stream of electronic data multiplexed through the umbilical cable relayed my commands into the underwater machine. The horizontal thrusters came to life, their propellers driving the robot towards the shadows in the dark blue of the twilight zone we had entered. Through the video camera eye the shadows emerged as structural angles, deck railings covered with prolific sponges and deepwater corals. Telepresence transmitted our senses down through the water column, providing the ability to project our thoughts, our eyes and even our hands into the depths. We were there – we had arrived. As with those who had come before us, the *Niagara* was to capture our souls.

It was June 1988. Our charter vessel, the 14-metre *Norseman*, was tethered to the shipwreck below. The black umbilical cable snaked over the stern into the depths supplying life to the underwater Remote Operated Vehicle (ROV) now approaching the sunken liner. I had been warned about abandoned fishing nets draping sections of the wreck, so caution was required – we were approaching unknown territory.

Flying the ROV slowly over the stern section, the starboard wing of the stern docking bridge came into view. Angled towards the surface 325 feet above, it was the shallowest section of the wreck. Our lights revealed a blaze of colour from the marine growths that festooned the railings. The sleek form of a hapuku flashed a silver reflection as it slowly swam into the protective shelter of the wreck interior. Using the articulator claw jutting forward of the ROV, I grasped the encrusted railing of the docking bridge and relaxed. We were safe here from entanglement in the wreck. Using the pan-and-tilt mechanism of the video camera, we surveyed our surroundings.

Against a surface backlight, shoals of fish were scattered across the blue ceiling. Formations of inquisitive kingfish swam past, patrolling the open water above the wreck. Closer to the protective wreck structure, a pot-pourri of fish species milled around the sponge growths and black corals that sprouted from the steel plates. Lying out on the submarine plain of the Gulf, the *Niagara* had been transformed into an underwater city that beckoned us to explore further. The excitement of exploring the sunken liner and her secrets gripped all aboard as we descended into the scenes transmitted in real time from below. I released the ROV's hold on the railing and applying power to the vertical thruster descended into the darkness of the shadows.

Together with my old diving compatriots who joined me on our first *Niagara* adventure, I had begun diving beneath New Zealand seas in the early 1950s. Living in the southern city of Christchurch, our young minds were captured by the exploits of Hans Hass recorded in his book *Under the Red Sea* and Jacques Cousteau's *The Silent World*. The boy next door, Wade Doak, and I scraped together the money to purchase masks and snorkels and improvising on other requirements set out to explore the ocean depths.

Spearfishing dominated those early years. Holding our breath we would slip beneath the surface to stalk our quarry through forests of kelp and the submarine terrain of coastal Banks Peninsular and Kaikoura. Free-diving developed our knowledge of this new world. The continuous exertions as we strove to improve our diving technique to dive deeper or remain underwater longer honed our bodies to be at home in the sea. We learned how to handle the many temperaments the ocean would suddenly spring upon us, providing the survival skills we needed in later years to penetrate further into the depths. Today, commercial interests process large numbers of neophytes on short courses to become "certified divers". This is often after only one ocean dive – it is unfortunate for many that the free-diving apprenticeship of past years is now ignored.

Aqualungs arrived in the mid-1950s onto the shelves of local sports equipment retailers, though their cost was beyond the resources of many in our group of young divers. These compressed air systems were offered to the public without any instruction and with very little information on guidelines for use. Diving physiology was something we had not heard of, except that one could possibly get the bends if one remained too deep for too long. We were also aware of the danger of rupturing your lungs if you held your breath while ascending from the depths.

I started an engineering apprenticeship with the national airline and there met Jim White, an engineer from Ireland. Jim had developed a demand regulator similar to Cousteau's aqualung, and with access to the airline's engineering facilities we fabricated the required parts to produce a regulator for under $10. With Jim's war-surplus air compressor, once used to power a B29 aircraft gun turret, we pumped air into the pressure cylinders. The majority of early cylinders were ex-CO_2 fire extinguisher or war-surplus aircraft cylinders into which we pumped compressed air to pressures of 1800 psi. One intrepid diver had even manufactured his own cylinder. An engineer at the railways, he had welded end pieces to a steel tube making a beautiful job where it was hard to detect that the cylinder was not factory-made. On learning the origins of the cylinder, Jim would not fill it above 600 psi. Despite the non-existence of yet-to-be developed equipment such as buoyancy compensators, pressure contents and reliable depth gauges, we survived our ignorance. The door had been opened to dive deeper into the depths.

With the acquisition of factory-made equipment we ventured further afield, seeking new underwater adventures. With Kelly Tarlton, Wade Doak and others, I travelled to Stewart Island in search of better underwater visibility. In the Marlborough Sounds we dived our first shipwreck, the *Koi*. Fascinated by the sunken ship we excitedly explored her remains, taking underwater photos of divers peering out from her portholes similar to the images we had admired in Cousteau's *Silent World*. For Kelly, this first wreck dive was to lead to his fascination and exploration of numerous shipwrecks across the world.

Spearfishing was replaced by underwater photography as a major activity and our interest turned to diving the warm crystal-clear waters of the South Pacific islands. In 1959 Kelly led his Coral Seas Expedition to the Admiralty Islands north of New Guinea. Wade and I had started the diving magazine *Dive* and published Kelly's reports of his team's adventures. Stories of diving with sharks, riding on manta rays and deep dives on coral reefs fascinated the diving fraternity.

The expedition received *Porpoise* compressed-air diving systems from the Australian makers. These units differed from the Cousteau-Gagnan twin-hose regulators in that a single hose supplied a second-stage regulator gripped in the diver's mouth. These regulators were extremely easy to breathe and became the forerunners of future regulator design. Armed with such equipment and in clear waters, Kelly gained the confidence to dive to depths further than he previously reached. Relating a dive down the reef wall to 200 feet, he described his first experience of nitrogen narcosis. Under the pressure of the deep, the 79 per cent of nitrogen in the air we breathe has an intoxicating effect on divers – sometimes with fatal results:

> At 130 feet we began to feel the effects of nitrogen narcosis. We could feel a slight fuzziness in our heads as if we had two or three drinks. At 180 feet we were feeling quite light-headed. It was hard to imagine we were swimming down a slope, my brain kept telling me we were swimming across a flat bottom. Possibly my balancing organs were being affected by the narcosis. It was only by a concentrated effort that I forced myself to watch the hand on my depth gauge winding itself round.
>
> By now my tongue felt as if it was filling up my whole mouth. Birds were singing in my head. A vision of a grove of trees with a small creek running through it kept drifting in front of my eyes. I knew I should be keeping a look out for the big sharks that we occasionally saw swimming in these deeper waters but I could not be bothered to turn my head to look. Occasionally a worm on the bottom did not pull back into its hole as we approached and I found myself trying

> to poke them back with my finger. I suddenly realised that I must pull myself together and forced myself to look at my depth gauge. The luminous paint on the dial was glowing like a neon light with the needle passing the 200-foot mark. We had been down about fifteen minutes and I tapped Dennis on the shoulder and gave the signal to ascend. I fastened my eyes on a small bubble and followed it up. At 50 feet we levelled out and swam back to the anchor chain to decompress. It was not until I was nearly finished decompressing at 10 feet that the last of the narcosis finally left me.

Although still ignorant of the many physiological dangers of ambient diving breathing compressed air, these dives gave Kelly the confidence for future deep diving.

Following the return of the Coral Seas Expedition, Wade and I, accompanied by two other divers, travelled to New Caledonia on our South Seas Underwater Expeditions. It was a time before television when the media would report with great drama the dangers divers faced in the ocean. As earlier with Kelly, the media hype focused on where we would be diving in shark-infested waters. Although a great many people considered we were all insane, the publicity did assist us to gain sponsorship with equipment from manufacturers. Not all the equipment included diving equipment: some supplied footwear, others camping equipment or foodstuffs. On reflection, one now wonders if some suppliers considered that by association with our underwater ventures, they might gain unexpected media exposure, especially if we were to succumb to shark attack or other dangers that lurked in the depths. If so, they were disappointed.

The two expeditions whetted our appetites for underwater adventure in tropical waters. There followed in the early 1960s a succession of diving sojourns to New Caledonia. Underwater photography by now surpassed spearfishing as the major underwater activity. Kelly, Wade and my other close diving friends left Christchurch to live closer to the clearer warmer waters of Northland. The Poor Knights islands off the east coast were to become their diving Mecca. In search of further diving adventures I also moved, but further afield to Western Samoa.

The discovery of the clear waters of the Poor Knights with their abundance of marine life enticed divers searching for adventure to dive deeper. New knowledge of diving physiology, especially with deep diving, became available. Divers learnt to recognise the oncoming effects of narcosis and with heightened awareness kept it under control. United States Navy Diving Tables were now available to sport divers, giving some measure of safety against the bends. The barriers to greater depths were cautiously probed, lessons were learnt and on occasions a diving accident would be a harsh reminder of the dangers of challenging the depths.

In 1965 while on a spearfishing trip to the Three Kings islands off the northern tip of New Zealand, a group of divers including Kelly and Wade discovered the remains of the shipwreck *Elingamite* at a depth of 150 feet. In 1902 while en route from Sydney to Auckland the ship, carrying bullion to the value of £17,320 sterling and 194 passengers, was wrecked on the desolate islands while sailing in heavy fog: 45 lives were lost. Using standard helmet diving dress, early divers made attempts to recover the bullion, but after two had succumbed to the bends, further attempts were abandoned. Forming a salvage syndicate with other divers, Kelly and Wade went after the remaining bullion. Working in 150-foot depths with the aid of the newly developed decompression meter, the syndicate avoided the bends with their salvage of 10,000 coins.

The romance and adventure of diving shipwrecks, especially where treasure was involved, captured Kelly. He set about accumulating data on treasure wrecks both in New Zealand and foreign seas. The *Niagara* with her remaining gold captured his imagination, but she was beyond attainable depths using the diving technology then available to him. He turned his attention to more accessible wrecks and, with artefacts recovered on his successful salvage operations, established the Kelly Tarlton's Shipwreck Museum in the Bay of Islands. Displayed prominently among the exhibits were items recovered from the two *Niagara* gold salvage operations, together with mementos from survivors of the sinking.

The *Niagara* also continued to attract the attention of the public. The media occasionally featured the stories of Johnno Johnstone's deeds, which had also become the meat for many adventure magazine stories. To Kelly, the nearby sunken liner in her ocean grave remained the holy grail of New Zealand shipwrecks – a challenge to be conquered. Other divers also dreamed of the challenge to dive down into the depths to the legendary sunken liner and recover the treasure she held. But the wreck remained a dream.

Speculation abounded on the amount of gold that might remain on the wreck. In 1975, Auckland diver Lynton Diggle wrote to the Bank of

England seeking information on the lost gold and procedures for obtaining salvage rights to the wreck. In reply the bank confirmed the existence of five remaining gold bars and advised that Her Majesty's Treasury was prepared to consider a salvage contract. This would be under the proviso that all salvage work would be at the salvor's expense and HM Treasury would receive a "reasonable share" of any proceeds. Further, the Treasury would enter into a contract only if the gold was valued at the prevailing price, at that time £14.5833 per fine ounce.

Lynton in reply queried the bank's pricing of the gold, as the world free market price at that time was around $US175 per ounce. At the bank's quoted price, he commented, the remaining bars were destined to remain at the bottom of the sea forever. A reply curtly informed him that any agreement entered into by Her Majesty's Government required the gold to be sold to the government agent at the bank's stated price. A list of details including the serial numbers of the remaining bars and their weight revealed a total weight for the five bars of 2018 ounces.

With the Treasury's insistence that the salvor was to pay all costs and sell the gold to the government at a predetermined low official price, Lynton abandoned any ideas for a salvage attempt. His plans were to use expensive mixed-gas diving techniques – with the Treasury's conditions it would be impossible to find financial backing.

The *Niagara* continued to lie undisturbed in her submarine grave. Occasionally a trawl net would snag on the upper structure, wrenching stanchions and davits from their mountings. Abandoned, the ghost nets draped across the wreck continued to trap shoals of fish attracted to the submarine city. Caught in the mesh, the hapless creatures would die a slow death. Life also flourished with cup corals and encrustations sprouting from hull plating to encapsulate the liner in a shroud of marine growth. In the shelter of the promenade deck, bushes of black coral blossomed as the Gulf's tidal flow fed nutrients to the growing marine population. For the local line fishermen, the *Niagara* became productive grounds. Hapuku, a large goggle-eyed grouper, attracted to the cavernous wreck were a prime target. The wreck became festooned with lost hapuku fishing lines snagged around its many protuberances.

Meanwhile, the space race between the United States and Russia to land the first man on the moon spurred major advances in microprocessor technology. The microprocessor, or chip, allowed complex operating systems to be bundled into small packages, enabling complicated tasks to be accomplished from a distance by robotic remote control. Environments considered dangerous to humans were now accessible to direct human intervention. The underwater industry grasped the new technology to gain access to greater depths, unrestricted by the time constraints working in the pressure of the deep.

ROVs were developed with the ability to remotely explore the depths and accomplish various tasks underwater. ROV video cameras could transmit underwater images through a cable in real time to surface observers. Telepresence, a term coined by the industry for the real-time video images, transported the human senses down into the depths, creating the impression of being actually there. Man has only once physically descended to the deepest part of the ocean. In the 45 years since, he has never returned.

In January 1960, eight years before humans landed on the moon, Don Walsh and Jacque Piccard, encapsulated in the bathyscaphe *Trieste,* descended 35,800 feet to the bottom of the Mariana Trench – the deepest known place on our planet. At this depth their spherical chamber was subjected to a pressure of some 200,000 tons. It was not until 35 years later, in 1995, that humans again visited the deepest ocean. This time their return was not in person, but in the form of a Japanese-developed ROV named *Kaiko*. The vehicle's technology and cameras transmitting real-time images to the surface had replaced the requirement for human presence to carry out scientific tasks. As with the exploration of the far planets of our solar system, it is human intelligence, not human presence, that has resulted in the most spectacular discoveries.

In the ocean depths, ROVs provide humans the technology to explore deep shipwrecks without the hazards of diving in a dangerous environment. For example, in 1986, Dr Robert Ballard returned to the wreck of the *Titanic,* discovered the previous year with the aid of a remotely operated camera sled. Ballard and his crew descended 12,500 feet to the wreck in the deep-diving submersible *Alvin*. Carried on the front of *Alvin* was a small ROV dubbed *Jason Jr,* designed to withstand the 7000 psi. ocean pressure while operating in confined spaces. Parking the submersible on the deteriorating deck of the wreck, the ROV pilot flew the little robot out of its cradle into the bowels of the rusting liner. Manoeuvring through staterooms and the area of the grand staircase, *Jason Jr*'s lights and cameras probed the darkness transmitting images in real time to the *Alvin* crew.

The *Titanic* exploration, a milestone in deepwater shipwreck exploration, fired enthusiasm among wreck hunters to explore deep shipwrecks previously considered inaccessible. Once again, interest was reawakened in visiting and exploring the *Niagara*.

16

New Tools

ROV systems are expensive. Early systems were US-government funded for use by the military, and initial commercial development was slow. The underwater community was at first hesitant to accept the practicality of using tethered, free-swimming robots. Saturation diving and manned submersibles were the accepted tools for deepwater tasks until the late 1970s when the oil industry, recognising the benefits of the technology, spurred a period of rapid growth.

In 1981, Benthos Inc, an oceanographic company based in Falmouth, Massachusetts, contracted a young MIT engineer, Chris Nicholson. Benthos, which specialised in deepwater camera and communication systems, engaged him to build a ROV that would be smaller and lighter than the systems available at the time. Chris had a background of designing and building underwater systems and had developed ideas for a small compact system he had wanted to put into practice. The Benthos requirement, designated as a Remote Propelled Vehicle (RPV), gave him the opportunity he had been waiting for.

Working long hours under a tight schedule, he completed the vehicle within the four-month period Benthos had set for the project. Its unique features including the camera systems attracted the attention of a Canadian organisation that in the previous year, using a side-scan sonar system, had located the 1853 shipwreck *Breadalbane* sunk in the Arctic waters of Resolute Bay. The project involved the National Geographic Society which was anxious to obtain images of the lost ship preserved in the icy waters. They signed a lease and Chris with the newly completed RPV system was off to the Arctic.

Images captured by the RPV revealed the 128-year-old wreck in a remarkable preserved state. Still intact, the hull and superstructure covered with thick branches of orange and pink soft corals presented the explorers with a kaleidoscope of colour. The RPV cameras recorded equipment including lanterns and the ship's compass still in position as they were when abandoned by the crew when escaping the sinking vessel. *National Geographic* exposure of the lost ship beneath the Arctic ice captured worldwide interest. To obtain the film images, the RPV had remained underwater in the icy ocean at a depth of 320 feet for a number of hours. A diver attempting to carry out the same mission, in addition to surviving the cold, would have had to undergone many hours of decompression.

With the success of the Benthos RPV system, Chris set about designing a "low cost" ROV under the banner of his own company Deep Sea Systems International Inc. Working with the support of Benthos, he produced the MiniRover line of underwater vehicles capable of diving to depths of 500 to 1000 feet and selling at $US28,000 to $US38,000 for basic systems. The new small ROV systems were an instant success, attracting the attention of scientists, contractors, wreck hunters and treasure seekers among others.

In the South Pacific, the developments in underwater remote-operated technology were of great interest to Ian Lockley, head of the Fiji-based salvage company Salvage Pacific. I had met Ian while living in Samoa where a fellow aviation engineer and I operated a small diving company catering for visiting dive tourists and carrying out the occasional salvage job. Our largest salvage venture had been the raising of a dredge that suddenly sunk while dredging a new harbour on the island of Savai'i.

At Ian's invitation, I dived with his Salvage Pacific divers working on a contract to remove fuel oil from the wartime wreck of the liner *President Coolidge* in the New Hebrides (now Vanuatu). Working in depths down to 200 feet using compressed air, we needed to carry out long periods of decompression before returning to the surface. To facilitate this Ian designed a unique four-man submersible diving chamber (SDC). The sunken troopship lay on her port side, like the *Niagara*, allowing the SDC to be attached to the bilge keel of the wreck. Using a counter-weighted chain and block system, the divers were able to regulate chamber depth from 40 to 10 feet according to their decompression requirements while resting within the dry chamber. Comfort during long periods of decompression was further aided by music piped from the surface vessel above and hot meals transported in a pressure pot down to the chamber.

The team made salvage history with the pumping of 750 tonnes of fuel oil from the wreck to surface storage. The recovered oil was still usable after 34 years in the wreck and was pumped into the bunkers of a visiting P & O cruise ship. The success of the *Coolidge* oil recovery was followed by other successful Pacific salvage ventures as Ian turned his attention to the challenge of recovering cargoes from deepwater wrecks. He recognised the new remote technology as the key to unlocking the riches in the ocean depths. He purchased two Benthos RPV systems and set about developing a deepwater electro-hydraulic grab recovery system for working in depths down to 3000 feet.

Ian began researching possible targets for the new technology. Among the list of local prospects, the *Niagara* appeared an attractive proposition. Not only had gold risen in value, but he also identified other cargo of possible value having gone down with the liner in 1940.

He signed a salvage agreement with Her Majesty's Treasury for the gold bars and planned a survey of the wreck. It was now 1987, 34 years since the wreck had been last sighted, and its present condition was unknown. Perhaps it was now a collapsed pile of steel plating and machinery on the seabed. Unlike their portrayal in movies, shipwrecks do not remain in the state they were on the day they slipped beneath the waves. Born from nature's elements, shipwrecks in the ocean deep eventually return to the atomic particles and matter from which they originated. Even in the deepest ocean a sunken ship over a period of time biologically implodes. After 90 years, the *Titanic* at a depth of 12,500 feet is slowly being consumed by oxidising bacteria in the form of rusticle growths resembling stalactites. In the short period since 1986 when Robert Ballard first explored it, large sections of the wreck's mass has disappeared. It has been calculated that the rusticle growths are consuming at least 90 kilograms of iron per day and the rate of iron consumption is accelerating.

The *Lusitania*, sunk by a German U-boat in 1915, 25 years before the *Niagara* slipped beneath the waves, also lies on her port side. The years underwater have taken a toll – her superstructure has gone and her hull is collapsing. The decks were not designed to support the hull in the manner in which she lies and are sliding away. The wreck will eventually collapse into a pile of steel on the bottom, to be consumed over the next century or two until little remains of the once-elegant liner.

The question now arose – after 47 years underwater, what was the condition of the *Niagara*? Had the mine-damaged ship, her integrity further weakened from two salvage operations, finally collapsed onto the ocean bed? That would make future salvage operations and recovering the remaining gold bars an unprofitable venture.

Ian decided to carry out an initial survey using a small MiniRover-type ROV designed by Chris Nicholson. In the interests of promoting ROV technology in New Zealand, Benthos came to the party and supplied a system.

Joined by Chris and ROV technician Will Sellers, who had been with Ballard on the initial discovery of the *Titanic,* Ian contacted Lynton Diggle to arrange a local charter boat. Lynton's curiosity years earlier had confirmed the amount of gold remaining on the wreck. Not wanting to miss an opportunity to see the shipwreck of his dreams, Lynton made sure he was aboard the charter vessel when it departed the northern fishing port of Leigh.

The weather favoured the small party, allowing them to remain anchored over the *Niagara* for three days. Aided by a Klein side-scan sonar system, the wreck was not difficult to find and Ian wasted no time in launching the ROV into the depths. With Chris at the controls, the small robotic vehicle made a number of excursions over the for'ard area of the sunken ship. The area of hull breached by the Williams team to gain access to the bullion room and the sand sea floor below were examined with the ROV camera. Flying the vehicle out from the hull across the sand, part of an old salvage mooring was discovered, signifying how firm the bottom remained. Exploring further forward to the bow area revealed damage caused from test charges before the salvors attempted to blast their way into the hull to get to the bullion room.

The good water visibility around the wreck surprised the survey team. During the previous year, 1986, the Cousteau expedition to New Zealand dived on the wreck with the submersible diving saucer *Denise*. Operating from the research vessel *Calypso,* Albert Falco piloted the submersible with cameraman Michel Deloire down to the wreck. Falco reported finding the top of the wreck at a depth of 325 feet, but encountering a 1.5-knot current and poor visibility, he considered operating the submersible around the wreck to be dangerous. The French submariners confirmed that the wreck was lying on its side north-to-south direction – a huge hole in its hull was assumed to have been made by the early salvors.

Reports from earlier salvage records confirmed conditions of poor visibility regularly occurring, making operations around the wreck hazardous. Operating the diving bell in a minefield in such conditions added to the dangers the early salvors had to face. Now with the new remote controlled technology, Ian and his team remained safely on the surface as they surveyed the wreck. Except for fishing nets tangled on the wreckage at times causing some danger for the little robot flying around the wreck, the team found it a fun dive.

The ROV was not fitted with an articulator arm, preventing the operator grasping for tempting artefacts sighted on the seabed. Both the bridge and stern-castle areas were now collapsed across the sand with items such as the bridge telegraph and compass binnacle lying exposed among the debris. Wreck fever broke out among the team. Lynton, determined to retrieve a brass porthole, cajoled Ian and Chris to mount an extension with a hook on the front of the ROV. Following numerous attempts and despite Lynton's constant badgering of Chris, the ROV pilot, their attempts were without success.

With their extended stay anchored over the wreck, the stationary vessel did not go unnoticed. Reports of the team's presence in the area of the *Niagara* caused some alarm in the office of the local Receiver of Wreck at Whangarei, Nelson Connolly, who considered himself as guardian of the famous wreck lying in his patch, more so due to reports stating the wreck still contained an unknown quantity of gold bullion. Although Salvage Pacific had a salvage agreement with HM Treasury, and the British government had advised the New Zealand authorities of the salvage company's interest, the word had not got through to Whangarei. Believing that somebody was involved with illegal salvage activities on "his" wreck and stealing "his" gold, Nelson Connolly prepared for action. Enlisting the assistance of the local police force, he was about to set sail to apprehend the raiders when the story of the underwater exploration of the famous wreck featured in local newspapers. It was rather upsetting for the Receiver to learn through the media that the activities out on the Gulf were legal. The arrival of this new underwater technology making it now relatively easy to access shipwrecks was further cause for consternation. He considered that in future he would need to be alert to such incursions and increase his vigilance over the nearby treasure wreck.

17

Remote Intervention

Returning to New Zealand in 1987, following eighteen years working in Samoa and Singapore in the aviation industry, I decided to take the plunge and purchase one of the new small ROV systems. Over the past 35 years I had dived many areas of the Pacific and South-east Asian seas enjoying the clear tropical waters. At times, suspended off the edge of a coral reef that plunged into the cobalt blue of the abyss, I wondered what mysteries were hidden below in the deep.

Ian Lockley was back in Suva outfitting Salvage Pacific's new salvage vessel *Ocean Rover*. In addition to his recent survey of the *Niagara*, Ian had identified another promising target for the deepwater cargo recovery system he was developing. In 1975 the *Koyten Maru*, a Korean cargo vessel on passage from Melbourne to Korea struck the outer rampart of Lihou Reef some 200 miles east of Townsville. The stricken ship, abandoned by the crew, remained aground on the edge of the coral reef. Days later an aerial survey revealed that the ship had disappeared, having slid off the reef edge into the depths. Its cargo included six tons of zinc ingots. With rising world prices, the zinc cargo was then worth some $US6.5 million – a prize Ian considered as a worthwhile target for the new deepwater recovery system.

Visiting Lihou Reef on a chartered yacht, he took with him the newly acquired Benthos RPV system. Deploying the robotic vehicle down the face of the reef, he discovered a trail of zinc ingots leading down into the depths. Indications were the ship had broken its back, spilling cargo as it slid down the reef onto a sandy slope some 1800 feet below the surface. Restricted by the available length of umbilical cable the ROV was unable to reach the wreck, but by clever improvisation using a set of hedge clippers in the robotic arm, Ian recovered a few zinc bars from a depth of 600 feet.

The insurers of the cargo were sceptical about Ian's ability to recover the zinc from such a great depth until at a meeting following his visit to Lihou Reef he produced from his bag a recovered ingot. With the ingot lying on the desk before the surprised insurers Ian had proved his point – a recovery was possible. A salvage contract was signed and the challenge was on.

I contacted Ian in Suva for advice about purchasing a ROV system. Inviting me to Suva to familiarise myself with the new technology, he suggested I contact Chris Nicholson with a view to obtaining one of his MiniRover ROV systems, as he was about to sign a deal with Benthos for their purchase of the manufacturing rights. Chris offered me a system at reasonable terms and I set off for Suva to learn more about the new robotic systems that would take us into the depths beyond our diving limits.

The 1987 Rabuka military coup had taken place in Fiji five months previously, with a further coup occurring a few days before my arrival. Our flight path into Suva late at night took us over the deserted, glistening, rain-swept streets of a capital still under curfew. Armed soldiers were the only greeting party in the airport terminal, but this was Fiji and I saw a group of soldiers warmly greeting a Fijian Salvation Army officer arriving off our flight. A soldier boarded the airport bus and we set off on the drive through the darkened deserted suburbs into town.

Ian was waiting at the town terminal; he had been issued with a military pass permitting him to be on the roads during the curfew. We were stopped by armed troops at roadblocks on the drive to Ian's house, and our passes were checked before we were waved on. Everybody was very polite. Ian explained to me that the coup was the result of conflict between the old-guard Fijians and the new over changes in society eroding the power of the chiefs and the traditional ways. The elders had supported the coup as they considered the power they held was flowing into the hands of people with wealth. The Indian population was caught up in the conflict between the two sides as meat in a sandwich.

An air of depression now hung over a country that had until the coup enjoyed a booming economy. Now, Suva's buildings and roads showed signs of deterioration, interest rates had risen to 33 per cent and businesses were desperate to get their money out of the country. It struck me as rather ludicrous to be visiting a country in such turmoil to seek knowledge of a new technology to enable us humans to explore deeper into our oceans.

Ian lived on the outskirts of Suva, his home looking out over the lagoon to the expanse of the Pacific beyond. Moored in the lagoon adjacent to the house was the *Ocean Rover*. Her decks and workshops were a hive of activity as crew and technicians prepared the deepwater salvage systems for the recovery of the *Koyten Maru*'s cargo. I soon forgot the woes of Fiji as I immersed myself into this exciting new world of deepwater exploration.

The Salvage Pacific team was developing a cargo recovery system capable of operating in 3000 feet of water, under a pressure of some 1350 psi. The core of the robotic system, nicknamed *Scoopy*, was a commercial Palfinger hydraulic extendible crane, similar to units mounted on truck decks for handling cargo. An electronic brain, sealed against water pressure, was mounted on the crane along with a hydraulic power-pack, thruster motors to swing the jib, underwater cameras and lighting. The system would be operated remotely, like an ROV, by an operator at a control console viewing the underwater operation through the system cameras. In addition to transmitting the video signal, the umbilical cable carried electrical power and control signals to the electro-hydraulic machine. It was difficult to accept that such a system was being developed here in a small Pacific Island country undergoing the turmoil of a military coup.

The Benthos RPV systems were protected from the tropics in their air-conditioned control room. Resembling the robot R2D2 from the film *Star Wars*, the now-dormant vehicles sat alongside the control console racks of switches, instruments and monitor screens, which looked like a flight deck panels in a modern aircraft. Over the next two days I consumed every bit of information I could on underwater remote-operated technology.

Late into the night we discussed projects that were now feasible. The site of a possible sunken Portuguese caravel in 300 feet of water off the east coast of Australia was one exciting prospect that could even change history. An associate of Ian's was in possession of an old clay pot recovered from the site in a fisherman's net – now we had the ability to visit such sites to carry out robotic investigations. Valuable sunken cargoes around the Pacific and South-east Asia, previously inaccessible to salvage divers, were now feasible salvage prospects. Then there was the *Niagara*, a wreck well within the MiniRover's capability to explore. Salvage Pacific still held the salvage rights to the *Niagara* and it was decided that with the arrival of the MiniRover I would continue with the survey of the wreck. In addition to the remaining gold bars, Ian had information that suggested there could also be other cargo of interest. However, first he had to deal with the *Koyten Maru*. The zinc cargo offered the opportunity to perfect the deepwater recovery system with a good return that would finance development costs and future projects.

I departed Fiji, on the way to the airport passing soldiers searching the cars of the bewildered locals. Rabuka was still flying the Fijian flag, the curfew had been extended and rumours abounded, causing much consternation among the local populace. My thoughts went back to the colonial days when the *Niagara* was a regular caller at the once-popular port we now skirted.

Chris Nicholson and Benthos are based in the small Cape Cod town of Falmouth. Close to the Woods Hole Oceanographic Institute, the area has become home for a number of companies involved with underwater technology research and manufacture: it was from Woods Hole two years previously that Robert Ballard set out on his mission to discover the wreck of the *Titanic*. Falmouth was certainly the area to visit to gain knowledge on underwater technology.

Checking into the Falmouth Holiday Inn hotel I knew I had come to the right place. Above the check-in desk hung a large colour photo of the wreck of the *Breadalbane*, taken by Chris with his ROV. The MiniRover was in the final stages of assembly and I had come to Falmouth to learn more on the intricacies of the system. New Zealand was a long way from Cape Cod and when things went wrong it would not be easy to communicate about the technicalities of a problem – email was still in the distant future.

It snowed the first night and I awoke to find my rental car buried under a large mound of snow. Chris picked me up and on our way along the picturesque snow-covered route to Benthos he told me Falmouth was one area where a person could ski the beach in winter and swim off it in summer. This quest for knowledge on ROV technology was taking me to some bizarre places. A few days earlier it had been a military coup on a tropical South Pacific island and now a snowbound countryside where people skied on the beach.

The Benthos facility was equipped with a large test pool in which a number of MiniRovers were being tested. Lined up alongside the deep pool, clad in their bright yellow composite shells, the little underwater vehicles with their acrylic moon faces gave the impression they were not machines but living entities, especially when they were darting around the pool following the orders transmitted to them. It took some practice controlling the vehicle with only a two-dimensional image on a video monitor screen. The ROV camera becomes your eyes in the deep as your senses are transmitted underwater through telepresence. You feel as if one with the machine. But with only two dimensions the perception of distance to an object is at first difficult to grasp, especially when attempting to pick up an object from the bottom using the articulator arm. Chris had been working on a system using two cameras to supply a three-dimensional image to the operator wearing special glasses, but for now it was a matter of practice makes perfect.

Impressed with the MiniRover's performance and having observed the final stages of assembly of my system, I returned to New Zealand. A message from Ian awaited me – *Scoopy* had been tested successfully to 2000 feet, and the *Ocean Rover* had now departed for Lihou Reef.

18

Robotic Dive

The ROV arrived a few days before Christmas. Following the expected Customs clearance problems for goods that did not seem to fit any description in the tariff listings, I finally positioned the system at Tutukaka, close to the Poor Knights islands and the site of the *Niagara*. It was New Year's Eve and we looked forward to 1988 when we would explore the depths around the Poor Knights. Until now the deeper sections of the cliffs that plunged into the depths had remained beyond our diving limits.

The summer months were occupied learning the skills of operating the MiniRover, and as we gained confidence we probed deeper into the twilight of the depths. Divers have a better affinity with operating the underwater vehicle than non-divers. Through telepresence the operator's eyes become part of the system, conveying the operator's senses into the depths. With their past underwater experience, divers control the vehicle as if they are swimming through the depths, exercising the same cautious approach but aware of the trailing umbilical cable, whereas a non-diver would initially tend to charge around the bottom colliding with the topography and at times getting the cable tangled around protuberances.

By May I felt confident we were ready to tackle the *Niagara* and would not lose the vehicle in the process. The latest marine charts indicated that the wreck was now on the border of a no-anchoring, no-fishing zone extending up the Gulf from Auckland to protect underwater telecommunications cables. This presented problems, as we needed to anchor our vessel on-site to ensure the umbilical cable was not dragged through the wreckage. And then there was Nelson Connolly, Receiver of Wreck. We did not want to get on the wrong side of officialdom and I thought it would be prudent to visit the gentleman in person and explain what we were up to.

Salvage Pacific's salvage agreement with British government was still in force. Armed with a telex from the Treasury confirming this, and a fax from Ian stating we were continuing a survey of the wreck on his company's behalf, I met with Mr Connolly. At first there was suspicion. He was no doubt thinking we were about to rob the bank of its gold. As I continued to explain the capabilities of the ROV and that our primary interest was only in filming the wreck, the atmosphere warmed. He asked, "Could I have a copy of the video?"

"Er, yes."

He was most interested in our operation announcing that he would arrange to come out on the pilot boat to observe the ROV in action.

"Er, well, that might not be advisable as we would have the ROV cable in the water and I am sure you would not want to tangle the cable around your boat propeller."

"Yes, that could be a problem, but the video copy would be appreciated."

"No problem."

The fact was we did not want any official party to visit us, as to get around the anchoring restriction we intended to anchor onto the wreck not the bottom, but as this was a grey area I decided the less said the better.

In Samoa we once carried out the salvage of equipment from a Chinese fishing boat that had ended up on the barrier reef close to Apia. Although the vessel was partially awash and badly holed, the Samoan police, not conversant with salvage law, charged us with stealing the boat. The case was dismissed after the prosecution's evidence had been heard. I did not want a similar experience and with the possibility of a posse of the local constabulary led by the Receiver of Wreck arriving on the scene now out of the way, we proceeded with our preparations.

Phil Bendle, who operated the *Norseman*, a Tutukaka dive charter boat, was keen to see the *Niagara* and offered his services practically at cost. Old-time dive buddies Wade Doak, Jaan Voot and Quentin Bennett joined as crew, all keen to see the wreck that had become a legend and the ultimate challenge for New Zealand wreck divers. Missing was our old diving mate Kelly Tarlton, who had passed away three years earlier. His wife Rosemary arranged for me to look through his *Niagara* files. Kelly's interest in the wreck was evident and no doubt he would have embraced the new technology to expand his wreck-exploration exploits.

Up to then I had been recording underwater images on VHS videotape, a format not suitable for commercial TV production. The previous ROV visit with Ian and his team had recorded on video equipment that resulted in problems with the recordings. Realising there was no film available of the famous wreck, I hired a Hi-Band video recorder, a suitable format for use by production units. Curtis Doby, a video technician, came with the recorder and would look after video recording of images from the ROV.

We departed Tutukaka on 1 June, nearly 44 years since the *Niagara* had gone to her grave. Under a spectacular sunrise over the Poor Knights, Phil set course south into a 15-knot wind towards the Hen and Chickens and beyond into the channel towards the distant Moko Hinau islands. An air of excitement prevailed as the image of the wreck grew on the *Norseman*'s echo sounder screen into a large red mountain rising from the bottom. Phil had placed us over the *Niagara* following a series of short search transits calculated from distant landmarks. With some difficulty we managed to hook two anchors into the wreck and by early afternoon launched the ROV for its journey down to the sunken liner. At the time I only had a vague idea of the events around the sinking and the subsequent salvage operations. Details of the ship were also sketchy as we had only a photo in a book to refer to. So when the first images of the wreck ghosted onto the monitor screen we were unsure of the area of vessel onto which we had landed.

Releasing the ROV's articulator hold on the railing we had first approached, I flew the vehicle slowly down the platform until our lights illuminated an encrusted ship's telegraph. We were on the stern docking bridge which was now angled some 80 degrees towards the vertical. Lying on her port side, the *Niagara* disappeared towards the bow, pointing south back towards Auckland, her last port of departure. A cautious probe forwards revealed trawl nets draped across the hull. Exercising caution on this first dive we returned to the stern area. Our lights reflected off the silver grey body of a hapuku as it glided down into the darkness of the shadows below. The barrel of the ship's gun pointed upwards towards the surface, locked in position as it was when abandoned by Ray Nelson and the gun crew. Gun components provided a foothold for skeletal shrubs of black coral and encrusting marine growth.

Stern portholes, encapsulated in a colourful blanket of marine organisms, winked reflections of the ROV lights from their glass orbs. The shape of an anchor secured to the stern plates slipped past as we descended into a cavern beneath the hourglass curve of the stern. A school of young hapuku emerged from the darkness beneath the rudder. Attracted by our lights they paraded across the screen teasing Phil, who operated fishing charters to these waters.

The seabed materialised onto the screen and the ROV touched down onto a firm sand bottom. The depth reading registered 398 feet – far short of the 438 feet claimed for the record salvage depth back in the 1940s. Objects were illuminated lying on the bottom in the debris field scattered around the wreck. The absence of soft mud was a surprise. Moving across the sand, our lights showed a ship's lantern. Fallen from the stern, it now provided shelter to a small fish that slipped into the casing as the ROV approached.

Determined to recover an artefact as a souvenir of our visit, I manoeuvred the ROV into position, opening the articulator claw for the final approach. Picking up an object in the darkness of the ocean depths by remote control, working with two-dimensional imaging, requires intense concentration. After some juggling of controls I had the ROV claw positioned to clasp onto the lamp body. All eyes were locked onto the monitor screens as I made the final approach. Suddenly, the screens went blank. With loss of the image, our telepresence link to the depths was broken – we were suddenly blind. The tension that had built within me collapsed and was replaced with a fear that disaster had befallen the robotic vehicle. This was followed by anger, then frustration as the source of the problem was quickly identified. Curtis had at various intervals switched the video recording of the dive between VHS and Hi-Band systems to record scenes considered of commercial interest. Now he had decided to switch at the last moment, thinking the capture of the lamp would make great footage. Unfortunately he picked an inopportune time not to relay his intentions. Disconnecting the monitor video feed broke the visual connection to the vehicle and, in turn, all sense of control I had over the vehicle. With our shouts and curses ringing in his ears, Curtis quickly remade the connection. Images were restored to the screens and we returned to the situation below. During the loss of visual contact the ROV had drifted away from the target and after some time fruitlessly searching the darkness under the stern we abandoned the search. There were mutterings that perhaps Curtis should be consigned to the deep along with the electronic gadgetry he had with him, but I shrugged off the disappointment of not making the recovery. The lamp would be there for the future.

Ascending into the clear blue of the upper water column, the ROV camera located the *Norseman* suspended on the surface ceiling as an inquisitive mako shark swam slowly beneath the keel. Comparison with the hull indicated the shark to be about 3.5 metres in length. The little yellow robot appearing out of the depths, its two lights stabbing shafts of brilliance through the water, immediately attracted the mako's attention. We watched the shark below our keel turn and dive towards the now stationary ROV hovering 30 metres below. The approaching shark grew in size on our monitor screens as it hurtled through the clear water towards the little machine. I flicked the control sticks to maintain the camera on the swiftly moving shark, wondering whether the MiniRover was about to become shark fodder. The streamlined body swept past, a dark beady eye above open jaws flashed across the screen. Pirouetting the ROV, I attempted to keep the shark in sight. In an instant it was back, hurtling past in the opposite direction. The reflected lights flashed off the mako's iridescent body before it disappeared from the screen. I turned the lights off. Manoeuvring the vehicle we probed the blue arena for the fast-moving beast, but saw nothing. I turned the lights back on. A shadow broke through the blue curtain – travelling fast. The head-on image of the mako grew as it accelerated towards the ROV. I quickly flipped the lights off. The shark altered course, passing within a metre before disappearing back into the visual veil. We continued to retrieve the ROV without further incident.

At intervals, while anchored over the wreck, we were conscious of the pungent smell of fuel oil. The ship below was still bleeding. Although not great in quantity, oil rising from the depths would, on reaching the surface disperse into a spreading sheen carried by the south-west wind across the Gulf waters towards the offshore islands. Fully bunkered with fuel for the voyage from Sydney to Vancouver, the *Niagara*'s fuel tanks contained 4200 tons of heavy fuel oil. Reports at the time of the sinking indicated a large amount of oil dispersed across the Gulf and washed onto nearby beaches. This would have originated from fuel tanks damaged by the mine blasts. The question now was, what quantity remained in the wreck? With the hull slowly collapsing, was there an ecological time-bomb slowly ticking away in the depths below us? In future, the continuing deterioration of the *Niagara*'s hull could result in a sudden collapse, releasing an eruption of trapped oil into the ocean. Newspaper articles on our *Niagara* explorations commented on the oil leaking from the wreck, but little interest was shown by the authorities in the potential danger the sunken oil reservoir presented to the Gulf ecology.

We had confirmed that the sunken vessel was lying at a depth shallower than claimed by Williams for a salvage record, which raised another question: why did the 1941 reports place the vessel considerably deeper? Williams and his divers must have known the depth was less than the claimed 438 feet. The only reason for this claim appears to be wartime propaganda. At the time, the record depth for salvage was the 396-foot *Egypt* salvage claimed by the Italians in 1932. Placing the *Niagara* deeper at 438 feet let the propaganda machine claim the British were now superior in the field of deepwater salvage to their Axis enemy, Italy.

Publications of the time reflect this claim. In *Niagara Gold* by R.J. Dunn, published in 1942, Chapter One is titled "The *Egypt* Feat Eclipsed" and states that "the *Egypt*'s salvage pales almost to insignificance compared with the achievements of the Australian Company . . . The achievement gives Britishers, whose Navy has long ruled the waves, the right to claim supremacy in submarine salvage." James Taylor, the reporter on board the *Claymore* during the salvage, records in his book *Gold from the Sea* that the *Niagara* had sunk 42 feet deeper than the *Egypt* – "438 feet as to 396 feet".

Compared with the *Egypt* salvage, there is no doubt that the *Niagara* was a greater feat, regardless of the fact that it was not deeper. Even though the Italians were far better equipped, they required more than five years with the loss of lives to complete the recovery of £1 million worth of specie. They were also aided by the shipwreck sitting upright on the bottom, whereas the Williams team, working under wartime conditions in the middle of a minefield on a far larger wreck lying at an angle, recovered a much larger quantity of gold within a fifth of the time and at a sixth of the cost – and no lives were lost.

Even today, media reports and books relating this historical salvage still record the salvage depth as establishing a world record of 438 feet (or 133 metres). When discussing records, however, it should be noted that although the wreck was on the seabed at 396 feet, with a beam of 60 feet and the hull inclined at approximately 80 degrees, the majority of the salvage work was carried out at a shallower depth of around 363 feet. The same situation applied to the *Egypt* sitting upright on the bottom. A group of technical divers using mixed-gas technology dived the *Egypt* in 2001. They found the wreck sitting at 412 feet, deeper than the 360–380 feet they had planned for.

19

For the Record

Following our initial ROV dives on the *Niagara*, media reports noted the discrepancy in depths with the claimed salvage record. In 1989 I met Ray Nelson at his home on Australia's Gold Coast. Having read the reports, he had taken me to task over my highlighting in a magazine article the error in depth with the record claim. Returning from Lihou Reef, 200 miles off the Australian east coast where I had spent a few weeks on the *Ocean Rover* with Ian and the Salvage Pacific team, I decided to visit Ray. The salvage attempt on the *Koyten Maru* cargo of zinc ingots had been proceeding slowly. Moored above the wreck off the edge of the reef in 2000 feet of water presented the salvage attempt with a number of unforeseen problems. Although ROV surveys of the wreck had been accomplished, *Scoopy*, the cargo-recovery system, had still not been placed on the wreck. Unpredictable strong ocean currents would suddenly assail the site then disappear. Moored above the wreck in a catenary of six moorings, the salvage vessel was unable to manoeuvre to relieve the sudden cable loading. Ropes designed for far higher loads failed, so that year's attempt was aborted and we returned to Gladstone.

Having driven down the coast to Ray's home south of Brisbane, it was with some apprehension that I knocked on the door of the *Niagara* veteran. Talking to Ray previously on the phone from New Zealand, I had formed an impression of the elderly veteran of the sea, but the man who greeted me belied this image. His demeanour was that of a far younger man and the twinkle in his clear blue eyes at my mention of the *Niagara* indicated the important role the lost ship had played in his life.

Following the *Niagara* salvage, Ray had served in the Pacific during the Second World War with New Zealand, Australian and US forces. He finally settled in Runaway Bay close to Surfers Paradise with his wife Cecily. No doubt having heard the story of the gold salvage numerous times previously, Cecily listened patiently as Ray enthusiastically related his experiences once more for my benefit. He produced a number of *Niagara* mementos, including a boxing trophy he had won while a member of the crew. Known then as "Stingray", he was proud of his feats in the ring. I recalled the sports evening programme on a voyage in June 1939 – the evening's entertainment included Lindsay Fabre presenting "his world famous animal *Aussie* the boxing Kangaroo". Ray did not mention boxing Aussie or if the animal won the bout.

We viewed a video recording of the 1941 film of the salvage filmed by American cinematographer J.M. Leonard. Watching this film sitting alongside one of those who had been there, I was able learn a number of facts that had not been published in the earlier accounts. Surely here were the ingredients of a fine tale for a television documentary. With Ray as a participant, the 1941 film and our ability to film the wreck with the ROV, we would have the material to attract a production company. This could also assist with finance for further exploration of the wreck and perhaps the recovery and preservation of artefacts for display.

I asked Ray why Williams recorded the wreck as deeper than it actually lay. Was this wartime propaganda or was there another reason? Surely the divers in the bell would have known what depth they were at. Ray seemed a little offended that this anomaly had been raised. His only comment was that perhaps it was due to using a sounding lead as was customary in those days. My raising the subject was perhaps questioning the integrity of Captain Herd. Although the captain had passed on, he still had family living in Brisbane and Ray considered it not proper to raise the subject. With that twinkle again in his eyes he remarked, "After all, the Italians only had the same method to record the *Egypt*'s depth." I decided to let the matter rest.

A television documentary of the salvage, *Niagara Gold*, produced by Melbourne writer Jeff Maynard, was later made. Featuring Ray and other surviving members of the Williams team, it included footage taken by Leonard and our 1988 ROV film. Narration was by the New Zealand actor Sam Neill. It screened by a number of television channels around the world including the Discovery Channel. For some reason it was not shown in New Zealand, the country of "the greatest gold salvage in history".

Returning to New Zealand following a period working in South-east Asia, I had the opportunity to continue exploring the *Niagara*'s sunken remains. The MiniRover system had been upgraded to improve its capability, including a scanning sonar system to help finding targets in the limited visibility of the depths. Previously, our first indications of the proximity of the wreck were the shoals of fish suddenly materialising from the veil of darkness. Now with sonar, we would see the wreck on the sonar monitor screen from a distance of up to 100 metres.

Salvage Pacific had encountered further problems with the *Koyten Maru* salvage, requiring additional finance to continue the project. Unfortunately, the world financial problems of the late 1980s caused the banks to rethink their policy on funding salvage projects in the ocean depths. This resulted in Salvage Pacific ceasing operations and their *Niagara* salvage contract with the Treasury expired. I decided to apply for the salvage rights for my company, SeaROV Technologies, as there was always a possibility of stumbling across one of the remaining gold bars with the ROV. Without a signed agreement the Treasury would take all. Negotiations with HM Treasury Solicitor's office took time, but I duly received the official document titled: "Agreement for Salvage of Gold from SS Niagara".

The agreement stated that the vessel carried at the time of her loss a cargo which included 590 gold bars, that the Treasury Solicitor believed that only five had not been recovered. A percentage of the value would be paid to the contractor according to the total number of bars recovered on a sliding scale from 70 per cent for one bar recovered to 50 per cent if five bars or more were recovered.

Armed with this document I approached the Maritime Safety Authority under whose jurisdiction the sunken vessel now came. The latest 1994 marine charts had repositioned the wreck from the western edge of the no-anchoring, no-fishing zone to well within it. It seems that not only did Williams and the salvors of earlier days have problems recording the position of the wreck, but so to do the marine authorities of today: a recent survey carried out by the RNZN using the latest survey equipment has recorded the wreck to be lying about 460 metres out of position to the north-west of the chart position – almost back on the protection zone boundary.

The MSA advised I would also require permission from Telecom, which was responsible for the cables in the Gulf. More applications, more waiting – but no reply. After a while I asked about progress on the application and was informed that my application had highlighted a problem. A new fibre-optic communications cable had been laid to the US recently and it had been decided, rather than run the cable up the eastern side of the Gulf and out into the Pacific, to run it up the Gulf close to the western side before crossing to the eastern side. The new cable had been laid within 1000 metres of a shipwreck Telecom was not aware of until my application – the wreck of the *Niagara*.

"But surely not." I said. "All the local marine charts show a wreck and it is a well-known one!"

"Well, the cable-laying ship's charts didn't show a wreck, and neither did the side-scan sonar survey that was carried out."

"What are you going to do about it?"

"We haven't decided."

Eventually I received the permits with the proviso that we were only allowed to anchor onto the wreck and not on the surrounding ocean bottom. I thought of the large debris field now scattered around the wreck and the structure torn from the wreck by the gold salvors and dumped nearby.

Since our first visit to the *Niagara* I had located the wreck of HMS *Puriri*, the minesweeper that had been blown apart by one of the *Orion* mines in 1941, killing five of her crew. The ill-fated vessel lay closer to Whangarei at a depth of 98 metres/323 feet. Small amounts of fuel oil still bled from the remains on the seabed, appearing on the surface as circular colour-banded wreaths marking the grave below. With the MiniRover we explored this naval vessel, a forgotten victim of war in our waters.

Flying the ROV across the bottom towards the wreck, we passed over ballast stone scattered across the bottom. Reports of the *Puriri*'s sinking mention the large amount of ballast stone that was flung high into the air by the explosion. Approaching the upright stern section, I was careful to avoid abandoned fishing nets draped across the hull, shrouding the wreck in a ghostly veil. Adding to the spectral scene, a light winked from the shadows as if somebody was beaming a light towards us. It was the ROV's lights reflecting back from the glass of a porthole.

Ascending to above the aft deck, the outline of the stern gun came into view cloaked in a fishnet shroud. Moving forward, the stern structure abruptly ended in a tangle of twisted steel beams and plating, the complete forward section had been blasted way. The seabed was a mass of torn wreckage: the bow section, separated by the blast, was nowhere to be seen. Penetrating this jungle of steel required a cautious approach but even then the ROV was caught twice. Once when the forward claw was jammed beneath a beam, and again when the umbilical cable caught under an overhanging structure. It was not a place for a machine and we cautiously retreated.

On a later dive it was not so simple to extract the vehicle from the devastated wreck. A beam that had been standing upright collapsed across the umbilical after the vehicle passed. It didn't fall completely – an extension from the beam down forming a passage between beam and bottom that was too small for the ROV to reverse back under. After some initial probing it appeared that the vehicle was trapped.

Closer investigation using the claw revealed that the extension was a section of steel cable heavily corroded and encrusted with marine growth. Gripping the cable in the claw I worked the ROV backwards and forwards, flexing the cable and breaking the encrustation free. After more than an hour of intense effort, the passage beneath the angled beam was larger. With thrusters on full power, the vehicle was aimed at the gap and driven forwards, squeezing through the opening to reach the safety of open water. The tension washed from our bodies as the vehicle ascended towards the surface. Telepresence is not always a relaxing medium.

On the way to the surface we passed an old trawl net suspended 30 metres above the wreck. A section of the net buoyed by floats had broken free but remained attached to the wreck as a twisted tower extending up into the water-column. We glimpsed the silver body of a tuna trapped within the netting; the fish had not been there long. I veered the vehicle way from the swaying column of mesh. This was not a good wreck for fish or machine.

Author's Collection

Maria Letiza Galleazzi

Author's Collection

Above Left: Author inspects the United Salvage Company diving bell at the Castlemaine museum, Australia.

Above Right: A Galleazi diving bell as used by Risdon Beasley Ltd.

Right: Launching Salvage Pacific's Benthos RPV at Lihou Reef.

GARTH BURLEIGH

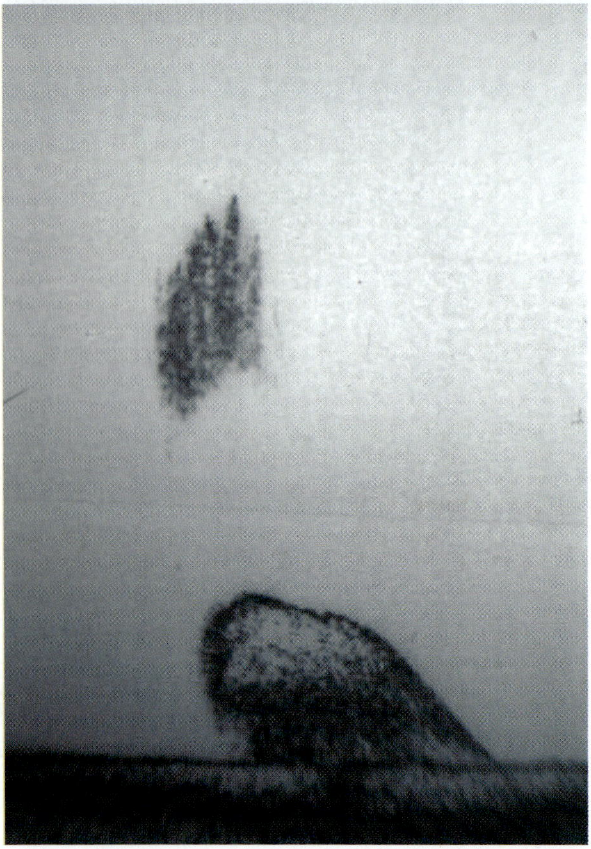

LYNTON DIGGLE

Above: Cousteau's research vessel *Calypso* at the Poor Knights islands. The submersible Denise used nearby on the *Niagara* dive is on the stern deck – 1986.

Left: The *Niagara*'s image on an echo sounder. A shoal of fish above.

LYNTON DIGGLE

AUTHOR'S COLLECTION

Above: Chris Nicholson and Will Sellers prepare a Benthos ROV to explore the *Niagara* – 1987.

Right: Allan Kircher and the author ready the MiniRover ROV for a dive at the Poor Knights islands – 1988.

Quentin Bennett

Left: The MiniRover is launched from the *Norseman* for our first dive on the *Niagara* – 1988.

Below: The MiniRover on descent to the *Niagara*.

Quentin Bennett

Author's Collection

Above: A herd of young hapuku emerge from the *Niagara* to inspect the ROV.

Below: Shark bait. The mako shark sweeps past the MiniRover.

Author's Collection

Author's Collection

Author's Collection

Above: 1988 ROV team. Keith Gordon, Quentin Bennett, Wade Doak, Curtis Doby, Jaan Voot, Phil Bendle.

Left: Memories. Ray Nelson relates past adventures for a film crew – 2000.

Illustration by Ego Guiotto reproduced courtesy of *Australian Geographic*

Author's Collection

Above: Dressed for the deep. A technical diver with an open circuit breathing system and camera equipment.

Right: Dave Apperley prepares for his first *Niagara* dive assisted by Brian Oxenham – 1999.

Author's Collection

Author's Collection

Above: Tim Cashman and Dave Apperley relax at Tutukaka marina after their historic first dive to the *Niagara*.

Left: Author with the MiniRover modified for deep dives and sonar.

20

Deep Descent

During the 1990s a revolution was occurring in sport diving. Breathing a mixture of gases, divers were reaching depths previously beyond the accepted limits of sport diving. Termed "technical diving", the new techniques overcame many problems involved with diving on compressed air. To extend time underwater down to depths of 40 metres/132 feet, the nitrogen content of air is partially replaced by a larger percentage of oxygen. For deeper dives, the inert gas helium is blended with reduced percentages of oxygen and nitrogen (or the total elimination of nitrogen). To understand the dangers of diving deep and why the *Niagara* remained outside the limits of sport diving for so long requires some technical explanation.

The air we breathe at sea-level atmospheric pressure consists primarily of 21 per cent oxygen and 79 per cent nitrogen. When breathing air under pressure, nitrogen dissolves from the lungs into the body's blood and soft tissues. The deeper and the longer the dive, the more nitrogen is absorbed. Returning to the surface from depth, the diver passes through diminishing pressure until the surface is reached where the pressure is 14.7 psi (1 bar). At 50 metres/165 feet the pressure exerted on the diver's body by the surrounding water is 88.2 psi, five times higher. To surface safely from this depth, a diver must follow a decompression schedule, allowing time for the nitrogen to dissolve back out of the blood and tissues into the lungs from where, as a gas, it is exhaled. As the diver ascends, the decompression schedule requires him to stop at calculated depths to allow the excess nitrogen to off-gas from the body.

Returning to the surface too quickly can result in nitrogen gas bubbles still in the blood system to cause blockages in the heart, brain or nervous system, which can be fatal. This is the bends, or decompression illness. The sudden release of the dissolved gas in a diver ascending too quickly is similar to what happens when you open a bottle of soft drink after vigorously shaking it.

The US Navy decompression schedule for a diver spending 30 minutes at 180 feet requires 5 minutes to ascend to the first stop of 6 minutes at 30 feet, a 17-minute stop at 20 feet and 27 minutes at 10 feet. A total decompression time of 56 minutes is required for a 30-minute dive at the bottom depth.

Another problem with breathing nitrogen under pressure is the narcotic effect it has. Cousteau termed the effect "the rapture of the depths"; pioneer American divers compared the effect with drinking a glass of martini on an empty stomach for every 50 feet of depth. Termed the "Martini Law", the analogy dictates that a dive to 150 feet has the same effect as downing three straight martinis. In such a "narced" state, a diver's ability to think clearly and concentrate is greatly impaired. By replacing some nitrogen with additional oxygen in the compressed air, technical divers found they were able to extend their dive time without requiring long decompression times and also overcame some of the narcotic effects of nitrogen. This oxygen-enriched air was called "enriched air nitrox", often termed EAN or "nitrox". The percentage of oxygen in the compressed gas blend is indicated – for example, "nitrox 32" denotes 32 per cent of oxygen in the compressed gas, higher than the normal 21 per cent in the air we breathe.

However, oxygen too can be dangerous when breathed under pressure. At 10 metres/33 feet, at a pressure of 29.4 psi, pure oxygen is toxic. This presents problems with diving to depths exceeding 66 metres/218 feet breathing air, as the 21 per cent oxygen in compressed air will become toxic. At this depth the oxygen content of air reaches a partial pressure oxygen (PO_2) of 1.6 bar (atmospheres), and the consequences are likely to be fatal. A PO_2 limit of 1.4 bar is the safety limit recognised by sport divers. At these deeper depths, divers breathing compressed air are exposed to the same danger from a toxic hit as they would be from breathing oxygen at depths exceeding 10 metres. This is all explained by Dalton's Law of Gases, which states that each gas in a mixture of gases exerts a pressure proportional to the percentage of the total gas it represents. The oxygen-toxicity effect on the central nervous system (CNS) can cause a diver to convulse, lose consciousness and drown.

Shipwrecks such as the *Andrea Doria*, lying at a depth of 72 metres/235 feet, were an attraction for sport divers as they pushed the envelope in seeking new adventures. A number succumbed to the dangers of exceeding the accepted limits for diving on air. The increase of fatalities from narcosis, the bends or drowning at depth following an oxygen CNS "hit" accelerated the development of alternate gases for sport diving. By breathing a combination of gases known as trimix and switching gas mixes at different depths, technical divers following computer-generated schedules began to push the envelope ever further.

Helium is less dense than nitrogen, making it easier to breathe, so it is used at depth to replace some or all of the nitrogen in the breathing gas. The inert gas does not have the narcotic effect of nitrogen, enabling the diver to maintain a relatively clear mind at depth. To reduce the danger from oxygen toxicity, the percentage of oxygen in the gas mix is reduced. A typical trimix gas for the deeper portion of the dive might consist of 10 per cent oxygen, 60 per cent helium and 30 per cent nitrogen. Switching to air and/or nitrox on the ascent maintains the correct PO_2 and reduces decompression times. Switching to 100 per cent oxygen at 6 metres/20 feet aids further in flushing any residual nitrogen from the body.

I followed the advancement of technical sport diving with interest. Although sport divers were still not diving wrecks as deep as the *Niagara*, the indications were it was only a matter of time. Attending a technical diving conference in San Francisco in 1995, I met Billy Deans who operated technical dive training courses in Florida and Dr. Bill Hamilton, a physiologist and computer programmer who specialised in mixed-gas decompression schedules. Both men were recognised experts in deep technical diving. Billy had dived a number of deep wrecks including the *Andrea Doria* and the Civil War vessel *Monitor* at a depth of 70 metres/230 feet. Bill had been involved with developing the mixed gas and decompression schedules for a number of deep dives. My thoughts were – if it were possible to carry out a technical dive on the *Niagara*, perhaps we could finance the cost of bringing a team of divers experienced in deep diving to New Zealand by filming a television documentary.

Both men agreed a mixed gas dive of 20 minutes on the wreck was possible using a decompression schedule requiring around 3-hours to complete the dive. Billy commented that to dive to 122 metres/400 feet was really pushing the envelope for deep diving at that time and there would need to be a real good reason for such a dive. I returned to New Zealand from the conference now confident a dive to the *Niagara* was feasible and not a dream of the past.

Tim Cashman dreamed of diving the *Niagara*. The young Welshman arrived in New Zealand for some overseas experience working in the timber industry. An avid wreck diver, he had embraced technical diving to explore the many wrecks lying beyond the limits for compressed-air sport diving. For Tim, these unexplored wrecks were capsules of maritime history that captured his imagination and presented a challenge. He read the story of the *Niagara* gold salvage and, learning of my ROV incursions on the wreck, approached me in 1998 with a proposal to dive the wreck.

I recalled the words of Deans and Hamilton three years earlier that any dive to such depths was pushing the accepted diving limits. Advances in deep-diving knowledge had been made since then, but dives over 100 metres were still looked upon as a risk. Only accomplished divers with sufficient experience and training should attempt such an undertaking.

In New Zealand technical diving was not promoted by the dive-training agencies and was considered by many in the dive industry to be foolish. I was aware that Tim had accomplished deep dives in cave systems during his stay in New Zealand, but the *Niagara* in the open ocean and deeper was far different. However, it was possible, with the right approach and training with build-up dives using the latest mixed-gas computer programs, that the wreck dive could be accomplished by a competent team.

Tim's enthusiasm was infectious. We decided to proceed with a joint ROV/technical diver project early the following year. Tim would organise the team of support divers and seek divers with suitable experience to accompany him to the bottom. I would look after the logistical arrangements and ROV team. As a training dive for the support team, we decided to dive the wreck of the *Puriri*, which had not yet been dived, the only visits to her mangled remains being our excursions with the ROV. It would be good training for the *Niagara* as it would be within fifteen metres of the planned maximum depth for that dive. The additional depth was still a big jump. Tim was well aware of the physiological changes associated with the additional pressure, and considered the dive to the *Puriri* as a waypoint in reaching the deeper goal.

On 9 January 1999, I joined the dive team on the *Norseman*, the same charter boat we used for our initial ROV exploration of the *Niagara*. Using the co-ordinates I obtained on my earlier visits to the *Puriri*, Phil Bendle our skipper positioned the dive boat over the wreck. A pod of dolphins sliced through the surface of a calm sea, their welcome was considered a good omen. The bottom divers, Pete Mesley and Tim, would dive to the wreck with deep support provided by Geoff Payne and mid-water support by Willy Heatly. All were experienced deepwater divers. Brian Oxenham, a former British submariner the divers named "Captain Nemo", would run the dive programme and provide surface support. A run-time schedule had been formulated for each diver with gas mix and decompression stops dictated by computer-generated dive schedules.

With feelings of anticipation fuelled by thoughts of the unknown wreck in the depths below, the divers climbed into their dive suits. The two bottom divers, bedecked with additional equipment including side-slung gas cylinders, staggered under the weight to the edge of the dive platform. Dive computers strapped on their wrists would keep them informed on the status of their dive. As with the exploration of outer space, survival in the depths of inner space is dependent on these minute electronic circuits.

Plunging through the surface, the divers were immediately relieved from the burden of their equipment weight by being transformed into a state of weightlessness. Powerful strokes of their fins sent them gliding downward into the indigo depths. Vertical shafts of light danced past, beckoning them onwards into an alien world. The shot-line anchored to the wreck stretched down through the featureless void.

At 40 metres, the first signs of narcosis are apparent. The divers switch from breathing compressed air to their trimix gas supply. The mixture of 10 per cent oxygen, 50 per cent helium and 40 per cent nitrogen cleared the fuzziness that had begun to affect their thinking. Although the low percentage of oxygen would not sustain life on the surface or in the shallows above, they were safe in the ocean deep. Dalton's Law of Gases ensured their survival. With clear heads they pressed onwards into the diminishing twilight.

Twelve minutes after the two divers disappeared beneath the surface Geoff hit the water. Carrying a spare cylinder of air he quickly descended to 50 metres where he attached the cylinder to the shot-line. The visibility was great – reassured by the columns of bubbles rising from below, he relaxed. Silver orbs of exhaled gas rushed past, expanding on their journey to the surface above.

Following the shot-line, the two divers did not at first discern the wreck hidden in the gloom that enveloped the bottom. Suddenly a wall of encrusted steel materialised before them. The shot-line curved up over a gunwale and disappeared into a hatchway. Blindly casting the grapnel from above the surface, Phil had placed it squarely through the hatch. The divers checked their dive computers. They had planned only a short period on the wreck – fifteen minutes from the time they left the surface before they had to begin their ascent. They were unable to identify what section of the wreck they had landed on, but later by studying old photographs they determined it was a section of the stern.

Their lights stabbed into the liquid night – there was little suspension in the water allowing horizontal vision through the gloom for a distance of 10 metres. A small hapuku swam across the deck, disturbed by the divers' intrusion. Pete's light failed, a victim of the water pressure. The divers finned on, the twin beams from Tim's helmet lights probing the darkness. Hull plates, now separated, allowed a glimpse into the vessel's interior. Juvenile hapuku sheltering in the shadows were undisturbed by the divers. White cup corals and delicate silica sponges reflected the lights, presenting a contrast to the skeletal growths of black coral sprouting from steel hull plates. The hull section came to an abrupt end among a mass of buckled and torn steel.

The curtain of darkness pressed in from all sides, the divers hesitated, peering into the gloom, wanting to explore further out to where the twisted remains lay scattered across the bottom. A shoal of golden snapper hovered above, their bodies winking back reflections from the light beams. The silence of the deep was near complete: only the noise of the divers' exhalations broke the serene quiet. In the ghostly surroundings the divers' thoughts momentarily turned to Lieutenant Blacklaws and the four crew members who met their deaths when the *Orion*'s mine tore the minesweeper asunder – their bodies were never recovered. The divers felt they were intruders in a war grave. Now only twisted steel wreckage remained as a memorial to the sailors' passing. It was time to go. With strong fin strokes they began their slow ascent, and the wreck was swallowed by the darkness below.

Suspended 50 metres deep in the blue void, Geoff waited alone on the shot-line. Scanning the depths below he waited for the first appearance of the bottom divers, now scheduled to commence their ascent.

Shrouded by veils of shimmering gas bubbles, Pete and Tim emerged out of the gloom. They signalled all was well. To avoid hypoxia, the lack of oxygen in shallower depths, the divers switched to their air-travel gas at 50 metres. The change hit both with a crunch. The clear-headedness from breathing the trimix was replaced with fuzziness from the onslaught of nitrogen narcosis. But they were ready for the change – they had trained to control such physiological effects.

Satisfied they were okay, Geoff ascended the shot-line to 20 metres where Willie waited with a spare supply of nitrox 60 (60 per cent oxygen, 40 per cent nitrogen) as a back-up gas supply. Pete and Tim switched to the nitrox mix at 20 metres for the 20-minute ascent to nine metres, where they switched to 100 per cent oxygen to flush nitrogen from their bodies. Another 50 minutes with a stop at three metres passed before they finally broke through the surface to Captain Nemo's triumphant-submariner cry, "Diver on the roof!"

Over two hours had passed since they had descended to the wreck. For little more than ten minutes of bottom exploration, they had consumed over 7200 litres of gas.

Relaxing back aboard the *Norseman* in the warm sun, Tim gazed out across the waters to the Hen and Chickens and beyond to where the *Niagara* lay sleeping in her grave. With the dive to the *Puriri* now safely accomplished, he was confident the team was ready for the challenge of diving the sunken liner. Back ashore he phoned Dave Apperley in Sydney, who agrees to join the team as the third bottom diver. Tim had dived deep with him previously in the Pearce Resurgence cave system near Nelson.

An avid cave diver, Dave had developed his dive equipment for deep penetrations into cave systems and now used a closed circuit mixed-gas rebreather system rather than the traditional open-circuit system Tim used. With the open-circuit system, the diver exhales gas in large volumes into the surrounding water, where it burbles to the surface in a cloud of bubbles. With Dave's British-made Inspiration rebreather, the exhaled gas remains in the system recycling through a scrubber unit containing soda-lime granules to remove carbon dioxide. The modified gas then passes into the counter-lung, a flexible chamber exposed to the ambient water pressure. Oxygen in the breathing loop is maintained at a pre-determined partial pressure by a computer-maintained set point, controlling the percentage of oxygen according to depth. The diluent gas carried in a separate cylinder mixes with the oxygen to maintain the pre-programmed PO_2. For shallow depths, air is used as the diluent, providing a nitrox mix. On deeper dives, helium is used to replace the majority of air and its nitrogen.

Retaining the gas in a breathing loop, rather than exhaling into the water, allows the diver to carry less on-board gas. Dave had accumulated considerable experience on the Inspiration system with both deep and extended cave dives. On the *Niagara* dive, as a safety back-up in the event of rebreather failure, he would also carry an open-circuit system. As a precaution, both divers would carry additional gas supplies to be completely independent of the support team and the reserve cylinders of gas suspended in the water.

21

Gold Fever

Around the upper North Island, the summer month of January is often a period of strong winds generated by cyclonic weather systems in the Tasman and Pacific oceans. It can also be a period of calm sunny days with the beaches crowded with holidaymakers. Weather forecasting is unpredictable at this time of the year, causing difficulties when planning offshore projects.

I had organised the charter boat *Reel Passion*, a 14-metre fast catamaran, to transport both the dive and ROV teams to the *Niagara* site, a trip of just over an hour from Tutukaka where we were based. The large amount of dive equipment, including gas supplies crowded our facility in the tiny coastal village. Expectations were high as the dive team assembled and the word "gold" was overheard on more than one occasion as preparations were made for the deep dive.

Gas blends were mixed, decompression programs formulated and safety procedures established. The nearest decompression chamber facility was at the Auckland naval base, so it would take time to evacuate a stricken diver by sea and land. A helicopter rescue team was alerted: it could be on-site within a short time if needed to transport the diver to the naval base. With the required formalities in place to operate in the restricted marine zone, we were ready to roll.

The winds strengthened, turning the Gulf waters into a sea of white caps. We waited. The winds continued. Out in the nearby Tasman and Pacific oceans, four cyclone systems were vying for dominance. The days passed, the winds continued and the excitement of the moment diminished as we waited. Having been on a high with the expected dive, the waiting became a frustration for the divers. With continuing strong winds forecast, the dive team headed back to the bright lights of Auckland.

After fourteen days we finally had a break in the weather. I phoned Tim who rushed back to Tutukaka with Dave; there was no time to round up the support divers, who were still in Auckland. We decided to try the next morning with only the two bottom divers and surface support provided again by Brian Oxenham. To wait for the remainder of the team would mean the window of opportunity would be lost.

The *Reel Passion*, pushed along through the ocean swell by twin 370-HP Volvos, headed out into the Gulf tracking across the GPS screen to the target position of the *Niagara*. On board, in addition to the dive team and boat crew, were Jaan Voot and Wade Doak, who had accompanied me on our first ROV visit to the wreck, with Win Christie and Jim White, all associates from my old Canterbury dive days. Jim, the originator of our first aqualung regulators we made back in the 1950s, had often schemed of ways and means to get down to the wreck. Although showing signs of the years gone past, these diving veterans were still attracted by adventure under the sea and if required would provide in-water support for the dive team. The adventure they were now part of was only a dream back in their early diving days. Peter Thompson, a professional underwater cameraman, would operate the video-recording equipment; Curtis and the blank monitor screens on our first visit to the wreck was still a vivid memory.

The sweep of the ROV sonar cycled slowly across the screen, painting a narrow red target in midwater ahead. Our concentration switched to the video monitors as we waited for the camera to capture the target we were approaching.

Flying the ROV slowly through the twilight blue, I focused onto a dark shadow ghosting on the screen before me. The shape of a ship's mast materialised, stretched horizontal in midwater across the screen. The crow's-nest festooned with black coral growths signified we had arrived at the *Niagara*'s main mast. It was here, that fateful night 59 years before, that Reg Kerr had clung precariously as the mine blast below erupted into the darkness. Now the deserted platform stood silent, a sentinel guarding the remains below. Shoals of golden snapper reflected our lights as the lithe form of a hapuku glided past following the mast down into the shadows. We followed along the angle of the mast towards the deck. The remains of the foredeck, with the ship lying nearly on her port side, loomed out of the gloom as a dark vertical wall.

Features materialised first as shadows in the low light, then took on form as the ROV approached. Visibility was good. With our lights turned off we could see fifteen metres or more. As the camera tilted up to look across the deck, a solitary cruciform shape stood out against the blue, like a cross standing over a grave. Closer, our lights revealed a multitude of colours from jewel anemones and marine encrustations. Abandoned hapuku fishing lines entwined the outstretched arms like a spider's web to snare the unwary. Beneath the growths we discerned the shapes of pulley wheels and fittings, identifying the cross as part of the cargo-handling system.

Closer to the deck other features appeared. First, a skylight above the third-class dining and smoking saloons where Ray Nelson and his off-duty shipmates had joined the passengers for drinks at the bar. Now its frame twisted outwards with broken panes, a testimony to the blast that wrecked the forward accommodation. Passing cargo lifting equipment and deck machinery, we flew aft towards the remains of the forward superstructure. Deck timbers had rotted away, leaving behind lines of caulking to mark their former location. Large square-framed Georgian windows, more suited to a manor house than a ship, appeared ghostly in the blue light. A door onto the forward deck was open. Alongside, a large square window hung open, a steel beam piercing a glass pane. The door had once opened to the first-class accommodation reading and writing rooms. Now only blue water greeted us: the music room once above had collapsed with other upper structure, including the bridge, onto the sea floor.

The sight of the wreckage enveloped in the surreal blue light reminded Tim of the film *Titanic*. The sudden urge to go and see for themselves propelled the two divers into their dry suits. As they dressed, Tim's attention was drawn to a large black fin cutting through the surface nearby. Not wanting to believe what he was seeing, he indicated the nearby shape to the crew. The skipper, Bob Ash, confirmed Tim's fears. A large hammerhead shark was patrolling the dive site. His comment, "Don't worry, they are too well fed!", did little to put the divers at ease. Eventually the shark disappeared and they refocused on the task ahead.

The dive shot-line was positioned on the stern section of the wreck, some distance from where the ROV was operating. Dave led Tim down the taut line and the clear blue water closed in around them. The only points of focus now were the line and each other. At 50 metres, Tim switched from air to trimix. He passed Dave who, slightly slower, frequently checked that his oxygen set point was maintaining a 1.3 PO_2. At 60 metres a school of kingfish swept into view from the depths. The torpedo shapes circled the divers rapidly as another three came bolting up the shot-line.

A thermocline at 80 metres dropped the water temperature from 20 to 16 degrees Centigrade. Clad in dry suits with thermal underwear, the divers were further protected against hypothermia with a barrier of argon fed into the suits from a small cylinder of the compressed gas. Helium is a very poor insulator and causes heat loss on a diver immersed in the gas. Argon, a denser gas, reduces the conduction of heat and provides a form of insulation.

Below, the divers could see the liner lying on her side. Dave's first impression was of the huge size of the wreck, his second the rows of portholes disappearing along the hull into the distance. Landing close to the stern they swam slowly forward, conscious of old trawl nets tangled around the stern docking bridge. Disintegration of the upper wooden superstructure let in enough ambient light to make Dave's penetration through the area relatively easy. His main concern was the net strung five metres overhead. Any escape would require an exit out through the side.

Swimming across the vertical wall of the aft deck area, they halted at the entrance to a large cavern. It was the opening into No. 5 hold, now missing the hatch covers which had been dislodged during the sinking. Dave peered into the darkness, his cave-diving instincts attracting him to the unknown. Using his torch beam he could detect neither floor nor walls, indicating the enormity of the hull interior. His curiosity was now aroused. He checked his remaining dive time – nine minutes to go. Deciding there was just enough time for a quick look around, he reached for the penetration reel clipped to his harness. It was then he suddenly realised where he was – 110 metres down with a closed-circuit rebreather he had never used to such depths before. The gas mix he was breathing gave him an equivalent narcotic depth of 41 metres – the clear headiness he experienced had, for an instant, brought on a feeling of complacency. He did not feel as if he was at 110 metres: everything was just perfect. He resecured the reel to his harness and turned away from temptation.

Nearby, Tim was gesticulating at a fully intact deck light, semi-spherical with a protective brass cage over the frosted glass. Always on the lookout for a memento, Tim was pulling at the securely attached lamp, uttering his frustration into his regulator, "Where's my tool bag?" Without tools to dislodge the assembly from its mounting, he abandoned his efforts and joined Dave for the swim back to the shot-line. As he began the swim he looked up and recognised the remains of the docking bridge, but their completed time was now fourteen minutes of the planned fifteen minutes of bottom time on the wreck – it was time to go. Starting their ascent, the divers recognised the shape of the stern docking bridge telegraph I had seen on the first ROV excursion, a prize that would have to await their return.

The wreck faded back into the depths as the two divers made their way slowly back up the shot-line to commence their long decompression schedule. The first stop was at 78 metres for one minute. All the deep stops were of the same interval until around the 30 metre mark, where they settled in for the 100-minute decompression obligation.

They carefully monitored themselves for signs of bends symptoms. Tim was alarmed when at 21 metres Dave indicated he was seeing orange spots before his eyes. He had been gesturing to Tim on something he had seen on the wreck when, on turning back to the shot-line, his whole field of vision was taken up by the tiny bright orange spots. His immediate thought was he was experiencing the onset of oxygen toxicity. Instinctively he looked down for the diluent flush button, and the dots disappeared. Raising his vision they immediately reappeared. To his relief he realised what the problem was. The shot-line had been prepared with depth markings using a fluoro-orange paint. This was now rubbing off, causing small particles of paint suspension in the water. Tim, realising Dave was not in any danger, found difficulty keeping his mouthpiece in place as he broke into laughter.

Dave surfaced some 20 minutes before Tim, his decompression time shortened as he was using the Inspiration rebreather gas schedule; Tim, on open-circuit equipment, required longer. For fifteen minutes down on the wreck, Tim's total dive time was 140 minutes.

While the divers were descending to the stern area, I flew the ROV over to an area adjacent to the opening ripped in the hull's side by the salvors in their quest to recover the gold bars from the bullion room. As we approached the opening we came across debris strewn across the adjacent hull plates. From reports I had studied, I knew there was a strong possibility of one or more of the remaining gold bars lying exposed on the hull plates. The debris had fallen from the grab as it was being extracted from the interior and, on at least two occasions, gold bars had also fallen from the grab. Johnstone had reported to Risdon Beasley that a bar dropped during the 1941 salvage was exposed lying in a fold of a hull plate. Despite numerous attempts with the grab, the elusive bar trapped in the confines of the fold escaped the grasping jaws. With the knowledge we were approaching gold country there was a noticeable change in the demeanour of those crowded around the monitors. Gold fever was beginning to infect the crew. Jim White cried out: "There's a gold bar!"

Busy concentrating on manoeuvring the ROV around the debris field, I was not giving close attention to the various pieces of debris that were scattered around on the hull plates. Jim was adamant he had seen a shape of a bar of gold, but despite my backtracking the ROV I was unable to determine what he had seen. Later examination of the video also failed to reveal a bar of gold. This did not deter Jim from his assertion that we had passed over a bar of gold. Gold fever can play strange tricks on people's minds. Nevertheless, the debris area on the side of the hull adjacent to the bullion room workings certainly required closer examination.

Returning the ROV to the surface, I flew the vehicle across to the shot-line. Tim and Dave were now at nine metres, breathing 100 per cent oxygen. Brian had the inflatable tender boat positioned above and frequently checked on the decompressing divers, who indicated all was well.

With the divers safely back aboard it was a time for celebration. A barrage of questions was directed at the two divers as cameras and dictaphones recorded the moment. At last, using self-contained breathing apparatus and diving free from a surface tether, Tim and Dave had achieved our dream of the past 40 years – they had dived the *Niagara*.

22

Spectre from the Past

By June 1999, six months after Tim and Dave's pioneering dive, we were back anchored over the *Niagara*. On board the *Reel Passion*, in addition to the ROV team, was a film crew from the television documentary show *60 Minutes* prepared to film another *Niagara* pioneer. Through the medium of telepresence, he would revisit a ghost from his past. Ray Nelson, still sprightly in his mid-70s, had flown across from Queensland to feature in a programme recording his experiences as *Niagara* crew and a participant in what has become known as "the greatest gold salvage in history".

Tim Cashman was also along for the ride. I observed the young diver sitting alongside Ray: although from different generations, they shared a common bond. I reflected on the differing technologies, spanning 60 years, the two men had used to visit the lost liner. Ray had been lowered by cable, encapsulated at atmospheric pressure in a steel tube to protect him from the pressure of the depths; Tim, breathing a cocktail of gases concocted by a computer program, his body exposed to the increasing pressure, glided down through the depths free from surface bondage.

The *Niagara*'s grave was discernible as we approached, thanks to a large surface stain from oil still escaping from her. This aroused the interest of the film team in featuring the danger of a sudden release of the trapped oil creating a possible environmental disaster for the nearby marine reserves. We collected surface samples, which indicated the oil was lighter than one would expect from heavy fuel oil. Following our initial 1988 visit, we had noted surface oil slicks on occasions when visiting the wreck site. Local media highlighted reports of oil leaks, raising the possibility of an ecological time-bomb ticking away in the depths. Maritime Safety Authority officials had taken an interest in the reports and had contacted me on the possible implications of the surface oil. With the knowledge that the vessel fully bunkered for a Pacific voyage could carry 4200 tons of fuel oil, and that a large amount of fuel had been lost at the time of her sinking, what remained in the undamaged fuel tanks some 60 years later was questionable. I had proposed to the MSA that we carry out a ROV survey of the wreck to determine the state of the fuel tanks and estimate the amount of fuel oil that could still be trapped. My offer was declined. The official thinking was the oil reaching the surface was only of a light viscosity and presented no danger, while any heavy fuel oil would remain in a semi-solid form in the cold temperatures at depth and were unlikely to exit the hull. This is questionable, as we have found that the water temperatures down on the wreck vary from around 15 to over 20 degrees Centigrade, not low enough for the oil to convert to a semi-solid state. (On a later dive project, we observed small globules of heavy fuel oil rising to the surface. Sticky black spheres underwater, the globules would break up on reaching the surface, dissolving into a light multi-coloured surface sheen. There was no doubt that the hull still retained a large amount of fuel which in time, with the deterioration of the wreck, would suddenly be released into the Gulf waters.)

Ray's excitement increased as the ROV descended through the depths for a rendezvous with a spectre from his past. We touched down on the bottom at 120 metres alongside the wreck. Aware of Ray's strong feelings about the old claims of a salvage depth record, I did not bring this depth to his notice. I flew the ROV up over the collapsed superstructure, past the remains of lifeboat davits marking the area where Ray had made his leap into the darkness as he grabbed for the falls of No. 3 boat. His thoughts returned to his descent to free the jammed boatload of frightened women and children. Now a shoal of kingfish, their bodies shining silver in our lights, patrolled the scene of that night to remember.

Further forward, we flew across the bridge area. Now collapsed along with Captain Martin's cabin onto the seabed, the large square window frames of the first-class library remained as the only reminder of the command post that once stood above. To Ray, transported down through the depths by telepresence, the wreck scenes rekindled memories of those halcyon days of his youth. To the night when a war on the far side of the world invaded our seas, the mine explosion, the moment of terror as he was thrown from his bunk, abandoning ship in the night and watching from a lifeboat as his ship reared up before slipping into the ocean depths.

The excitement of the salvage returned. Memories of Johnno climbing into the bell, recovering the first gold bar and celebrating with Captains Williams, Herd and the rest of the *Claymore* crew as they danced on a carpet of gold. Gazing at the remains of the *Niagara* on the monitors, Ray recalled for the camera crew those events of 60 years ago.

Sitting with the others listening to Ray recount his adventures, I realised what a major part the ship resting below had played in his life. It was a nostalgic experience at this time in his life to return and revisit the ship that over the past decades had been only a memory. For us who shared his return and memories, it was a moment to remember.

Others from the past had also been drawn back to the *Niagara*. Captain William Martin passed away following a short retirement in 1946. Following his wishes, a USSCo vessel carried his ashes across the Tasman to be scattered on the waters close to the resting place of the ship he had considered his favourite. Mementos and memories of the *Niagara* survive in both Australia and New Zealand. The diving bell used by the Williams gold salvage in 1941 is in the Castlemaine Museum, the Victorian town where it was constructed. Kelly Tarlton's Museum of Shipwrecks in the Bay of Islands featured a number of *Niagara* mementos and artefacts, and other New Zealand museums have collections of photographs and documents pertaining to the history of the ship and the gold salvage. The door from the bullion room, now inscribed with details of the 1941 gold salvage, is in the possession of the Johnstone family in Australia.

Visiting the Castlemaine Museum, I was most keen to examine the interior of the diving bell. I had taken a number of exterior photos of the bell standing upright in the museum, but needed a ladder to reach the open hatch. Explaining to the receptionist my connection with the *Niagara* and my wishes to photograph the interior, I was directed to the museum manager. A young woman dressed in a smart business suit, her hair knotted neatly in a bun, studied me through her designer glasses as she listened to my request.

"Yes, we do have a ladder available, but I am afraid it will be impossible for you to use it."

"Why?"

"Well, we would require an approval for you and the ladder under the occupational safety regulations, and I am sorry as we do not have that, we are unable to let you use the ladder."

I gazed at the nearby video screen on which Jeff Maynard's documentary *Niagara's Gold* was being screened non-stop during the day. A scene of Johnno Johnstone emerging from the bell filled the screen. The thought passed through my mind – if those guys set out today to do what they did back then, they probably would never have been allowed to leave the wharf.

Perhaps one of the most unusual *Niagara* artefacts I have come across is a lifeboat that rested on the banks of the Awanui River in the New Zealand far north. Jack Ward, a resident of Kaitaia, came across it while searching for a suitable craft in which to install a steam engine that had originated from a pinnace off the steamer *Iris*, which had laid the first Pacific communications cable and, like the *Niagara*, had played cat-and-mouse games with the Germans across the Pacific during the First World War. She narrowly escaped a German raider at Fanning Island in 1914 and later pursued a scow commandeered by the escaping prisoner Count Felix Von Luckner, ending in his recapture. Jack mated the components from the two ships, naming the vessel *Iris*. With Jack at the helm, the little steamboat, now painted a bright yellow, would steam down the Awanui and out onto the ocean – a descendant of two famous ships from the past.

I talked with Jack, then aged 93 years, about the fate of the little boat I had discovered down an isolated road alongside the river. Although hindered by the effects of a stroke, his enthusiasm to sail her once more down the river was evident. However, under the watchful eyes of his wife and restricted by his failing health, the *Iris* was now out of bounds for him. His hope was for the vessel to eventually find a home in a museum.

23

Vertigo

Now the path to the *Niagara* had been opened for recreational divers using mixed-gas technical diving technology, further dives were to follow. Each one resulted in a longer bottom time on the wreck, furthering our knowledge on the ship and its rate of deterioration.

Tim and Dave carried out two dives in the summer of 2000. Both divers, now using Inspiration closed-circuit rebreathers, were able to extend their bottom time to 20 minutes. Carrying an underwater video camera, Dave recorded one dive when they explored the remains of the forward superstructure. Unfortunately, due to the video light imploding under the pressure of a previous deep dive in the Pearce Resurgence cave system, the video was recorded in natural light. Without artificial light, colours at the depth of the wreck are predominately blue. The true colours of the wreck were only momentarily exposed when the divers' helmet-mounted lights swept across the scene.

Dave aborted the second dive when he noticed that a repair he had carried out on a computer was not secure. Remaining at 60 metres he waited as Tim continued on down to the wreck. The breach in the hull came into Tim's view. Peering down into the darkness of the cavern, he could discern the twisted beams and a mound of debris where salvage grabs had grasped for boxes containing the gold bars. It was clear that any bars remaining in the bullion room would require a major excavation to find.

In July 2001 we returned to the wreck with a film crew making a documentary for the National Geographic Channel. The theme was technical sport diving and a dive down to the *Niagara* was the goal for the deep-dive segment. Tim, who had returned to Wales, flew out to join Dave and Pete Mesley as bottom divers. Natural History, a New Zealand film company, was contracted to produce the film. The cameras filmed both topside and underwater but for the deeper scenes a special camera interfaced with a back-mounted video recorder was installed on Pete's helmet. Dave also operated an underwater video-camera system modified for filming in the greater pressures. In addition, the ROV followed the divers recording their exploration of the wreck.

The resident school of kingfish circled the diving trio as they descended onto the wreck. Beams of light cut through the twilight void seeking out the sunken liner and were captured by the ROV waiting on the wreck. On our shipboard monitors the shafts of light heralded the divers' approach. They appeared on the screens as silent intruders, without the plumes of exhaust gas trailing above that are a signature of open-circuit breathing systems. All three were equipped with rebreathers and inhaled a trimix gas blend of 10 per cent oxygen, 60 per cent helium and 30 per cent nitrogen.

Following the instructions of the film director alongside me, I endeavoured to maintain the ROV at a distance to cover all three divers simultaneously with the camera. The diver-operated cameras recorded wreck features and close-up scenes of the exploring divers. Our lights combined in sweeping the darkness, highlighting machinery on the foredeck, for example an anchor secured forward of the collapsed superstructure that would no doubt in time tumble from its vertical perch to the seabed below.

The open door between the deck and the library spotted on my earlier ROV dives attracted Dave. As he squeezed through, his lights illuminated a wall-mounted electric fan and lamp now covered with marine encrustations. The wash from the lights flooding the foredeck area gave Tim the confidence to explore further into the shadows below. Descending to the seabed alongside the port gunwale, he discovered sections of superstructure that had detached over past years. Falling to the bottom they added to the growing debris field around the wreck. He noted a structural section that had indications of recent detachment, signifying that the wreck was continuing to decay. Looking upwards he absorbed the surrealistic scene in which he was immersed. Light-beams traversed the darkness above like laser beams in a science fiction movie. His diving companions hovered above like astronauts on a space walk as the little yellow robotic ROV zoomed around them in the dark void of inner-space.

Swimming forward, the divers discovered that the upper bow section had been blown away with explosive charges. The damage had originated from the early salvors testing the strength of their explosive charges before attempting to breach the bullion room. The gaping hole provided access into the forward crew accommodation area. The interior cavern was an enticing invitation for Dave the cave-diver. Exploring the darkness with the beam of his light, he discovered a solitary teacup lying on a beam. Retrieving it he found it to be cracked though still intact, the green emblem of the Union Steam Ship Company still discernible in the glazing. Perhaps it was a cup seaman Harris had been preparing for the end of shift cuppa when the mine struck, hurling both Harris and crockery across the room.

Missing hatch covers blasted into the heavens by the mine together with Mrs Wise's car enabled the divers to make a short penetration into the forward holds. Inside the sheltered confines of the hull, the absence of tidal currents had caused a large amount of silt to accumulate. The divers moved with care. Water visibility in the confines of the hold would quickly become zero from silt if stirred up by careless fin movements. A large conger eel slipped from the shadows attracted by the invasion of movement and light into its lair.

All too soon the planned bottom time of 25 minutes had elapsed. The increase in bottom time from their previous dives was not accomplished without a penalty. Additional time decompressing on ascent to the surface was required, varying between the divers who had chosen different decompression schedules. Pete, using a more conservative staging programme, completed a total of 320 minutes underwater. Dave, using different decompression calculations, completed his dive in 276 minutes. The three divers using rebreathers with their PO_2 set at 1.3 bar reached 100 per cent CNS oxygen exposure after about 180 minutes. To avoid oxygen toxicity they carried out five-minute breaks on air every 20 minutes. There is still much to learn about human physiology in the ocean depths.

Pete Mesley returned to dive the *Niagara* in the winter of 2002 with

Simon Mitchell, an expatriate Kiwi then living in Sydney. Pete had changed his dive apparatus to the Inspiration closed-circuit rebreather while Simon used a more expensive military-style Biomarine Mk15 rebreather. Previously director of the New Zealand Navy diving medicine unit, and now a doctor working full-time in diving and hyperbaric medicine, Simon was a knowledgeable person to have along on a mixed-gas deep dive expedition. With Willy Heatly and Geoff Payne again as support divers, the dive team was complete.

Once again inclement weather haunted the dive team, forcing their boat to shelter at the nearby Hen and Chicken islands. The team were close to abandoning any attempt to dive when an unexpected short weather break came. We had learnt not to place too much faith in the weather forecasts for this Gulf area and adopted the attitude of nothing ventured, nothing gained. Otherwise, planning a *Niagara* expedition on the basis of weather reports would be fraught with indecision and procrastination.

As the two divers descended they knew they were in for a great dive. With excellent water visibility allowing a high level of ambient light to penetrate the depths, they sighted the wreck stretched out below when at 80 metres. The shot-line hung off to one side of the hull, but with the excellent visibility they departed the line and descended onto the area amidships where the two smoke stacks had once stood. Collapsed from the wreck a long time past, the funnels now lay on the bottom alongside the hull among remains of the promenade and boat decks. Gone too was the large glass cathedral dome that once featured over the first-class vestibule. The circular opening which had once accommodated the dome now provided an entrance for the divers.

Shafts of ambient light penetrated the ship's interior, enticing the pair to explore further. In the bright conditions their torches were of little effect except to investigate darkened corners. Entering the first-class dining saloon they were confronted by the ravages of the deep. Once decorated in Louis XVI style, the former elegant saloon where the rich and famous had wined and dined was now reduced to a decaying shell slowly dissolving into the surrounding ocean. Some features were still recognisable to Pete from his study of old photos of the liner's glory days. A ceiling fan hung from its cord still attached to the now-vertical ceiling; ornate columns once ascending to the ceiling extended horizontally across the liquid space. Table legs, attached to the floor to prevent tables sliding with the ship's movement, protruded stump-like from the decaying deck. Devoid of their tops, which had rotted away, they were the only reminder of the accommodation that had once seated 190 diners.

Shoals of fish flitted through the silence where once floated the sounds of music from Patrick Watters and the ship's band, their instruments now buried in the accumulated silt and debris. Shadows flickered around the columns and table remains where waiters glided as they served from glittering silverware, now also buried among the debris of the time capsule into which the divers had ventured.

A stack of white discs some 25cm in diameter attracted Pete's attention. Thinking he had discovered a pile of crockery dishes, he picked one up. It broke in half in his hand. He squeezed the disc; it contracted like a hard sponge; perhaps it was a type of marine creature now living in the saloon. Cup corals, sponges and other exotic marine growths cover the exterior of the wreck. No doubt its interior also provided shelter for other organisms, some possibly having fed on the rich interior furnishings. In the end it would all result in the wreck being reduced back to carbon, the element from which it had been born.

The dive had proceeded smoothly. The divers, breathing an 8 per cent oxygen and 60 per cent helium mix, had not exceeded a depth of 112 metres. Remaining clear-headed they began their ascent back up the dive line, careful not to exceed the planned 25-minute bottom time. With past experience of the sudden onslaught of narcosis when switching from trimix to air at 50 metres, Pete delayed the gas change until his ascent to 32 metres.

While decompressing at six metres on oxygen, he was suddenly overcome by vertigo. Grasping the shot-line he closed his eyes, desperately attempting to stop the world spinning around him. The rotational vertigo continued, creating a bout of nausea. Pete was conscious that whatever happened, he must maintain his decompression schedule. Although he was so close to the comfort of the boat, to surface now would most likely result in a painful death. The sudden change in ambient pressure would result in the nitrogen remaining trapped in his body, to erupt through the blood vessels into his brain. The support divers, aware of his predicament, provided in-water assistance.

The continuing vertigo and nausea made Pete vomit. This presented a further predicament, as he needed to maintain his grip on the mouthpiece of the closed-circuit rebreather. To keep the breathing circuit free from vomit contamination, when he felt another bout of vomiting coming he switched to his back-up open-circuit system. The regulator exhaled into the open water and could be kept clear by purging gas. Continuing in this manner Pete completed his decompression schedule. On the surface he was stripped of his equipment and placed on pure oxygen while transported to the Navy decompression chamber in Auckland. Initial treatment there was carried out at a pressure equivalent to a depth of eighteen metres, but as he still felt dizzy he was taken down to 30 metres on a heliox mixture of 50/50 helium and oxygen. He emerged from the chamber with no after-effects. Simon diagnosed the problem as a random inner-ear decompression illness event (see Appendix 3). Diving the *Niagara*, as for any deep dive over 40 metres, requires specialist skills that can be obtained only through intense training and experience. The majority of fatalities resulting from deep diving are not caused through equipment failure but from physiological or "people" factors. Panic is the number-one danger.

On the day and time Pete and Simon were exploring the *Niagara*, I was across the Tasman on the Gold Coast visiting Ray Nelson. As in the past, I was again made most welcome and entertained by Ray with recollections of his crew days on the *Niagara* and working with Captain Williams on the gold salvage.

Following the salvage, with the entry of Japan into the war, the Australian government formed the Commonwealth Marine Salvage Board in 1942. Captain Williams, with his past success of the *Niagara* salvage, was appointed director of the new salvage operation. Many of the crew from the *Claymore*, including Ray, joined him. With a small fleet of salvage vessels including six tugs and an ancient salvage vessel, the salvage group was responsible for returning 600,000 tons of sunk or disabled Allied vessels back to active service. Ray was most proud of these efforts, which were often carried out in harsh conditions or under fire from enemy aircraft.

At the time of my visit Ray was preparing to give a presentation at the local branch of the Second World War mariners' RSL , including a showing of the *Niagara's Gold* documentary film. The local newspaper had run a story on Ray and his involvement with the gold salvage. The sunken liner had certainly been a major part of Ray's life and even now at the age of 80 it still played a major role.

Asked about the mine-sweeping paravane system installed in Sydney before the *Niagara*'s last departure, Ray remarked, "We didn't use the paravanes coming into or leaving Auckland as we weren't used to using them, having only tried them once when we left Sydney. But you know, if we had used them, the ship probably wouldn't have bloody well sunk!" But then I would have probably never met Ray. Or descended into the depths to seek the *Niagara*'s gold.

24

The Smell of Oil

The depth sounder indicated a flat featureless seabed. Studying a sketch of distant landmarks drawn by Jaan Voot back in 1988 during our first visits to the *Niagara,* I realised the GPS position we had arrived at was incorrect. The alignment of distant land features did not coincide with Jaan's drawing and indicated we were positioned too far to the north. The team of international divers on board our charter vessel *Pacific Hideaway* were restless. Some had travelled halfway around the globe to dive the famous shipwreck and found our inability to locate such a large wreck a frustrating anti-climax to their long journey and associated jetlag.

Gareth Jones, our skipper, had logged the wreck's position into his GPS two weeks earlier when he transited the site. Its absence on his depth-sounder screen was puzzling. The US was preparing to invade Iraq and we had heard rumours of GPS satellite signals being manipulated by Uncle Sam to confuse the Iraqis. Perhaps this was the cause of the wreck's absence.

With our space-age navigation technology in doubt, we reverted to using the landmarks recorded by Jaan. It was ironic that in this day and age we had to rely on methods used decades before by Captain Williams and Risdon Beasley to locate the wreck. I recalled an old chart John Williams had drawn highlighting land features to aid the positioning of the salvage vessel over the wreck – he had marked a large tree on the mainland as a bearing. The mainland was a distant shadow on the horizon, making it impossible to find the tree even if it still existed. Perhaps the atmosphere was a lot clearer back in those days, but no doubt the tree, like many of the salvage team, had long gone.

It was March 2003 and with the threat of war in the Middle East the price of gold was on the rise. With gold fetching around $US350 an ounce, the five remaining gold bars on the *Niagara* were now valued at around $NZ1.4 million – a prize well worth challenging the depths for. I had even received an email from HM Treasury wishing us all the best for our endeavours; it was also a reminder that it still laid claim to its lost treasures.

The team assembled in Tutukaka. Their expectations for deep adventure and, with a bit of luck, success in finding a gold bar or two were high. Tim Cashman had returned from England eager to extend his previous explorations of the wreck. Three highly experienced deepwater wreck divers accompanied him: Christina Campbell and Chris Hutchison, the team leaders of the Starfish Enterprise Dive Team – a UK group who had dived on a number of classical shipwrecks including RMS *Lusitania* and RMS *Brittanic*, sister ship of the *Titanic* – were accompanied by Keiran Hulme, another avid wreck-diver. He had dived the *Egypt* and was familiar with the story of the *Niagara* salvage. Tim had also now dived the *Egypt* and his stories of diving on the *Niagara* were like nectar to a bee to Keiran, who needed little encouragement to travel to New Zealand to dive the scene of the epic salvage once reported to have eclipsed the record depth for salvage on the *Egypt*.

Dave Apperley had organised the dive project from his home in Sydney. Coordinating the logistics had presented numerous problems in assembling the vast amount of required support equipment in Tutukaka. With months of frustration and preparations now behind him, Dave was eager to get on with the dive, as were the two other Australians who had joined the team. Craig Challan and Karl Hall were accomplished cave divers. Deep underground, they had both been instrumental in making significant discoveries with their explorations of the submerged cave systems under the Nullabor Plains. Their experience in diving overhead environments where there was no immediate escape to the surface qualified both to explore the vast confines of the *Niagara*. To aid their explorations they had brought diver-propulsion vehicles with them. These electric-powered tow vehicles, specially designed for deepwater operations, would enable Craig and Karl to cover extensive areas of the wreck in the limited bottom time available.

We motored slowly across the calm sea, bringing the distant land features into line as shown on Jaan's drawing. The pungent odour of fuel oil invaded the crisp smell of the ocean. I could tell the wreck was near even though it was concealed beneath 120 metres of water. The shine on the surface of the sea ahead was unmistakable: all we needed to do was follow the slick and our noses. The bottom line on the echo sounder climbed the screen, imaging a large protuberance on the seabed. We had arrived over the wreck.

The surrounding ocean was peppered with spreading halos of colour as black spheres of oil broached the smooth surface. The smell was unmistakable as the released oil spread across the surface as a thin sheen to be carried off towards the distant islands. Although bleeding, the wreck was not yet haemorrhaging and the oil being released would eventually evaporate into the atmosphere. The amount of oil now rising to the surface significantly exceeded the volume I had previously observed escaping from the wreck. Over the following two weeks the fuel oil was constantly rising to the surface. This indicated that the wreck had now deteriorated so much that now there is danger of a major eruption of the oil trapped in it. On one trip we came upon a surface slick running some fourteen kilometres from the wreck site.

Gareth manoeuvred the *Pacific Hideaway* until the echo sounder indicated that the wreck was directly below. Acting on his signal, Dave cast a light grapnel into the ocean. It quickly snaked into the depths, and the attached orange buoy floated on the calm surface marking the pathway to the sunken liner. Tim and Kieran in their Inspiration rebreather systems broke through the liquid portal separating two worlds, their jetlag torpor quickly cast aside now they were finally in the water. The delays locating the wreck had taken us well into the afternoon before the first divers entered the water. The plan was for a 25-minute bottom time, requiring nearly four hours in the water with decompression requirements. The delay had taken us close to a time limit where the dive would have to be cancelled if we were to avoid the divers surfacing close to evening.

At 120 metres the divers arrived onto a seabed of sediment and broken shells, but no wreck. A furrow across the seabed pointed the direction from whence the grapnel had come. Tim realised that the grapnel had pulled from the wreck and would be at the end of the trail in the seabed. He clipped his dive reel line to the shot-line and the two divers set off across the bottom in search of the wreck they knew lay obscured somewhere in the surrounding gloom. Except for sighting a solitary section of railing on the bottom, they still had not reached the wreck after swimming for fifteen minutes. It was obvious that the tidal current had dragged the grapnel for some distance. The dive was aborted. Ascending the shot-line the disappointed bottom divers met Craig and Karl descending with their scooters, unaware of the predicament below. The message was conveyed and the descending divers returned to the surface without needing to undergo three hours of decompression that Tim and Kieran now settled into.

Before departing, to ensure we would not have a recurrence of problems with finding the wreck, a heavy mooring was anchored into the wreck and also another down line. We departed the scene with the two marker buoys floating on the calm surface. A day of perfect weather conditions had been lost and it was a rather dejected team that returned to Tutukaka.

A series of lows swept across the Tasman Sea and a tropical cyclone to the north turned the seas into a maelstrom, keeping us in port for the next eight days. The La Nina weather pattern we had been experiencing over summer was still causing strong winds that made it impossible to dive the *Niagara*. Although once the divers were at depth they would not be affected by the surface conditions, we required winds of less than fifteen knots to recover the equipment-burdened divers safely from the water. Finally the seas abated and with the forecast predicting dropping winds we returned to the wreck site. The tempest over the previous week had carried away the buoys we had left marking the wreck, so once again we went through the process of hooking a shot-line grapnel into the wreck. Conditions were still marginal, but as the forecast was for dropping winds and improved weather, we decided to proceed with the dive.

Karl and Craig headed for the bottom riding their underwater scooters only to discover once again a barren expanse of sediment and no wreck. The force of the surface swell on the buoy had bent the light hooks tearing the grapnel from the wreckage. They rode their scooters across the seabed searching for the lost shipwreck. In the storm-reduced visibility their task was made more difficult and they finally gave up the search to return to the surface.

Disappointed, we settled in for the long wait while Karl and Craig went through their decompression schedule. The large orange buoys suspending the diver decompression lines with the back-up gas supplies drifted with the wind and swell. Visits by a surface support diver to the two divers off-gassing in the water column ensured all was going to schedule.

Rather than dropping as forecast, the wind increased. A three-metre swell developed with waves cresting across the surface. Time passed and the divers had not surfaced. On the surface there was rising consternation among the team as sea conditions were deteriorating. Below at six metres, Craig had felt a slight pain in his shoulder. It could have been a muscle strain but he decided to remain submerged for extra time as a precaution against a possible bends hit. To add to his problems, the scrubber unit on his rebreather had taken in water from a slow leak. The reaction of seawater with the scrubber's soda-lime chemical could cause a caustic cocktail in his breathing loop, resulting in the burning of tissues in his throat air passages. As a precaution, he switched across to his open-circuit oxygen system to complete the prolonged decompression.

Finally, after four hours submerged, the divers were on the surface. Gareth kept the boat headed into the rising seas as the two divers, clutching onto haul lines, were pulled aboard the surging stern platform. Again we had failed to hook into the wreck and four divers, although they had reached the bottom, had failed to sight even the shadow of the elusive liner. Time was running out. Only two days diving remained before team departed for distant shores.

The following day we arrived back on site determined that our elusive quarry would not escape us this time. The weather had improved and we were armed with a heavy grapnel and chain attached to the shot-line which, after Gareth carefully positioned the *Pacific Hideaway* over the sonar image from below, was cast into the depths. Dave, who had put the project together and enticed the other members of the dive team to travel long distances and at considerable expense, felt bad about their failure to reach the wreck. He dived first with Tim to ensure that the shot-line was securely tied to the wreck; the others would follow once the signal float hit the surface.

Descending below Tim, Dave came upon the mooring line we had set on day one floating in mid-water. The frayed end told the story why the marker buoy had been lost during the storm. He halted his descent to secure the floating line to the shot-line then continued his journey into the depths. Tim, having now passed Dave, realised by the depth he had reached they were again not on the wreck but continued on down to the seabed. Dave could see Tim's light below him and knew the wreck must be somewhere close. Turning his lights off to avoid chasing shadows, he peered into the darkness surrounding him. Deciding the wreck lay ahead he tied his reel line to the shot and swam ahead three metres. A vertical flat steel wall covered with marine growth appeared from the dark. The featureless bottom of the *Niagara* soared upwards. Aware of the other divers waiting on the surface, Dave set about heaving 110 metres of shot-line complete with surface buoy across to the wreck, seeking a tie in point.

In the silence of the depths Tim could hear Dave grunting into his mouthpiece as he struggled dragging the load over to the sunken hull. Swimming upwards they came upon the bilge keel as the vertical wall curved onto the flat, near-horizontal expanse of the starboard hull section. Portholes, recessed among the encrusting marine growth, stretched into the distance. Straining under his burden, Dave cast around the smooth hull surface for a suitable tie-in point. It was obvious why the grapnels had not held on this section of the hull – further forward, the shattered hull plates would have offered secure anchor points. For the team waiting on the surface, the delay with the signal float to appear was starting to look ominous, but I knew that Dave and Tim wanted to ensure the disappointments of the past two weeks were not repeated and this time the shot-line would be secured to the wreck.

A heavy cable stretched across hull plates disappearing in both directions into the visual curtain. With no other suitable feature around, Dave forced the shot-line under the cable and knotted it securely. The signal float was inflated and accelerated through the diminishing pressures to the surface. By now, I was resigned that the gremlins were at work again once more and our efforts to secure the shot-line into the wreck had been thwarted, so there was a sense of relief all round when the orange float finally broke the surface and the second team of Christina, Chris and Kieran disappeared into the depths.

Down on the wreck Dave and Tim, having spent 20 minutes of their precious bottom time securing the shot-line, were now free to explore and set off across the hull towards the decaying superstructure. They swam over to deck level and dropped down into the slot between the promenade and boat decks. Tim carried a digital video camera in a pressure-proof housing and had filmed the dive continuously from the time they had left the surface. They were now on the area close to the stern I had first documented with the ROV camera back in 1988. Comparing the two videos later, the deterioration of the wreck over the span of time between was obvious. Square brass-framed windows reflected the divers' lights but the interior secrets they masked remained hidden from view. Portholes and other metallic fittings lay loose on ledges where they had fallen from the decaying superstructure. Exercising care so as not to stir the sediment blanketing the wreck, the divers swam forward brushing past growths of black coral that sprouted from the steel plates. Corridors leading off the walkway descended as black shafts into the ship's interior providing avenues which Dave noted for possible future penetration dives.

The second team followed a similar route, with Chris also filming as he followed Christina along the canyon formed between the decaying decks. Kieran's first sight of the sunken liner will remain etched into his memory: rows of portholes stretched in both directions until swallowed by the twilight veil of the deep. The wreck seemed to him huge and relatively intact – a sight to stir his wreck-diving juices.

The divers swam through the upper realms of the wreck. Teak decking, now slowly disintegrating, marked the avenues where passengers and crew had hurried to their lifeboat stations. The solitary remains of the davits that witnessed the departure of the lifeboats with their human cargo projected above the crumbling decks. Now surrounded by shoals of pink mao-mao fish and festooned with lost hapuku fishing lines, they were a reminder of the escape from an unseen enemy. Breathing either trimix gas, with a minimal percentage of nitrogen, or heliox containing no nitrogen at all, the divers remained clear-headed, absorbing the sights as if they were on a surface stroll along the seashore.

Dave surfaced first after completing the decompression schedule he had computed before the dive. However the schedule did not take into account his exertions at depth hauling on the shot-line. Back aboard, he was to soon feel the effects of this oversight – a deep pain in his right shoulder indicated all was not well. The deep struggle to tie-in the shot-line was no doubt causing the discomfort he now felt. In an effort to overcome the problem, he began breathing 100 per cent oxygen.

Christina also encountered a problem during her decompression. She had worn an additional dive computer, which did not now agree

Natural History Ltd

Graphic image of the *Niagara*'s stern section, the area of our first ROV explorations.

Natural History Ltd

Preparing for the dive – Dave breaths the dive gas combination.

Author's Collection

Above: Chris Hutchison and Christina Campbell wearing Megladon rebreathers wait the clearance to dive.

NATURAL HISTORY LTD

The ROV descends down the shot-line.

CHRIS HUTCHISON

Keiran Hulme passes a black coral bush sprouting from the wreck.

NATURAL HISTORY LTD

Dave ties onto the shot-line.

TIM CASHMAN

Dave hovers above the promenade deck railings.

CHRIS HUTCHISON

Christina explores the upper wreck.

NATURAL HISTORY LTD

Computer image of the *Niagara*'s bow section.

NATURAL HISTORY LTD

First class library Georgian style window frame.

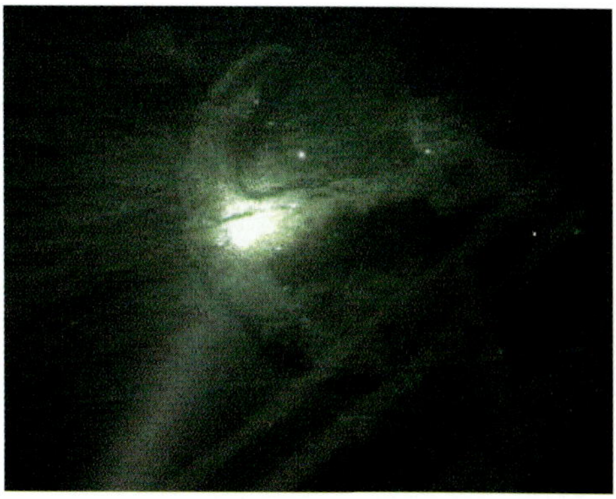
NATURAL HISTORY LTD

A spare anchor still remains secure on the foredeck.

TIM CASHMAN

Empty lifeboat davits festooned with lost hapuku lines.

NATURAL HISTORY LTD

Pete Mesley inspects a cabin interior.

NATURAL HISTORY LTD.

Divers communicate at 110 metres during filming of the wreck.

NATURAL HISTORY LTD

Pete gestures with the cup recovered from the crew's quarters.

Chris Hutchison

Christina hesitates at the dome aperture entrance into the first class lounge.

Chris Hutchison

Inspecting the remains of the first class lounge area.

Chris Hutchison

Artefacts from the past litter the first class lounge.

Natural History Ltd

A fan which once provided comfort in the library.

Author's Collection

Keiran Hulme carries out pre-dive checks.

Author's Collection

Author's Collection

Above: Heavy with equipment Christina is assisted to the stern.

Right: Christina – a leap into the deep.

AUTHOR'S COLLECTION

Left: The author with Dr. Deither Schmidt inspect Kurt Weyher's paintings and records at the Insitute.

Below: The Institute for Shipping and Naval Information, Hamburg.

AUTHOR'S COLLECTION

Wissenschaftliches Institut fur Schiffaharts-und Marineschichte

Above: HSK *Orion* deploying mines in Hauraki Gulf, June 1940. A painting by Captain Kurt Weyher.

Below: HSK *Orion* steaming out of Hauraki Gulf, the Whangarei Heads and Hen and Chicken islands in the background. A painting by Captain Kurt Weyher.

Wissenschaftliches Institut fur Schiffaharts-und Marineschichte

Wissenschaftliches Institut fur Schiffahrts-und Marinegeschichte

Above: Kurt Weyher's painting depicting RMS *Niagara* sinking following the mine explosion.

Below: Craig Howell and Gavin Grant prepare to dive the *Niagara* assisted by Peter Snooks and Mark Brown – 2004.

Author's Collection

with the other onboard computers she carried. Although she realised the computer was at fault, she too decided as a precaution to extend her underwater decompression time. Chris remained submerged with Christina while she waited for the errant computer to register it was safe to surface. Finally, after over five hours underwater, the pair surfaced and staggered aboard. Christina, the first woman to have dived the wreck, collapsed to the deck exhausted after her long submarine excursion. The excitement of the dive and what she had seen below soon negated the fatigue she felt.

In the meantime, Dave had come off breathing oxygen and reported that the pain in his shoulder had diminished. Although he suspected otherwise, like many divers when affected by early signs of the bends he hoped that perhaps it was possibly only a niggle or a muscle strain. However, on the journey back to shore the pain returned and he knew he had a problem and it wasn't muscle strain. Arriving at the marina he grabbed his basic dive gear and with a cylinder of oxygen submerged to the shallow muddy bottom below our mooring. But he was clutching at straws and only delaying the inevitable.

In the early hours of the morning the pain intensified. Dave knew he was in trouble and phoned the Devonport naval base to report his predicament. Without disturbing the others he made the short trip to the village green where a helicopter air ambulance made a night landing and whisked him off to the naval decompression chamber. The flight south to Auckland was maintained at a low altitude to minimise the effect of the trapped bubbles of gas in his body, but to Dave it seemed to aggravate the pain now stabbing through his shoulder. It was with a sense of relief that he entered the chamber with a medic and the hatch clanged shut, sealing them off from the atmospheric world. Compressed air hissed into the chamber building up ambient pressure as if he was descending back into the depths. The expanded gas bubbles trapped in his body's tissues were squeezed smaller.

At a chamber pressure equating to eighteen metres of seawater, the pressure was stabilised for one hour. The trapped gas bubbles were forced back into solution and Dave felt the pain in his shoulder diminish. He relaxed on the couch as the pressure was further decreased to nine metres. He knew he was in good hands but was annoyed with his indiscretion that had got him into this predicament, causing so many people to be disturbed in the small hours of the morning.

Over the next four hours the chamber pressure was staged at 20-minute intervals back to the surface. The gas dissolved slowly from Dave's bloodstream in a controlled manner into the tissues of his lungs from where it exited his body. The decompressing diver was administered breathing oxygen at the shallower pressures to eliminate nitrogen from his system. He finally emerged from the chamber tired and sore from his ordeal. Dave's treatment for a Class One bend was successful in eliminating the pain from his shoulder joint. He remained in the navy hospital for another night – time to reflect on the ordeal he had undergone. He would also miss the last day of diving on the *Niagara*.

Back at Tutukaka the team awoke to find Dave gone. Only a note he had left told them of his ordeal and his decision to seek treatment. He had not wanted to waken any of his fellow divers and cause them to lose sleep over his misfortune. He knew they needed all the sleep they could get as only one more day's diving remained. It was a subdued team that assembled on the *Pacific Hideaway* and headed back out to the wreck site, aware that Dave had pushed himself harder than he should have on a deep dive. His exertions were single-minded as he wanted to ensure all divers would reach the wreck they had travelled so far to see. But he had paid a price.

Although the inclement weather had been a major factor in disrupting the diving, Dave felt somewhat responsible for the failure of the previous dives in reaching their goal. He wanted the last day's dive to proceed without his presence. I had contacted the naval hospital and been informed that Dave, although somewhat sore, was okay and now resting. Buoyed by the news that Dave was safe, Craig and Karl descended into the depths, towed by their propulsion vehicles. It was their last chance to see the *Niagara* and the underwater scooters gave them the platform with which to explore a large area of the wreck. They swooped down along the hull towards the stern, the electric motors of their vehicles humming in the silence of the deep.

The starboard wing propeller materialised from the gloom supported on its strut in mid-water. Festooned with corals and sponges it was a stationary reminder of the power that had once driven the *Niagara* across oceans to travel further than any other ocean liner of her time. The size of the propeller surprised Karl. He had imagined the propellers would have been larger – but then, with triple screws, the *Niagara* had all the propulsion required to power her at speeds of eighteen knots through the ocean. The diving duo motored forward along the hull towards the bow over 160 metres away. Solitary hapuku caught in the beams of the approaching scooter headlights slipped back into the shelter of the surrounding twilight. Shattered hull plates announced their arrival at No. 2 hold. They shone their lights into the jagged breach, but the searching beams were lost in the cavern of night.

I was interested to discover what cargo may still be hidden in the dark confines of the holds, but I have yet to find a copy of the cargo manifest or loading plan. This is possibly due to wartime security surrounding the consignment of munitions that had been loaded under secrecy before the ship departed Auckland. Also, the gold bullion aboard would have restricted circulation of the full manifest at the time of sinking and during the gold salvage.

Letters between Williams and the USSCo reveal that the small-arms ammunition was stowed at the after end of No. 1 and No. 2 Holds, and during the first salvage Williams had been asked on the possibilities of recovering the munitions. However, Williams had thought such a recovery would be high-cost and fraught with danger to his divers as the cargo would have rolled to the low side. He also remarked that at the depth the wreck lay, the pressure was approximately 178 psi, so unless the cartridges were pressure-tight to that extent they would be full of water.

Other information we have discovered has presented a question mark as to the contents and value of other items of cargo. During his research on sunken cargo for possible recovery by Salvage Pacific, Ian Lockley found reference to a shipment of "gold residue" loaded on the *Niagara* in Sydney for her last voyage. Enquiries to the Reserve Bank of Australia uncovered records that confirmed the loading of a consignment consisting of "casks" of gold concentrate consigned to the American Smelting Company of Tacoma, Washington. Ian made further inquiries to the Salvage Association in London who revealed that the residue was contained in 21 casks weighing a total of 7 tons 2 cwt, and was insured for £4709 sterling at the time of insurance settlement. Loading plans were unavailable, and into which hold the consignment had been loaded was unknown. What did the gold residue consist of, and why was it being shipped to Washington for processing? What would be the value of the consignment today? Ian was unable to find answers to these questions.

Perhaps the casks had been loaded in No. 2 Hold into which Craig and Karl were peering. If so, there would be little left of the consignment following the blast which had ripped through the hold. Other items of interest were also hidden in the holds. Into which hold had Mrs Major's heirlooms been consigned? And what about Mrs Livingston's gold cups and silverware, Bill Sparrow's bowls, the Chalmers family's effects and young Wally Guthrie's bike? These personal effects along with the belongings of other passengers and crew lay somewhere hidden in the interior of the sunken liner. Perhaps in the future these relics from this time capsule on the bottom of the sea will see the light of day to tell a story from the past.

Craig and Karl moved on. Manoeuvring their tow vehicles, they flew up over the damaged bow across the foredeck to the shattered structure surrounding the bullion room where Johnno Johnstone in his suspended diving bell had voiced directions to Williams on the surface. A fortune in gold had been wrenched from these depths: now only ghosts from the past remained. Unfortunately, our weather-restricted diving programme did not allow us the time required to continue the search for the remaining five gold bars. Johnstone had reported gold bars dropping from the grab – perhaps Craig and Karl passed over the lost bullion on their scooters as they swept along the hull. The gold remains there for the present, its value fluctuating with international markets driven by global turmoil and changing economies.

Aided by their scooters, Craig and Karl circumnavigated the wreck. They had covered a greater expanse of the lost vessel in one dive than all the previous dives combined. Until four years earlier in 1999, when Dave and Tim first dived the *Niagara*, the wreck had remained just an image in divers' dreams. Now, with advances in underwater technology, it was slowly giving up its secrets to robots and human divers. But with the sunken liner in a state of continual decay, how long the hull will remain relatively intact before collapsing inwards to become a mountain of rubble on the seabed is unknown. The time is close – perhaps within the next ten years or less.

Is the *Niagara* a ticking time-bomb hidden in the depths, waiting in silence on a countdown to the trigger point when the collapse of her hull will unleash a black tide of oil into the ocean? Will an ecological disaster follow as an eruption of fuel oil from the depths surfaces to sweep across the Gulf to the nearby marine reserves? We now have the technology to discover if such a danger exists – and if it does, we have the technology to recover the fuel oil. At the time of writing, a survey to determine if there is a danger of the oil remaining in the *Niagara* has yet to be carried out. From time to time the media reports on oil slicks in the Gulf and occasionally notes the possibility of danger of oil from the *Niagara*, but little investigation has occurred. Karl informed me that during their transit he didn't sight the main mast extending horizontally out from the wreck. If correct, the collapse of this major member we had seen on our 2001 dives would confirm that the wreck is now in rapid decline.

While the two divers traversed the wreck on their scooters, Chris and Christina dived to the aft section of the ship for their second dive. Restricted to using muscle power, they continued their exploration forward along the deck area, documenting the dive on video. Their images captured the ravages that salvors and time had inflicted on the vessel. The past quest for gold and the continual onslaught from the ocean's elements and her inhabitants had taken a toll. Their bottom time exhausted, the last divers ascended back through the shoal of patrolling kingfish into the comforting luminescence of shallow waters. Above, Craig and Karl had settled into their long decompression schedules. Below, the veils of darkness closed back over the *Niagara*. Hidden in the depths, ambient ocean pressure guards the liner until the next intervention when humans will again challenge the deep to unlock her secrets.

Percy Ginders watched fascinated as video images from the deep were replayed. A resident of the Tutukaka coast, he had joined us for the last trip out to the *Niagara*. As a man of the sea, he has more than a passing interest in her and the events surrounding her sinking. The epic voyage of the *Orion* had fascinated him, and on a visit to Germany in 1997 he had made enquiries about contacting survivors from the Pacific raider. To his delight he discovered that a crew member lived close to where he was staying. With his German host acting as interpreter, Percy met and talked with Hinrick Fick, who was 26 when he joined the *Orion*. He had been chosen as a crew member due to his experience in the merchant marine.

Now 82, Hinrick was excited to meet his first New Zealander and recalled his wartime raid on Percy's homeland. At first he apologised for the German ship's raid into the Pacific, and the damage and loss of life that had resulted. Percy, wanting to put the old sailor at ease, replied it had been a time of war between their countries and was now long past. He expressed his admiration for Captain Weyher and his crew's fortitude in accomplishing their mission by sailing 112,337 miles around the world in 511 days at sea. Hinrick told Percy of the *Orion* crew's amazement when, sailing into the waters of a country they were at war with, they discovered that New Zealand openly broadcast information that was helpful to the enemy. Even the music the Germans heard on the radio was a comfort so far from home. Kurt Weyher passed away in 1991 and was buried at sea. Hinrick said that the *Orion*'s commander had been a keen artist and had made a number of paintings depicting incidents and scenes on the voyage.

On the dive trip, Percy brought photographs of some of Weyher's paintings. The collection included the capture of the USSCo vessel *Holmwood* off the Chatham Islands while en route to Lyttelton. One painting in particular caught my eye, causing me to look up and out over our wake towards the Hen and Chicken islands as we sped back towards Tutukaka. It depicted the *Orion*, her black hull sailing bow-on across a calm sea as smoke curled from her yellow funnel into a sunlit sky. In the background, the high peaks and outlines of two islands stood out. The land features were unmistakable and drawn exactly as the scene I now looked upon – the Northland coast with the Hen and Chickens.

To record the detail in the painting, I thought, Weyher must have observed the scene in daylight. The *Orion* is shown sailing northwards away from New Zealand, at the approximate position where HMS *Puriri* struck a mine and sank. Her mines deployed, the raider is making her escape out of the Gulf. Records state it was 0236 hours when the last mine was deployed, so it was still dark when the vessel departed. With the late winter sunrise, Weyher's painting indicates that either the German raider remained in the Gulf for longer than reported, or he absorbed the local topography on arrival at twilight. Either way it is interesting that as commander of a warship on a mission to deliver a cargo of destruction, he still had time for artistic thoughts.

The oceans of the world hide the remains of thousands of ships lost since humans first ventured out onto the liquid surface that covers 70 per cent of our planet. They remain hidden in the depths as time capsules of human history. A few are remembered today for their moment in history when they played their role on the world stage. Names such as *Titanic, Bismarck, Monitor, Central America, General Grant, Lusitania,* and *Andrea Doria* conjure up images of tragedy, conflict, heroism, and treasure in the deep.

The *Niagara* is remembered in New Zealand today not for the role she played in over 25 years of plying the Pacific as a major vehicle of commerce serving the far reaches of the British Empire, nor for the enemy action that resulted in her sinking, but for the treasure of gold bars she took into the depths and the epic salvage ventures that followed. The fact that a German ship of war sailed halfway around the world undetected and mined the approaches to Auckland harbour is little known by the majority of today's younger generation. Her sunken remains are a reminder of the exposure of small, isolated nations to the threat of undetected attacks from the surrounding oceans. Today, in these times of the terrorist, even sophisticated satellite surveillance and submarine-detection systems are unable to prevent vessels in disguise from deploying cargoes of destruction into coastal waters of unsuspecting maritime nations.

The *Niagara* is also a timely reminder of the danger contained in the numerous Second World War shipwrecks scattered across the Pacific. Hidden in the depths over the past 60 years, these vessels are victims of time and are slowly being consumed by ocean chemistry and bacterial elements. During this transformation from solid steel into mounds of decayed rubble, the sunken vessels collapse like a stack of cards. Vulnerable to these processes, fuel-storage bunkers lose any remaining ability to retain their deadly contents. With this structural collapse, large quantities of fuel oil will erupt from the ocean depths. Spreading out across the surface, the oil will be swept by wind and current in a destructive black tide into coastal ecological systems.

The increase of oil we have noted escaping from the *Niagara* is a warning that other wartime shipwrecks hidden in the Pacific depths are similar time bombs ticking away. Until recently, this potential threat has gone relatively unnoticed by the authorities, but the recent appearance of oil slicks in Pacific areas such as the Solomon Islands are giving cause for concern. Whether the marine reserves in the Hauraki Gulf, such as the Poor Knights islands, are in danger from the oil remaining in the *Niagara* is at the time of writing still unknown.

The five remaining gold bars, until discovered, will continue to be a magnet for underwater explorers. But it is not only the gold that glitters in the depths – the ship herself is a treasure. The *Niagara* and everything that went down with her is a time capsule. For those who challenge the depths to reach and explore her remains, a preserved past era awaits.

Even for those who are unable to venture into the depths, technology similar to that used to explore outer space and the planets can now transport their senses into inner-space to visit the *Niagara*. Using video cameras on robotic vehicles, telepresence enables the non-diver to explore and probe deep secrets in real time. Artefacts and passenger effects recovered by divers or ROVs, when treated and displayed, will tell the story of the ship, of those who travelled on her, and of those who challenged the depths for her gold.

PART FOUR

Revelations

25

Secrets

The austere edifice of the Bank of England towered above me. Resembling a walled fortress in the heart of London, the windowless lower concrete walls angled in both directions to circumnavigate the city block. The Grecian columns and facade of the impressive building dominated the surrounding neighbourhood like an impregnable fortress, a place where one would feel safe in depositing one's treasures. Established on Threadneedle Street in 1760, this repository of an empire's riches has withstood the conflicts of war and monetary disasters. Now it guards the wealth of a nation involved with a new war – a war against terrorism. I was to find that this financial bastion also guards her secrets from the past.

It was April 2004 and I had come to London in an attempt to discover more about the salvage of *Niagara*'s gold. The city had changed in many ways from my last visit over a decade before. The United Kingdom had now joined the European Union and London's pavements were crowded with pedestrians speaking a pot-pourri of European languages. Another seven East European countries were about to join the EU and England was bracing herself for a further influx of people seeking work and fortune.

The people milling past me on the crowded streets took little notice of police cars speeding past sirens blaring, their occupants clad in bullet-proof vests. Warnings on buses and the Underground advised of the dangers of unattended bags and the need to be alert. Video cameras peering down from overhead gave the impression that Big Brother was watching my excursions around the city. Descending bleak white-tiled passageways leading into the Underground, my thoughts would turn to images of the Madrid train bombings two weeks previously. Although it was time-consuming travelling on a stop-go bus journey, I felt more at ease travelling above through the crowded streets on a bus.

A war 64 years ago had brought me to the confluence of the six roads where the Bank of England stood. I was in London to search for answers to wartime secrets surrounding the sinking of the *Niagara* and the salvage of her gold. Secrets, I was to discover, that the bank would not give up easily. I had made an appointment to visit its archives. Following the security checks that were now part of everyday life around the city and confirmed I was not carrying a bomb, I was passed on to my escort. With the assistance of one of two women entrusted with guarding the bank secrets, I perused the computer index listing the *Niagara* files – there were six. I found however, that only one file was available for public viewing. The other five were still restricted until 2019 to 2061. This surprised me – what secrets did the bank still guard? More than 60 years after the first salvage, surely there was little to hide. Confidentiality of such records for a period of 100 years seemed a little over the top, even for the British.

Despite my overtures to the guardians, they were adamant the restricted files could not be released to me. Perhaps, they said, the problem was that the files might contain other sensitive material. Finally they conceded that perhaps one other file could be released to me. But first it would have to be vetted by a representative from the Bullion Division. By the time of my departure from England, over a week later, this had still not occurred. I left London none the wiser as to what insights this file might contain.

In the meantime I resigned myself to being permitted access to only one file, thinking I certainly would not be around when the restricted files were finally released. The file I could read relates to what had happened to the salvaged gold bars following their recovery in 1941 and 1953.

In January 1942, the New Zealand government was concerned about the possibility of a Japanese invasion and distributed gold reserves around the country for storage in trading bank strongrooms. A secret cablegram was sent to the Bank of England asking if they required a similar arrangement for the *Niagara*'s gold. It is ironic that after all the efforts and risks taken by Williams and his salvage team, the gold from the *Niagara* played no further part in the war. It remained locked in New Zealand bank vaults until after the war ended. This retention belies Churchill's reply to the Opposition question put to him back in 1942, when he answered that the *Niagara*'s gold was much needed for the war effort. If the salvage operation had been left until after the war, it would have been conducted without the danger of working in a minefield and with a vessel and salvage equipment more suited for the recovery mission.

The gold was finally shipped to England in 1946. In February that year, 555 gold bars packed in 278 sealed cases were transported under naval escort by train from Wellington to Auckland. There the consignment was delivered to HMNZS *Gambia*. In addition to the gold, four boxes of coins were included in the shipment. The gold transfer note listed the bullion as 223,701.170 fine ounces, at a value of £172 0s 3d per fine ounce, a total value of £1,926,638. On arrival in London the gold was reweighed at 223,692.071 fine ounces, a shortage of 9.099 ounces, which was finally written off. Reading the report I smiled, thinking of Ray Nelson dropping bars he was cleaning and gathering chips of the metal for his gold ring.

The file also recorded details of the gold recovered by the 1953 Risdon Beasley salvage. A list of the 35 bars remaining before that salvage listed their serial numbers and weights. A note following the salvage certified that the 30 bars recovered, and then held at the Reserve Bank of New Zealand, had a total gold content of 12,089.85 fine ounces. A reconciliation of the recovered gold noted a discrepancy of minus .007 ounces. It would appear that Alan Martin and the English lads on the *Foremost 17* had not been as resourceful as Ray and his colonial mates.

Unable to glean any further information from the bank's archives, I walked to Guildhall nearby. Built in the 1400s, Guildhall reeks of history. Its ancient walls survived the Great Fire of 1666 and the Blitz inferno of 1940. Looking around the medieval architecture I recalled the assurance the old-world buildings of England had given Johnno Johnstone during his quest for assistance to recover the remaining *Niagara* gold. The focus of my visit was the library located in the Guildhall West Wing and the Lloyds List shipping records that were stored there.

Following their removal from Lloyds' London office, the records were photocopied and the originals then destroyed. The reason for my interest in them was to see if they included a copy of the cargo manifest for the *Niagara*'s last voyage. Attempts in New Zealand to locate this manifest had so far proved fruitless, but I was still keen to find the details of the cargo the *Niagara* carried to her grave. Besides the gold bullion, I was aware of the reports of the mysterious shipment of "gold residue" and also the shipment of small-arms ammunition, but so far I had been unable to determine what other cargo the vessel had aboard. The elusive manifest had most probably been withheld from release at the time of sinking due to wartime censorship, and was now buried in some dusty archival storage. With Lloyds' connection to marine insurance, I considered it was worth checking the Guildhall records. Again I proceeded through a gauntlet of security checks: when they were satisfied I was not carrying any explosive device or other offensive weapon, I was admitted to the library.

A check of Lloyds War Losses revealed that the *Niagara*'s cargo included canned fruits, gelatines, rabbit skins and gold and silver residues. No details of quantities or a loading plan were given, neither was there mention of munitions or gold bullion. Next I examined the Lloyds Cards pertaining to the vessel. These contain handwritten notes on shipwrecks and newspaper cuttings referring to the subject vessel and cargo. One card noted that fifteen lifeboats had been recovered following the loss of the *Niagara*. The boat that Jack Ward of Kaitaia had installed a steam engine into would have been among these recovered vessels. Newspaper clippings reported the 1953 salvage. One stated the wreck lay in 470 feet of water, another that the cargo was worth £284,000 and another that the *Foremost 17* was equipped with a "secret scientific device with arms and legs which will be able to grope its way about the wreck". A further report noted that "a secret robot will try to wrest the gold [from the wreck] estimated at £1,200,000".

Such information in so-called official records illustrates how stories of sunken treasure can be embellished for the purpose of attracting investors in parting with money for salvage schemes. Or how would-be treasure hunters, believing in such false reports, could spend their lifetimes and fortunes in chasing rainbows. I emerged from Guildhall not much the wiser about the *Niagara*'s cargo. Deciding to be brave, I joined a throng of commuters and risked the Underground train journey back to my hotel.

Roy Martin had been with Risdon Beasley as their manager for South-east Asia in the 1970s. Now retired, he lived close to Southampton. Although it was before his time with the firm, he had among his records material from the 1953 *Niagara* salvage and had been most helpful in providing me with information. These days he spent a lot of his time researching old records on shipwrecks at the National Archives (formerly the Public Records Office), just out of London at Kew Gardens. He offered to meet me at the Archives to assist in my quest for further information on the two *Niagara* salvage ventures.

Arriving at Kew Gardens station, I walked the short distance along streets lined with Edwardian terraced houses to the National Archives. Having become somewhat accustomed to the historical bastions of London where many of the nation's historical documents were buried, I was pleasantly surprised by the complex that confronted me. Resembling a modern commercial company headquarters, the National Archives was fronted by a large man-made lake complete with ducks and a fountain. Trees still in past autumn colours surrounded the small plaza that led me to the foyer of the concrete-and-glass structure where Roy was waiting for me. Under his guidance I completed the formalities required for the issue of a reader's pass then, following the inevitable security checks, entered the reading room where secrets from the past awaited me.

Government and legal documents held in the Archives span a thousand years of British history, from the Domesday Book to the present. If you wish to research a shipwreck with British connections, then this is the place to come. Roy had previously listed for me the files held in the Archives concerning the loss of the *Niagara*, which saved time researching indexes on computer. Following a wait of 30 minutes, I collected the files I had ordered and settled down at a desk in the crowded reading room.

Roy, carrying a large stack of files, joined me at the next desk. He was researching information requested by another New Zealander, concerning a British motor-torpedo boat sunk during the war in the North Sea by the Germans. The reason for the search I did not know. Silence was the order in the reading room and conversation was not permitted. I felt as if I was a schoolboy again sitting exams. I turned my attention to the files in front of me and to secrets I might discover.

One file I was interested in was not available. Roy's inquiries earlier had revealed that it had been issued to a government department and had not been returned. Subsequent requests had received replies that it was still with the department concerned. Finally Roy was informed the file had been "lost". This was still the case and what information the file contained or why a government department had suddenly taken an interest in the *Niagara* was a mystery. Perhaps the answer might lie in a query I had earlier sent HM Treasury. Although I knew the Treasury still laid claim to the remaining gold, I was not sure who actually owned the wreck or the cargo it still contained. I had put the question to the Treasury Solicitors Office. I had also reported that the wreck was now leaking fuel oil in increasing amounts, so ownership of it and responsibility for the oil it contained was a question of interest. The Treasury Solicitor replied they were looking into the matter and they would get back to me. So far I had not received any clarification on the issue. Perhaps the question had rung liability bells.

The files I now read revealed the concerns that officialdom had expressed regarding the 1941 salvage. Matters such as how much the salvage syndicate should be awarded for their efforts, contract negotiations, the question of censorship on the salvage operation and the accusations that followed between the British and Commonwealth governments. The initial response by the British government when informed of the loss of the *Niagara* and the gold on board was to write off the amount of metal involved. It was the first such loss the Bank of England had suffered and to have lost some £2 million worth in what one official described as "the Tasman Sea of all places" was difficult for London to accept. Then a glimmer of hope had arrived with a secret cablegram from Sir Henry Sheehan of the Commonwealth Bank of Australia. He reported it was thought the vessel was lying in a depth of 60 fathoms (360 feet) and there was a possibility of salvage. Enquiries were being made locally in Australia with likely owners of equipment that could work at such depths. A further communiqué from Australia advised that the Navy Board had received only one satisfactory reply and that was from a Captain John Williams, manager of United Salvage, who claimed he had the specification for suitable salvage equipment which could be manufactured in Melbourne within five weeks. The question was then raised, what would it cost for such a salvage operation? Sheehan was informed, for his knowledge only, that the gold was uninsured and therefore a claim could not be made on the loss.

Investigations into the integrity of United Salvage were carried out and

London was informed the company was found well backed with shares being held by the group William Cosby & Co., McDonald Hamilton & Co. and Gibbs Bright & Co. Sheehan was instructed to proceed with exploring salvage possibilities with Williams.

Meanwhile Mr. B.G. Catterns, the deputy governor of the Bank of England, contacted the Admiralty regarding the amount of remuneration to pay to a salvage contractor. He informed Sir Richard Hopkins at the Admiralty, that he had discussed the subject of paying a percentage award with the chairman of Lloyds. The chairman admitted to having had little experience with deepwater salvage but quoted percentage awards for two recent salvage operations. The highest award had been for the *Egypt* salvage, which received payment of 55 per cent of the value of the bullion recovered. He proposed that for the *Niagara* a payment of 20 or even 25 per cent based on the amount of gold recovered. Catterns pointed out that with such a percentage, a total recovery would result in a very large reward and this would need to be discussed with the Admiralty.

Back in Australia, Williams, unaware of the figures being discussed in England, proposed that the salvors be paid £27,000 plus the costs for estimated outgoings. He would make no charge for use of the equipment should the attempt be unsuccessful, and if it was successful a percentage of the recovered gold was to be paid. A vessel, the *Claymore,* had been found in Auckland and the owners were prepared to sell the vessel for £1000.

On receiving Williams' proposal, the bankers realised that he was not aware of the value of gold involved. One Treasury official suggested that perhaps the salvage operation should be left for the Admiralty to carry out when they would be available. However, due to the state of the British war chest at the time, it was considered the salvage should not be postponed. Catterns cabled Sheehan to offer Williams £28,000 for outgoings and 2.5 per cent of the value of the gold recovered. Transport of the gold to Sydney would be at the Bank of England's expense and the cost for all gear and general stock-in-trade was to be borne by United Salvage.

A salvage contract was drawn up. For unknown reasons the Bank of England required that a clause referring to the Commonwealth Bank of Australia as its representative be deleted. The Australian bank was instructed that the Bank of England's name and its interest in the contract were not to be disclosed. The contract was signed between the

Commonwealth Bank of Australia and the United Salvage Syndicate that comprised the four shareholding companies of United Salvage and John Prothero Williams. For what was stated as domestic reasons, the salvage company desired to undertake the salvage work in the name of the Syndicate.

Reading through the communiqués between the English and Australian bank officials, it became evident that Williams and the Syndicate could have negotiated a more rewarding contract, especially in light of the percentages that had originally been discussed in London. Twenty per cent would have been by far a better deal than the 2.5 per cent agreed upon. The Bank of England certainly got the better deal – but then things have not changed much today when it comes to dealing with banks.

But all was not lost. In April 1942 following the completion of the salvage, the Bank of England received a cable from the Commonwealth Bank reporting that Williams was requesting that a bonus of £A10,583 be paid to the Syndicate to cover special risks, overtime and special pay. It was noted the salvage crew had signed up on a fixed-payment basis on the understanding that a substantial bonus would be paid if gold was recovered. This bonus was to be paid on the following basis:

Chief Diver	£15 5s 0d	
Second in Command	£7 10s 0d	
Second Diver	£3 10s 0d	
Engineer	£1 10s 0d	
Crew	£9 17s 9d	
Total	£38 2s 9d	per box for 277.5 boxes.

The Bank of England in turn sent a huffy memo to the Admiralty. Those colonials had a cheek! The syndicate was now asking for reimbursement of a special bonus amounting to £A10,583 over and above the original £27,000 that had been contemplated. The memo commented it would be difficult to resist making this payment and did the Admiralty agree to it? The memo concluded with a warning that further demands might be presented on behalf of Williams. The bank eventually, but somewhat reluctantly, paid the amount requested.

The question of releasing the story of the salvage to the public had been raised during the operation. The three countries involved – England, Australia and New Zealand – had agreed upon strict censorship of the story. The press, aware of what was happening, agreed to this restriction. However, in November 1941 an Australian correspondent named Baume managed to get his story about the salvage past the censors in England, a method of bypassing local censorship sometimes used by Australian reporters to get their stories published. When Baume's ruse was discovered it caused a furore among government departments. The British Ministry of Information, in an attempt to play down the situation, said they saw no problem with the story as it did not reveal the location of the salvage. Others were concerned about how to explain to the Australian government how Baume's story got past British censorship and how to prevent the story being published by US interests over which Britain had no control.

In December, a cablegram from the Bank of England to the Reserve Bank of New Zealand advised that Whitehall had made arrangements to prevent publication of the story and would see that no messages about it would be cabled abroad. With the completion of the salvage, Williams and the Syndicate wanted the censorship of the gold recovery lifted so they might benefit from the sale of the official story and film images. They put pressure on the Australian authorities to release the story. The New Zealand government was against publication and urged both the British and Australian governments to maintain censorship. But seeing an opportunity for political kudos, the Australian Prime Minister, John Curtin, wanted to break the news to the public. On 21 February a cablegram was sent to Britain's Secretary of State for Dominion Affairs and New Zealand's Prime Minister, Peter Fraser, stating that because of the lapse of time since the gold salvage, and with the view of recording the achievements of Captain Williams and his crew, the Australian government considered that no good purpose would be served by withholding publication .

The New Zealand government was rather nervous about holding such a large amount of gold bullion, especially now that Japan had entered the war and German raiders were known to be still active in the area. Fraser responded with a cablegram to Curtin and the Secretary of State. He advised that due to possible repercussions, especially with the location of the gold, it was urged, pending further communication from himself, not to publish the proposed statement. Or, if it was already published, to take all possible steps to limit publication to Australia.

No doubt Curtin saw this reply as an opening to give the story to the Australian press. The bureaucrats in London were horrified at his intentions. To them it was not cricket and he was accused of coming out with the whole story with "a flourish of trumpets". The British considered Curtin's release to be "very shocking" and bad luck for their own press whose lips were sealed. The London *Daily Telegraph* published the story on 23 February some hours later than the *Sydney Morning Herald* due to the time difference between the two countries.

The New Zealand government in turn viewed the whole matter over the publicity with some distaste, and a strongly worded telegram from Fraser was sent to both Curtin and the Secretary of State for Dominion Affairs. The communiqué noted that in view of the wide publicity accorded the statement regarding the *Niagara*, the government felt obliged to release the details in New Zealand, despite vehement protests from the authorities responsible for the disposal of the gold. The Prime Minister's message went on to say:

> Quite apart from this aspect of the matter, which is source of much apprehension to us, I really would like to call to your serious attention the grave embarrassment which such ex parte disclosures, of which there have been many instances in the past, create for us. In this case the incident related to a New Zealand-owned ship sunk off the New Zealand coast, the gold recovered from which was the responsibility of the New Zealand Government. It had been generally understood between ourselves, London and Canberra that no publicity was to be given to this incident until the appropriate moment. We do not think that this was the appropriate moment but whether this was so or not we feel that we were at least entitled to prior consultation before publication was given to a matter which affected the New Zealand Government at least as much as, if not more than, any other government. As a minor but nevertheless embarrassing aspect, the New Zealand press who have of course been fully aware of the proceedings throughout have very loyally maintained silence on the understanding that they would be given as early an opportunity of publishing as the press of any other country, and I am sure you will agree with me that publication in Australia without notice to us puts us in the most invidious position with the New Zealand press. I do beg that you will give personal attention to this matter in view to preventing such embarrassments in future.

What Curtin's reply was I have been unable to establish, or even if he did reply. As previously noted, when Churchill replied to a question in the House the following month regarding the *Niagara* salvage, he took Curtin to task for releasing details of the salvage. With the amount of political flak the Australian Prime Minister received over the *Niagara* incident, it perhaps has a bearing on the only accolade he later bestowed on the crew of the *Claymore*. In a short letter of reply to James Herd dated 17 March 1942, Curtin states: "I am most appreciative of the great difficulties involved with the operations and it is gratifying to know that Australians were associated with such a magnificent achievement."

Having gleaned the information that was available to me in London about the *Niagara* salvage, except for the "lost" file and others that would not be available for another 20 to 60 years, I departed England and headed for Hamburg. I was interested in finding out more about the visit of the *Orion* to New Zealand and what revelations I might discover in Germany about Captain Weyher and his ship.

26

The German Factor

I had been intrigued by the photograph Percy Ginders had shown me of Kurt Weyher's painting depicting the *Orion* underway in Hauraki Gulf during the 1940 minelaying operation, and how he had accurately depicted the coastline even though his attack was at night. Except for Weyher's book *The Black Raider* published in 1955 and brief mentions in war history publications, there had been little published about the incursion of the German raider into New Zealand waters. I was curious to know more about Weyher and why the Germans had targeted the approaches to the port of Auckland: why did the Germans sail halfway around the world to deposit their entire complement of mines in the Hauraki Gulf? Why did they consider the approaches to this particular harbour an important military target? Admittedly, the harbour was relatively unprotected. The New Zealand population at that time was complacent about the possibility of an enemy attack. The distance from the war in Europe gave some comfort, and one would not expect the enemy to make such an audacious attack, especially on a port involved mainly with shipping farm produce. Was Weyher aware that the *Niagara* was scheduled to pass through these waters within a few days carrying a shipment of gold destined for payment of England's much-needed war materials? Or was there another factor?

I was also interested to know more about the man who commanded the *Orion*. After causing havoc among Allied shipping in the South Pacific, the German commander successfully brought his ship and crew safely home from a voyage of 511 days around the world. What other images had he painted of a war as seen through his own eyes? Were there other paintings depicting the raid into New Zealand waters? If so, they would be unique as it was most unlikely any other enemy commander had recorded his wartime action in this part of the world in such a manner.

The development of websites and email has greatly aided the search for historical information about the Second World War. After searching the web I had found and contacted a German Naval Association. In answer to my queries for information on possible survivors of the *Orion*'s crew, I was put in touch with Kurt Weyher's son, Hein-Peter Weyher. He in turn advised me that his father's wartime effects were now with a private institute, and referred me to Professor Peter Tamm at the Wissenschaftliches Institut fur Schiffahrts-und Marinegeschichte (Institute for Shipping-and Naval Information) in Hamburg. A German businessman now in his 70s, he had played a major role in the post-war reconstruction of Germany. His keen interest in German naval history had led to his establishing the maritime institute. He had become a prominent figure in publishing after the British occupying force at the end of the war granted him permission to publish Germany's only newspaper.

I wrote to Professor Tamm who replied confirming that his institute did hold the collection of Weyher's wartime memorabilia – including his paintings. He agreed to make available to me a transparency of the *Orion* painting I had seen in Percy's photo. He also told me the collection included two other paintings of the naval action in the Gulf, including, a fantasy painting of the *Niagara* sinking. This revelation aroused my curiosity as to what other *Orion* information the institute might hold – so I decided to visit Hamburg.

Dieter Hablie, an old friend from my days in Samoa, drove along the shores of Alster Lake and into the early morning traffic of central Hamburg. Sitting alongside him I tried to decipher the unfamiliar city roadmap in an attempt to take us towards the River Elbe where the institute was located. As we drove through the city, I recalled that Hamburg had been heavily bombed during the war. In July 1943, following a heavy bombing raid, a firestorm devastated 21 square kilometres of the city centre, killing 42,000 civilians. The majority of the buildings we now passed in the central district were of recent construction as not many buildings had survived the inferno. It was a grey overcast spring morning, and following a few excursions in the wrong direction we finally arrived on the Elbechausee, the avenue we were seeking.

Although inland, Hamburg is a major seaport spread along the banks of the River Elbe. As we drove along the avenue I was fascinated by the amount of shipping and maritime activity along this famous waterway some 120 kilometres from the sea. The river led out into the North Sea and to the Kiel Canal, which cut across an isthmus to the Baltic Sea. The *Orion* had sailed this route in 1940 at the start of her voyage to the South Pacific and around the world. On the opposite riverbank was the site of the Blohm and Voss shipyards where the mighty battleship *Bismarck* had been launched.

As we progressed along the avenue, trees now heavy with spring foliage closed in above us. Beyond their leafy screens, nineteenth-century villas and stately mansions, once the homes of shipping barons, gave the area an air of past grandeur. I began to wonder whether we had strayed off the route to our destination, thinking a maritime institute would be more likely to be situated among dockside buildings. We finally pulled up outside a grand mansion. There were no signs indicating the address was a maritime institute. Only the street number announced we had arrived at our destination.

Dieter spoke into the entrance speakerphone alongside the closed doors; they opened, admitting us into the foyer of the impressive old building. I was grateful for Dieter's company: my knowledge of German was virtually zero, so he would be most helpful with translation. He was curious to visit this maritime establishment too, saying it was still not easy for Germans to study this period. He considered this a pity as, after all, the war had happened and was now history.

Dr Diether Schmidt greeted us. Although it was his day off, he had made himself available to attend to our visit. The amiable Dr Schmidt spoke English fluently and put me at ease, explaining he had already prepared material for our visit. The foyer opened onto a magnificent stairwell, and the walls and open landings above displayed numerous paintings depicting maritime history from the eighteenth century to Second World War U-boat warfare. He said the institute housed over 5000 maritime paintings, all originals. A large model of a sailing ship, the replica of a vessel once owned by an ancestor of Professor Tamm, hung suspended in the centre of the stairwell. The mansion had been built in 1864 as the summerhouse of a shipping merchant, then from 1886 until the end of the First World War it was a hotel, recognised as one of the finest establishments in the area. Professor Tamm had acquired the magnificent old building to house his expanding maritime collection, which now covered many facets of German maritime history, both in peace and war. We could easily have spent a full day absorbing the many interesting displays, but our time was limited and we needed to concentrate on the main purpose of our the visit – the *Orion* and her visit to the Pacific.

Dr Schmidt was most knowledgeable about the German raiders and chatted continuously about their war operations as he gave us a quick tour around the display halls. The floor of what had once been the ballroom was now hidden beneath a vast display of model ships encased in glass cabinets. The model of an aircraft carrier attracted my interest, as I was not aware the Germans had such vessels during the Second World War. Deither explained that the *Graf Zeppelin* was to be the first of eight such carriers, but Hitler ordered the cancellation of the project before the first vessel was completed. A model of the *Bismarck* stood out and we paused for a closer inspection. I was familiar with the story of the battle that had sunk both the *Bismarck* and the British battlecruiser HMS *Hood* with great loss of life on both sides. Recently both vessels had been explored and filmed deep in the Atlantic using ROV technology. I could sense the pride in Deither's voice as he described how the ROV exploration had supported the thesis many Germans held, that the sinking of the *Bismarck* was not caused by British firepower but was from scuttling action by her own crew. It was evident that many people of Hamburg still harbour a strong association with the famous battleship that was constructed nearby on the banks of the River Elbe.

We made our way to the upper floor where displays on the Pacific raiders of both wars were located. A large display case was devoted to Captain Weyher and the *Orion*. Memorabilia included Weyher's uniform and military decorations alongside a model of the *Orion* complete with the dummy funnel used to disguise the ship. Crew belongings included items they had made or used to entertain themselves on the long voyage around the world. Old photos depicted the young men far from home on what appeared to be more of a grand adventure rather than a war that was to last far longer than many of them would have thought at the time. Studying their young faces, I wondered how many of this crew survived the war.

Diether pointed out a photo of Weyher in uniform and remarked on the way he wore his hat – jauntily on the side of the head. This unconventional method of dress had amused his fellow officers and earned him the nickname "Bubi" Weyher – meaning young man, a bit of a lad. The photo did give an impression that perhaps Weyher was a person who did not adhere strictly to Kriegsmarine conformity.

Diether commented that for most commanders and crews of the raiders, it had been an adventurous war. Of the ten auxiliary cruisers that had set out from Germany, only three were lost to enemy action. The *Komet*, disguised as the Japanese vessel *Manyo Maru*, joined the *Orion* in the South Pacific in 1941. The two raiders captured and then sank the *Holmwood* on her passage from the Chatham Islands to Lyttelton; 48 hours later they sank the 16,737-ton *Rangitane* east of the North Island. The *Holmwood* had not transmitted a warning signal before capture and the unfortunate ocean liner, unaware of the Germans close by, fell victim. The raiders relied on disguise, often as Japanese vessels, to aid with their survival while prowling the Pacific seeking targets. Supplied at secret rendezvous by German supply ships operating out of Japan, they continued to evade searching ships and aircraft of the British forces. At the time, Japan had not entered the war but, unknown to the Allies, had given the Germans the use of two Pacific Islands, Lamotrak and Alinglapalap, as operating bases.

The *Komet* had undertaken a dramatic voyage to reach the Pacific. Departing Germany she sailed 3500 miles across the Bering Sea above Russia, through the Bering Strait then south to join the *Orion*. In June 1941 while cruising off the Chathams, the *Komet* offloaded mines onto a captured Norwegian whale chaser, one of a fleet captured in the Antarctic by the German raider *Pinguin*. Renamed *Adjutant*, the vessel set a course for Lyttelton harbour, arriving off the entrance in the early hours of 25 June. Unseen by the Godley Head battery guarding the harbour, the little whale chaser laid ten magnetic mines in a zigzag pattern across the entrance. The following night the German crew laid a further ten mines in a double row off the entrance to Wellington harbour: again the shore battery guarding the harbour were unaware of the close presence of the enemy. Mission accomplished, the *Adjutant* set sail to the northeast of the Chathams where she rejoined the *Komet*.

In recognition of their bravery on this audacious mission under the guns of the enemy harbour defences, both Lieutenant Commander

Hemmer and Lieutenant Karsten of the *Adjutant* were awarded the Iron Cross First Class. The mines lay dormant at both harbour entrances and despite the passing of hundreds of ships they failed to explode. The New Zealand military were not aware of their presence until after the war. Captured German documents revealed details of the *Adjutant*'s raid and the number of mines that were laid – the mines are still there today.

The displayed artefacts told a fascinating tale of the exploits of the German raiders and their crews in the Pacific, but our time was limited. The main focus of our visit was to uncover additional information on the *Orion*'s visit to New Zealand, and we turned our attention back to that task. Photographs of the *Orion* on fire and sinking caught my attention. It was 5 May 1945 and following an order in January, the vessel (which upon her return from the Pacific had been commissioned as a training ship and renamed *Hektor*) had reverted back to her old role as a auxillary cruiser and the name *Orion*. The Russians had surrounded East Prussia and the Third Reich army was in retreat: the only escape from a Red Army bent on revenge was by sea. Operation Hannibal, with a mixed fleet of over 1000 naval and civilian vessels, evacuated more than two million civilian refugees and soldiers fleeing the advancing Russians. Many did not survive the Baltic gauntlet of Russian bombers and submarines. On 30 January the liner *Wilhelm Gustloff* was sunk by torpedoes. It is estimated that more than 8000 lives were lost in the sinking, the greatest maritime disaster in history. Sailing from Swinemunde (now the Polish port Swinoujecle) with some 4000 persons on board, the *Orion* was hit by a number of bombs and was soon ablaze. Fortunately other boats were close by and only about 150 lives were lost. Even totally burnt out the old raider remained afloat and was finally sunk by German gunfire. A marine chart was annotated with two positions in close proximity where the sunken vessel was thought to now lie. I queried Diether on this as I had previously been told that the vessel had been cut up by a Polish salvage company. He replied that to the institute's knowledge it had not been salvaged and still lay undisturbed. I made a mental note to check further on the fate of the old raider. If Diether's information was correct, then to find and dive the wreck could be an interesting project for Tim Cashman and his British divers.

Weyher's painting of the *Niagara* sinking was on display along with relics of the voyage. I was keen to view other paintings he had painted during the voyage. Diether led us downstairs to the cellar area, now a vast storeroom of documents including logbooks, personal notes and diaries that had been donated by ex-servicemen or their families. Boxes containing Weyher's effects included model ships he had fashioned in his retirement years, and we even found marine charts of Hauraki Gulf and the approaches to Auckland harbour. The charts of his old wartime target dated from the 1980s and I thought of the old mariner reliving his wartime adventures in his later years. Weyher, who finished his service in the Kreigsmarine with the rank of Konteradmiral (Rear Admiral), passed away in 1991 at the age of 89.

Diether said that during the war, crews of German naval vessels were not permitted cameras and the only film images to be recorded were by official military photographers carried on the vessels. (The institute had a collection of over 2000 of these films, now converted onto non-flammable materials. The contents of many have still to be viewed by institute staff and have created great interest from historical documentary filmmakers.) It was mainly because of such restrictions that Weyher took to painting many of the incidents and scenes on his voyage. The results present us with a record that no photographs could have captured: 41 paintings from August 1939 to August 1941 record the scenes as seen through the eyes of the commander of a German auxiliary cruiser. Seven of the paintings are of the action in New Zealand waters, and three are directly associated with the mine-laying operation, including the fantasy painting of the *Niagara* sinking. Weyher did not witness the actual sinking of the vessel, but his painting of the liner plunging to her grave is in fact a fairly accurate depiction of the *Niagara*'s last moments.

Diether held up the painting which had initially aroused my curiosity and led me here to the institute: the *Orion*, sailing in the Gulf, with the rugged coastal features of the Hen and Chicken islands accurately reproduced in the background. For Weyher to have painted such coastal detail, I asked Diether, was there a possibility of his being in the locality during daylight hours? Diether commented that as there were bright moonlight conditions the night the mines were laid, it was most probable that the crew could clearly define the outline of nearby coastal features. I pictured in my mind the *Orion*, without a light showing, her crew at battle stations, zigzagging across the moonlit waters while dispersing her deadly cargo. It seemed rather surreal that at such a time, when there was constant danger of discovery by the enemy, that the captain would turn to his artistic talents and sketch details of the shadowy coastline.

Turning the painting over, Diether revealed a handwritten inscription in German. Weyher had described the scene he had painted and recorded the action on that night of 13 June 1940. There was also an official stamp and signature dated 16 December 1943. Diether explained that this was a security clearance authorising the release of the painting. Sketches, paintings, official photographs and films originating from the raiders and U-boats operating in distant waters would be sent back to Germany on supply vessels returning to the homeland. Such material was placed under censorship control or used for propaganda purposes.

Unable to read Weyher's annotation, I asked my German friends for their translation. As the words were read to me in English, my interest intensified – especially when the last sentence was read:

> The main mine laying operation underway. Sunset 1633 hours. Absolute high-pressure weather conditions. Cloudless sky. Clear moon, first quarter. Visibility about 12 nautical miles. Wind around SW 1. Due to the extraordinary good visibility in this early evening we cannot approach Cuvier lighthouse closer than 8 nautical miles. Slowly the sky becomes cloudier. Start deployment 1925 hours at the east entrance of Colville Channel. In Auckland harbour – according to FT observations – one British cruiser and one auxiliary cruiser.

It was the reference to the British ships that caught my attention. The cruiser would have been HMS *Achilles* and the auxiliary cruiser HMS *Hector*. Weyher's inscription confirmed he was aware both warships were in Auckland at the time of his mine-laying operation. Were these two ships the main target of the German attack? If so, how did the Germans know they were in the port of Auckland? What was meant by "according to FT observations"? Had this information been passed on to the Germans from a spy operating in the Auckland region? Weyher's reference to this knowledge raised a number of questions in my mind and I in turn raised the possibilities with my companions.

Deither explained to me the term "FT". In the early stages of the war, the German Naval Command, Seekriegsleitung (SKL), had set up an operation to secretly monitor enemy communications originating in distant parts of the world. The SKL was at the time proficient in cracking enemy codes and together with other information monitored from radio broadcasts was able to gain knowledge of shipping movements around the globe. This intelligence was assimilated and then transmitted to the commanders of U-boats and raiders operating in distant areas. This secret monitoring programme was known as Funk Telegraphie or FT.

The commanders of German vessels were ordered that, if captured, they were not to disclose that their source of information was from Berlin through this secret FT operation. Under interrogation by the enemy, they were ordered to give the impression that their information had originated from spy operations. This was the case with the captain of the raider *Kormoran*, which sank off Western Australia following the action in which the Australian cruiser HMAS *Sydney* was lost with all hands. When interrogated following his capture, the captain told his captors that intelligence he received on shipping movements had originated from spy operations.

The presence of HMS *Achilles* in Auckland was well-known to the New Zealand public. The march through downtown Auckland by the crew to celebrate their victory at the Battle of the River Plate had been reported in the media. Whether Berlin had gained knowledge of the warships in port through monitoring New Zealand radio broadcasts or from intelligence supplied by an agent was immaterial. It was obvious that Weyher had prior knowledge of their presence through FT information from Berlin. The two ships would have been considered a prime target. The Germans would have seen the presence of the warships as a threat to their raiders operating in the South Pacific. Also, with her involvement in the loss of the *Admiral Graf Spee* at the Battle of the River Plate, sinking the *Achilles* could have possibly been promoted as payback by the German propaganda machine. The targets would certainly have been considered worth deploying the *Orion*'s full complement of mines. The fact that the *Niagara* struck one of the mines was perhaps luck for the Germans. It is possible the prime targets of the night raid escaped the deadly mine barrage.

Placing the *Orion*'s mines across the entrance to Auckland harbour at that early stage of the war was a risk that could have caused major problems for Germany – problems similar to those experienced in the First World War from the sinking of the *Lusitania* by a German U-boat. The United States had yet to declare war on Germany, and until June 1940 the Pacific Ocean, far from the battle in the Atlantic, was considered relatively safe for shipping. The US-owned Matson Shipping Line passenger liners *Mariposa* and *Monterey* made regular runs to the South Pacific, including to Auckland. If one of these American liners had struck a mine and sunk with loss of American lives, there would have been great pressure on President Roosevelt to take punitive action against Germany. The sinking of the *Laconia* off Ireland six months previously with the loss of American lives had caused strong condemnation in the US media and forced Hitler to order U-boats to avoid sinking passenger ships.

The *Niagara*, although a passenger/cargo ship, was armed and her cargo included the secret consignment of munitions destined for the war in Europe. Her sinking did not solicit any major media outcry that might have been expected with the loss of a passenger vessel at that early period of the war. Her sinking was the first maritime loss due to enemy action in the Pacific; luckily no lives were lost.

It was a strange experience to be in the Hamburg cellar with Deither and Dieter, studying Weyher's paintings of a time of war between our two countries. The coastal features Weyher depicted in his painting of the *Orion* in Hauraki Gulf were of the same coast I could look out upon from my home on the other side of the world. His painting of the *Niagara* sinking, her stern reaching for the sky, summoned images of the sunken liner's remains now resting on the ocean bottom.

This ship, the Queen of the Pacific, the creation of an uneducated lad who hailed from a remote Scottish isle, has touched many lives in both war and in peace. For some she provided a home, a way of life, transport to a new world. To others, the *Niagara* has been a catalyst for adventure – an adventure that lives on.

Epilogue

While writing this book new information would come to hand or events occur that would give me cause to reflect on what had been written and to consider whether changes were required or new material added to the story. This has been done in some instances, but if I had continued researching and kept continually updating the story of the *Niagara*, I would never have finished the book.

Divers returned to the wreck in July 2004. Weather again disrupted the planned two-week expedition and only two days were suitable to visit the wreck site. Pete Mesley, ascending from the wreck with his buddy Dave Maddox, suffered a recurrence of vertigo from inner-ear DCI problems. He again maintained his composure during a difficult decompression and repeatedly switched breathing systems to keep his rebreather circuit clear of vomit. Gavin Grant, using a diver propulsion vehicle, reported sighting the main mast still in position and not collapsed as had been thought by divers the previous year. On a second dive accompanied by Craig Howell, he scootered across the wreck to the area blasted open by salvors and carried out a quick inspection among the surrounding debris but they came away without gold.

The sinking of the *Niagara* has remained a traumatic event in the life of Lucy (Kit) Riches and one that until recently she has been reluctant to talk about. Reading news reports of our explorations of the shipwreck rekindled old memories. She was then the young pregnant Mrs Frank FitzGeorge travelling to Suva to join her husband, an instructor with the

Fiji Defence Force. Sleeping alone in the large steerage cabin, she was woken by the explosion to find herself lying on the floor. A stewardess, her face smeared with blood, arrived and ordered the frightened soldier's wife to don a lifejacket and get upstairs. She had no idea where to find one and, nearly in hysterics, frantically searched the cabin. Finally she hauled one down from an upper bunk and fled barefoot to the upper-deck lifeboat station. Through her life she has kept her memories of that night's trauma to herself. Now in the later stages of her life, she feels compelled to seek out other survivors of the sinking and put her ghosts to rest.

For Jenny Woods, then the young Jenny Chalmers, her short trip on the *Niagara* and escape from the sinking ship has remained a vivid memory. However, she has no recollection of when or how she and her family finally returned home to Suva – the drama of the sinking and the shock to her young mind at the time has erased this from her memory. No doubt there are others who have similar untold stories of that night but now, 65 years on, there are not many left.

Kelly Tarlton's shipwreck museum is no more and the *Niagara* memorabilia it displayed was dispersed through the auction of his museum collection. Jack Ward has passed on and in accordance with his wishes his *Niagara* lifeboat is with the Whangarei museum.

Like the *Niagara* and the *Orion*, the salvage vessel *Claymore* was sent to the bottom of the ocean by instruments of war. In 1953 she was loaded with condemned explosives and towed out past the *Niagara*'s grave to deep water, where as target practice she was sunk by gunfire from HMNZS *Black Prince*.

At the time of writing, August 2005, none of the five remaining gold bars have been recovered from the wreck. It is most probable that one day in the near future a diver fossicking among the debris strewn across the hull adjacent to the bullion room will come across one or more gold bars dropped from the salvage grabs. A major international dive expedition to the wreck is planned for mid-2006 and will include a team of bottom divers all experienced in diving deep shipwrecks. Their success will be determined not by technology alone but more so, as in the past, by the weather, sea conditions and some luck. These have always played a major role in finding and recovering the *Niagara*'s gold.

Appendix 1

RMS Niagara *Specifications*

Official number: 135193.
Built 1913 at Clydebank, Glasgow by John Brown & Co. Ltd for the Union Steam Ship Company Ltd of New Zealand.
Port of registry: London.
Length: 524.7ft (159.3m).
Breadth: 66.3ft (20.1m).
Depth: 34.5ft (11.4m).
Tonnage: 13,415 gross, 7582 nett.
Engines: 12,500hp indicated. Combination of two four-cylinder triple-expansion engines and a Parsons low-pressure turbine.
Fuel: oil fuel.
Total bunker capacity: 4324 tons.
Propellers: triple screw, two four-bladed 16ft-diameter wing and a three-bladed 10ft-diameter centre.
Sea speed: 16 knots average, 18 knots maximum.
Accommodation: 667 passengers in three classes, 237 officers and crew.

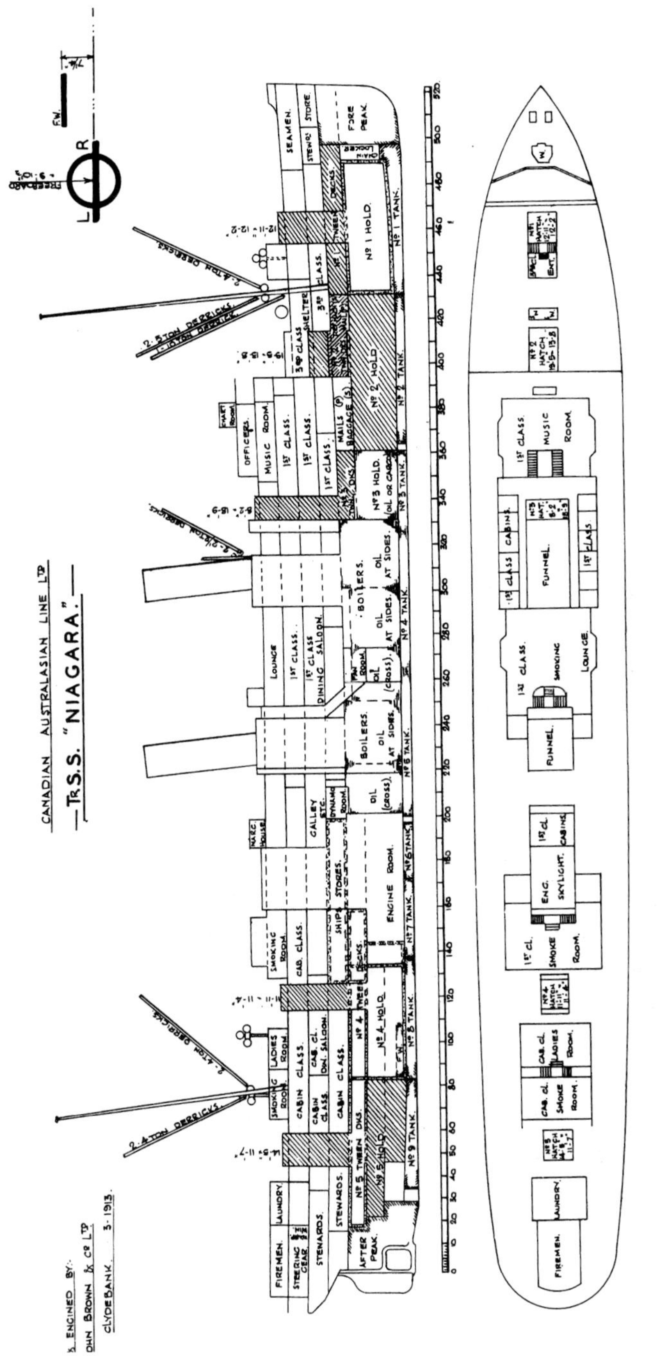

Museum of Wellington, City and Sea

1936 plan of *Niagara* showing layout of accommodation, holds and engine room.

Appendix 2

The Remaining Gold

Her Majesty's Treasury records the remaining five gold bars remaining in the wreck of the *Niagara* as follows:

BAR NO.	GROSS WEIGHT (OUNCES)	ASSAY	FINE CONTENT (OUNCES)
AU 7849	403.400	9953	401.504
AU 7887	403.405	9964	401.997
AU 7929	403.700	9967	402.367
AU 8412	401.300	9956	399.534
AU 8432	406.200	9961	404.615
	2018.050		2010.017

Note: 1 ounce = 28.35 grams

At the time of writing, August 2005, the price of gold was in the region of $US440 per fine ounce, resulting in an estimated value of the remaining gold of around $US880,000 – equivalent to approximately $NZ1.24 million. However, the intrinsic value of a Niagara gold bar as historical memorabilia would no doubt far exceed the gold's market value.

Appendix 3

Inner-Ear Decompression Illness

Dr Simon Mitchell diagnosed the cause of Peter Mesley's problem as a random inner-ear decompression illness event. This "pure" form of inner-ear DCI (that is, where the only symptoms arise from involvement of the inner ear) is rare in air diving but is well recognised in mixed-gas diving. It arises primarily because current decompression algorithms do not adequately account for the unique anatomy and gas flux properties of the inner ear on deep dives, and allow its ear tissues to become supersaturated with helium during the ascent.

Supersaturation is, in turn, responsible for bubble formation. This problem may be compounded when switching from gas mixes containing helium to gases containing nitrogen and no helium, such as air or nitrox during ascent. Under these circumstances, the sudden arrival of nitrogen in the sensitive inner-ear tissue combines with helium diffusing rapidly out of adjacent tissue compartments to temporarily worsen the supersaturation, thus further promoting bubble formation.

Both Simon and Pete switched the diluent gas in their rebreathers from helium-based trimix to air during their ascent to shorten decompression. Subsequent research suggested that the depth where they made this switch probably coincided with the peak of normal supersaturation, and was the worst possible time to do it. Although it was a rare occurrence, Simon was aware of the problem and with his participation in the dive he was able to readily diagnose the problem and treatment required.

Glossary

atmospheric diving system
A diving system in which a diver is enclosed at atmospheric pressure and protected from outside ocean ambient pressure.

aqualung
A generic name given to self-contained underwater breathing apparatus derived from the original Cousteau-Gagnan Scaphandre Autonome system that was manufactured under the trade name Aqua-Lung.

asdic
A sonic underwater detection device.

atmosphere
Pressure of the earth's atmosphere at sea level, measured in bars: 1 bar = 14.7 psi.

bell
A tethered underwater chamber providing life support to the diver.

bends
A term used for decompression illness with pain in body extremities.

bottom time
The duration of elapsed time from leaving the surface to begin the dive until commencing a direct ascent to the surface.

closed-circuit breathing system
A breathing apparatus in which the breathing gas is recycled, carbon

dioxide is removed and oxygen is added to replenish the supply as needed.

CNS oxygen toxicity
The effects of high-dose/short-term exposure to oxygen affecting the central nervous system.

cwt
Hundredweight. An imperial measurement of weight: 1 cwt = 112 lbs (50.8 kg).

DCI
Decompression illness, a condition caused by the formation of inert gas bubbles in the tissues and circulatory system as a result of releasing pressure too quickly.

decompression
A reduction in ambient pressure which occurs when a diver ascends from depth.

fathom
Unit of measurement of ocean depth: 1 fathom = 6 feet (1.83 metres).

hapuku
Polyprion oxygeneious, a large New Zealand fish of the grouper family.

heliox
A gas mixture of helium and oxygen used at depth as it has little narcotic effect.

knot
Unit of speed: 1 knot = 1 nautical mile per hour.

nautical mile
Unit of distance: 1 nautical mile = 6076 feet (1852m).

nitrogen narcosis
Narcotic effect caused by breathing the nitrogen in compressed air at depth.

nitrox
A diver's breathing mixture of nitrogen and oxygen in various proportions.

oxygen toxicity
Caused by breathing high partial pressures of oxygen. Can affect

the central nervous system and result in the diver convulsing and drowning.

PO_2
The partial pressure of oxygen in a gas mix expressed in atmospheres.

psi
Unit of pressure, expressed as pounds per square inch.

rebreather
Closed-circuit underwater breathing apparatus.

recompression
Returning a diver to a higher pressure to treat the effects of decompression illness. Normally carried out in a decompression chamber.

ROV
Remote-operated vehicle, an unmanned, tethered, remotely operated vehicle used for underwater observation and work.

telepresence
The use of video imaging from an ROV to create a simulated presence at an underwater location.

trimix
A gas mixture for deep diving involving three gases, normally oxygen, helium and nitrogen.

Bibliography

Callan, Louise. *Shipwreck*. Hodder Moa Beckett, Auckland, 2000.

Churchouse, Jack. *Glamour Ships of the Union Steam Ship Company NZ Ltd*. Millwood Press, Wellington, 1981.

Dunne, RJ. *Niagara Gold*. AH & AW Reed, Wellington, 1942.

Heath, Eric. *Shipwrecks Around New Zealand*. Grantham House, 1994.

Hinds, Fergus. *Riches from Wrecks*. Brown, Son & Ferguson, Glasgow, 1995.

Ingram, CWN and Wheatley, PO. *New Zealand Shipwrecks*. AH & AW Reed, Wellington, 1961.

Johnstone, JE and Dawlish, Peter. *Johnno the Deep Sea Diver*. George Harrap & Co, London, 1960.

Kirk, Allan A. *Ships and Sailormen*. AH & AW Reed, Wellington, 1964.

Locker-Lampson, Steve and Francis, Ian. *The Wreck Book*. The Halcyon Press, Auckland, 1994.

Locker-Lampson, Steve. *New Zealand Treasure Wrecks*. The Halcyon Press, Auckland, 1995.

Mallmann Showell, Jak P. *The German Navy in World War Two*. Naval Institute Press, Annapolis, 1979.

Maynard, Jeff. *Niagara's Gold*. Kangaroo Press, 1996.

Taylor, James. *Gold from the Sea*. Australasian Publishing Company, Sydney, 1942.

Taylor, James. *Spoils from the Sea*. Australasian Publishing Company, Sydney, 1949.

Waters, SD. *The Royal New Zealand Navy.* War History Branch, Department of Internal Affairs, Wellington, 1956.

Weyher, Kurt (and Hans Jurgen Ehrlich). *The Black Raider.* Elek Books, London, 1955.

Williams, Captain Sir John. *So Ends This Day.* Globe Press, Melbourne, 1981.

Index